Fenland Riots and the English Revolution

Fenland Riots and the English Revolution

Keith Lindley

Heinemann Educational Books · London

For my parents

Heinemann Educational Books Ltd
22 Bedford Square, London WC1B 3HH
LONDON EDINBURGH MELBOURNE AUCKLAND
HONG KONG SINGAPORE KUALA LUMPUR NEW DELHI
IBADAN NAIROBI JOHANNESBURG
EXETER (NH) KINGSTON PORT OF SPAIN

First published 1982

British Library Cataloguing in Publication Data

Lindley, Keith
  Fenland riots and the English Revolution.
  1. Drainage—England—Fens—History
  2. Fens (England)—Riots
  I. Title
  631.6'2'09426   S621

  ISBN 0-435-32535-3

Phototypesetting by Georgia Origination, Liverpool
Printed in Great Britain by Biddles Ltd, Guildford, Surrey.

Contents

List of Maps

1 The Fenland undertakings

2 Geographical origins of rioters in the Hatfield and Ancholme Levels

3 Geographical origins of rioters in the Lindsey Level, the Holland Fen and the East, West and Wildmore Fens

4 Geographical origins of rioters in the Great and Deeping Levels

Dating and Abbreviations

ALL dates are given in the old style, except that the year is taken to begin on 1 January and not 25 March. The following abbreviations and short titles are used in the notes. The place of publication is London unless otherwise stated and the spelling, but not the punctuation, of contemporary titles and quotations has been modernised.

ABBREVIATION	FULL TITLE
A Breviate of the Cause	**A Breviate of the Cause depending, and proofs made before the Committee of the late Parliament for the Fens, by the inhabitants between Bourne and Kyme Eau, in the County of Lincoln** (1651).
A.P.C.	**Acts of the privy council.**
Agrarian History	**The Agrarian History of England and Wales: vol. IV**, ed. J. Thirsk (Cambridge, 1967).
Albright	M. Albright, 'The entrepreneurs of fen draining in England under James I and Charles I' in **Explorations in Entrepreneurial History** (1955), viii, no. 2.
Badeslade	T. Badeslade, **The History of the Ancient and Present State of the Navigation of the Port of Kings Lynn, and of Cambridge** (1725).
Bodl.	Bodleian Library, Oxford.
B.L.	British Library.
Cal. S.P. dom.	**Calendar of State Papers, domestic.**
Camb. R.O.	Cambridgeshire Record Office.
Camb. U.L.	Cambridge University Library.
C.	Chancery.
Commons' jn.	**Journals of the House of Commons.**

Darby, **Draining**	H.C. Darby, **The draining of the fens** (2nd ed., Cambridge, 1956).
D.N.B.	**Dictionary of National Biography.**
D.L.	Duchy of Lancaster.
E.	Exchequer.
Harris, **Vermuyden**	L. E. Harris, **Vermuyden and the fens** (1953).
H.C.C.	Hatfield Chase Corporation.
H.M.C.	**Historical Manuscripts Commission.**
Holmes, **Lincolnshire**	C. Holmes, **Seventeenth-century Lincolnshire** (Lincoln, 1980).
H.L.R.O.	House of Lords Record Office.
Hughes	J. D. Hughes, 'The drainage disputes in the Isle of Axholme' in **The Lincolnshire Historian** (1954), ii, no. 1.
Hunter, **South Yorkshire**	J. Hunter, **South Yorkshire: the history and topography of the deanery of Doncaster, in the diocese and county of York** (2 vols, 1828).
K.B.	King's Bench.
Lilburne, **Epworth**	J. Lilburne, **The case of the tenants of the manor of Epworth in the Isle of Axholme in the County of Lincoln** (1651).
Lincs. R.O.	Lincolnshire Record Office.
Lords' jn.	**Journals of the House of Lords.**
Notts. R. O.	Nottinghamshire Record Office.
Notts. U. L.	Nottingham University Library.
P.C.	Privy Council.
PROB.	Probate.
P.R.O.	Public Record Office.
Sharp	B. Sharp, **In contempt of all authority: rural artisans and riot in the west of England, 1586–1660** (Berkeley, 1980).
Sir William Killigrew his answer	**Sir William Killigrew his answer to the Fen Men's objections against the Earl of Lindsey his Draining in Lincolnshire** (1649).
Spittlehouse, **The Case and Appeal**	J. Spittlehouse, **The Case and Appeal of the Inhabitants, Freeholders, and Commoners of the Manor of Epworth** (1653).

STAC.	Star Chamber.
S.P. dom.	State Papers, domestic.
Stonehouse	W.B. Stonehouse, **The history and topography of the Isle of Axholme** (1839).
The Anti-Projector	**The Anti-Projector, or The History of the Fen Project** (undated).
The declaration of Daniel Noddel	**The declaration of Daniel Noddel, Solicitor for the Freeholders and Commoners within the Manor of Epworth** (1653), in J. Tomlinson, **The Level of Hatfield Chase and parts adjacent** (Doncaster, 1882), appendices, pp. 258–70.
The great complaint	**The great complaint and declaration of about 1,200 Freeholders and Commoners, within the Manor of Epworth** (1654), in Tomlinson, op. cit., appendices, pp. 271–6.
The Picklock	**The Picklock of the Old Fen Project: or, Heads of Sir John Maynard his several speeches . . . at the Committee for the Lincolnshire Fens, in the Exchequer Chamber** (1650).
'The 1636 Exchequer decree'	'A decree of the Honourable Court of Exchequer upon the award of Sir John Banks, Attorney General, June 18th, 1636' in Hughes, appendix A, pp. 35–45.
Thompson, **Collections**	P. Thompson, **Collections for a topographical and historical account of Boston, and the hundred of Skirbeck, in the County of Lincoln** (1820).
V.C.H.	Victoria County History.

Preface

THE subject of this book was originally suggested by a general interest in popular movements and disturbances in early modern England and a particular concern with the English Revolution. I owe a great debt of gratitude to Professor Brian Manning, under whom I served my apprenticeship; my interest in this field owes much to his inspiration and he has always been generous with his help and criticism. I have benefited considerably from conversations with Jane Cox, the late C. A. F. Meekings, Peter Seddon and John Walter. I also wish to express my appreciation for the help and courtesy I have received from the staffs of the various archives and libraries I have visited.

The completion of this book has been made possible by the generosity of the trustees of the British Academy, the Twenty-Seven Foundation and the Muirhead Hanna Publications Fund, and the willingness of The New University of Ulster to grant me two periods of study leave. The efficiency and accuracy of my typist, Valerie Campling, also helped make the final stages relatively painless. On a personal level, vital months of research and writing were made possible by the patience and hospitality of Kathleen and Hugh Olphert. But the greatest debt of all I owe to my wife for her support and endurance.

Keith Lindley
14 August 1981

Introduction

THE urgent fiscal needs of early Stuart governments gave birth to a number of money-making expedients which directly challenged established property rights and ultimately raised wider constitutional issues. A series of ambitious drainage schemes initiated or encouraged by the King, which impinged upon the livelihood of the inhabitants of approximately 1430 square miles of fenland in eastern England,[1] exposed an entire region of the kingdom to such a challenge. The large-scale enclosure of previously commonable fens, which accompanied these schemes, falls into the same category as ship money and other expedients which undermined property rights and demonstrated absolutist tendencies in central government. Those who stood to lose most were the mass of fenland peasantry who relied in varying degrees upon the rich resources of their commons, and who would be constrained to witness a transformation of the traditional fenland economy. These casualties of fenland enclosure give the final lie, if any were needed, to the benevolent paternalism of Charles I's personal rule when considerations of social justice and harmony swiftly evaporated if they conflicted with fiscal imperatives. On another level, although substantial local figures featured prominently in some drainage schemes, they were in effect a central intrusion into local affairs by courtiers and their associates, as anxious to have a share in the profits of the Crown's exploitation of the fens as they were in its disafforestation proceedings.[2] This book is concerned with two central themes: the course and character of the fenmen's resistance to drainage schemes and enclosure throughout the seventeenth century, and the contribution that the fenmen's activities make to our understanding of the causes, course and consequences of the English Revolution, especially in view of the way in which an originally regional problem intruded into the national arena in the 1640s and 1650s.

A great deal of controversy, much of it finding its way into print,

[1] Albright, p. 52.
[2] Sharp, pp. 84–5.

was sparked off by these schemes from their very inception. An animated drainage debate took as its principal concerns the necessity and desirability of general drainage and the feasibility of specific schemes and, although inevitably characterised by exaggerated claims and counter-claims, it none the less highlighted the issues involved and reveals much about the motives of the protagonists. Those who advocated general drainage in the first half of the century contrasted the allegedly barren and unprofitable nature of the fens prior to drainage with its fecundity and prosperity afterwards. The environment of the undrained Great Level was depicted as being un-wholesome both for man and beast – sheep and cattle not infrequently perished from 'the rot' (also known as the 'fen disease') leaving their owners impoverished, and the very air left the inhabitants prone to certain illnesses. A contemporary fenland proverb that traced the de-cline of a man's fortune ran, 'From the Farm to the Fen, from the Fen to Ireland.' Camden characterised the fenmen as 'a kind of people according to the nature of the place where they dwell rude, uncivil, and envious to all others whom they call Uplandmen', while another detractor maintained that 'the generality of the fen people were very poor, lazy, given much to fishing and idleness, who were very much against the draining because they feared their condition should be worse, which truly was almost impossible'.[3] The Hatfield Level was described as being not only flooded in winter but sometimes in the summer months as well, and local people were found to testify that the fens had been drowned for most of the year (except for extra-ordinarily dry summers) allowing boats to pass over them and the catching of fish. They also claimed that corn, hay and fodder had been destroyed by flood waters, either in the fields or in flooded barns, and that occasionally even the lives of the inhabitants and their cattle had been at risk.[4]

The drainers later boasted that they had transformed this hostile environment, replacing poverty with prosperity by bringing into cultivation formerly unproductive land, greatly increasing the yield of pasturage and providing work for idle hands. Drained lands, con-

---

[3] W. Camden, *Britain* (1637), p. 491; H. C., *A Discourse concerning the draining of Fens and surrounded grounds in the six Counties of Norfolk, Suffolk, Cambridge with the Isle of Ely, Huntingdon, Northampton, and Lincoln* (1629), pp. 3–4; P.R.O., S.P. dom. 16/480, f. 88; B.L., Harleian 5011, pt II, fols 537–8; Camb. R.O., R. 59/31/9/3, fols 5, 8.
[4] *The great complaint*, p. 274; P.R.O., E. 178/5960; ibid., 5412; E. 134/24 Chas. I/East. 4; ibid., 1649/Mich. 11.

verted to arable, produced crops of corn, rape- and cole-seed (for oil extraction) and flax, and the fenmen were left with dramatically improved commons. In Hatfield Level it was confidently asserted that land had trebled in value after drainage (hence the commoners were not prejudiced when allotted only one-third of their former fenland), and some estimates of improvement ranged as high as a tenfold increase. It was also argued that the commoners' portion maintained more stock after drainage than had the whole common previously, and that even greater benefit awaited them if they could shed their inertia and move over to arable farming. Similar claims were made for the Lindsey Level, where the commoners' grounds were said to have sustained an increased number of cattle and horses, as well as flocks of sheep for which the undrained commons had not been very suitable, and in the Great Level stock breeding had become feasible in formerly uncongenial areas.[5]

Fenland drainage was also presented as making a major contribution to the relief of local poverty and unemployment as local labour was engaged not only in the drainage works themselves, but afterwards on a continuous basis maintaining the works, engaging in a more labour-intensive arable husbandry, rearing stock and manufacturing linen cloth, all of which provided employment for ablebodied poor previously dependent upon charity. Apart from the greater certainty of employment and marked reduction in seasonal idleness, the poor enjoyed commons rendered suitable for grazing at all times of the year. In the Hatfield Level labourers were said to have received double the previous wage rates, and there may initially have been a deliberate policy of employing local labour at higher wages there to allay some of the early opposition. Sir William Killigrew, a leading Lindsey Level figure, boasted of employing 500 people for three months in one summer alone to harvest his crop of cole and rape, and the drainage of the East and West Fens was said to have 'much enriched' local inhabitants 'who before were very poor'. An account of the benefits accruing from an area of 28 000 acres of former fenland within the Great Level in a single year itemised £95 000 as having been paid out in wages to labourers, workmen and

[5] *The Case of the Adventurers in the East and West-Fens, on the North and North-East sides of the River of Witham, in the County of Lincoln* (undated); J. L., *A Discourse concerning the great benefit of Draining and embanking, and of transportation by water within the Country* (1641), p. 8; P.R.O., S.P. dom. 16/480, f. 88; E. 178/5960; ibid., 5412; E. 134/24 Chas. I/East. 4; ibid., 1649/Mich. 11; Camb. R.O., R. 59/31/9/3, fols 5–6.

others out of a grand total of £113600 in 'advantages which have accrued to the State, the Country and the poor'. This was over and above the value of the crops themselves which consisted of cole-seed, wheat, barley, oats and flax.[6]

Fenland drainage was also projected as serving national as well as local interests. England's rapidly expanding population, as one drainage apologist commented, had led both to the planting of colonies in Ireland and the Atlantic seaboard of North America and to internal colonisation, the bringing of fens, and other waste and marginal lands, into production.[7] Neither the enterprising nor the indigent need step a foot outside of England for, as the drainers' poet proclaimed,

> And ye, whom hopes of sudden Wealth allure,
> Or wants into Virginia, force to fly,
> Ev'n spare your pains; here's Florida hard by.
> All ye that Treasures either want, or love,
> (And who is he, whom Profit will not move?)
> Would you repair your fortunes, would you make,
> To this most fruitful Land yourselves betake.[8]

Thus the case for internal colonisation was couched in the same terms as that for external, as coincidently serving the national interest and satisfying the profit motive. Successful drainage enterprises brought in effect 'the addition of a new province to England'. National interests were served in a number of ways: drained fenland increased the area of tillage; it accommodated the surplus population of neighbouring regions; it increased the area of the country that could contribute to the taxes of Church and State; it contributed to national pride by freeing the kingdom 'from the imputation of laxi-

---

[6] Hunter, *South Yorkshire*, ii, 161; Stonehouse, p. 81; 'The State of that part of Yorkshire, adjacent to the Levels of Hatfield Chase, truly represented, by a Lover of his Country' (York, 1700) in W. Peck, *A Topographical Account of the Isle of Axholme* (Doncaster, 1815), appendix 5, p. ii; *Certain papers concerning the Earl of Lindsey his Fens* (1649), p. 7; *Sir William Killigrew his answer*, p. 15; Sir William Killigrew, *A Representation to Parliament in favour of the draining of Lindsey Level* (1655); *The Case of the Adventurers in the East and West-Fens, on the North and North-East sides of the River of Witham, in the County of Lincoln* (undated); *An Answer to a Printed Paper dispersed by Sir John Maynard entitled The Humble Petition of the Owners and Commoners of the Town of Isleham in the County of Cambridge* (1653), pp. 13–14; P.R.O., E. 134/24 Chas. I/East. 4; ibid., 1649/Mich. 11; S.P. dom. 18/37, f. 11III; ibid., 16/480, f. 88; B.L., Harleian 368, fols 169–70; ibid., 6838, f. 179; Camb. R.O., R. 59/31/9/3, fols 5–6; Notts. U.L., H.C.C. 9111, fols 15–16.

[7] H.C., *A Discourse concerning the draining of Fens*, p. 9.

[8] 'A True and Natural Description of the Great Level of the Fens' in *The History or Narrative of the Great Level of the Fens, called Bedford Level* (1685), pp. 80–1.

ness and want of industry' levelled at it by foreigners for allowing large areas of the country to remain nonproductive; and it made a significant contribution to national self-sufficiency. Enlarging on the latter point, the drainers argued that the manufacture of several kinds of linen cloth had been stimulated by a greatly increased flax production thereby freeing the country from reliance on foreign manufacturers, and that rape-seed provided an alternative source of oil so that England might proclaim 'Here grows proud Rape, whose price and plenty foils The Greenland Trade, and checks the Spanish oils.'[9] In view of all these benefits, the drainers' local opponents could be castigated as 'But Slaves to Custom, Friends to Popery, And ranked with those, who, lest they should accuse Their Sires, no harness, but the Tail, will use.'[10]

Opposition to drainage was not entirely seen as arising from the innate conservatism of the fenmen. Sir William Killigrew identified as 'the chief of our opposers' in the Lindsey Level those rich men who overstocked the commons while obliging the rest of the commoners to contribute equally to the repairing and maintaining of ancient drainage works. He levelled a similar accusation at his opponents in the Holland Fen where 'many rich men of Boston' and others bordering on that fen 'would have no draining, that so themselves with their great stocks may still continue to eat out the poor Commoners'. Thus Sir William and his associates posed as the champions of oppressed commoners and expressed themselves ready to consent to the operation of a stint for their benefit. But his opponents could easily turn this argument against him by deducing that if, as conceded, the fens had maintained large numbers of stock before the advent of the drainers, then this supported their contention that new works were unnecessary. Another source of opposition isolated by the Lindsey drainers was the supposed fear of neighbouring landowners that 'our new improvement should cry down the value of their up Lands and invite away their Tenants'. Some opposed the new schemes 'out of envy and malice' because they themselves had failed to become shareholders; others because they owned upland pastures for the use of which they could charge whatever they pleased when the low grounds were flooded; and some

---

9 Ibid., p. 78; Sir William Killigrew, *A Representation to Parliament; Sir William Killigrew his answer*, pp. 9–10; J.L., *A Discourse*, op. cit., pp. 7, 15; P.R.O., S.P. dom. 16/480, f. 88; ibid., 452, f. 32; B.L., Additional MS. 21427, f. 209.
10 'A True and Natural Description of the Great Level of the Fens', p. 74.

because they pastured their cattle on the commons without any entitlement. There were, therefore, drainers who were convinced that opposition to their schemes was originated and sustained by substantial local landowners who, for their own selfish ends, misled the mass of poor commoners into opposing their own real interests.[11]

The fenmen replied to these pro-drainage arguments by stressing the value of the traditional fenland economy and denying the necessity of new schemes that actually worsened the condition of the fens and seriously undermined their livelihood. The legality of the drainers' proceedings was also challenged but this point is more appropriately examined in Chapter 1 in the context of the schemes themselves. A principal pro-fenman tract, *The Anti-Projector*, struck at the roots of the drainers' case and redirected attention to the very real value of the fens for local inhabitants. 'The undertakers', it proclaimed, 'have always vilified the fens, and have misinformed many Parliament men, that all the Fens is a mere quagmire and that it is a level hurtfully surrounded, and of little or no value: but those which live in the Fens, and are neighbours to it, know the contrary'.[12] Recent research has largely confirmed the view that the fens, far from being barren wastes prior to drainage, supported a large population of small farmers who exploited its valuable natural resources in a way that enabled them to live tolerably well compared with the peasantry of other agricultural regions. This environment may not have been favourable for genteel living, as the paucity of gentry in the Holland division of Lincolnshire towards the end of the sixteenth century testifies, but it did provide a reasonable livelihood for a fenland society composed at the top of a substantial group of moderately wealthy yeomen and sloping gradually down to the poor landless commoners.[13] A speech delivered by Sir John Maynard, a leading upholder of the fenmen's cause, before the committee for the Lincolnshire fens in 1650, contains one of the best summaries of the value of

[11] J.L., *A Discourse*, op. cit., p. 6; *Certain papers concerning the Earl of Lindsey his Fens*, p. 6; *Sir William Killigrew his answer*, p. 16; *A Paper delivered and dispersed by Sir William Killigrew; A Reply to Sir William Killigrew's dispersed papers, by the Owners and Commoners in Lincolnshire* (undated); B.L., Additional MS. 21427, f. 207; Harleian 6838, f. 193.
[12] *The Anti-Projector*, p. 8.
[13] J. Thirsk, *English peasant farming: the agrarian history of Lincolnshire from Tudor to recent times* (1957), pp. 7, 27, 45, 47, 78; J. Thirsk, *Fenland farming in the sixteenth century* (University of Leicester, occasional papers no. 3, 1953), pp. 5, 9, 10, 25, 42, 44; *Agrarian History*, pp. 36, 39.

the traditional fenland economy. Lauding its pastures, Sir John argued that

> Our Fens as they are, produce great store of Wool and Lamb, and large fat Mutton, besides infinite quantities of Butter and Cheese, and do breed great store of Cattle, and are stocked with Horses, Mares, and Colts, and we send fat Beef to the Markets, which affords Hides and Tallow, and for Corn, the Fodder we mow off the Fens in summer, feeds our Cattle in the winter: By which means we gather such quantities of Dung, that it enriches our upland, and Corn-ground .... Besides, our Fens relieves our neighbours, the Uplanders, in a dry summer, and many adjacent Counties: So thousands of Cattle besides our own are preserved, which otherwise would perish .... So that Rape, Cole-seed, and Hemp, is a Dutch Commodity, and but trash and trumpery, and pils Land in respect of the afore recited Commodities, which are the Oar of the Commonwealth.[14]

Poetic celebrations of 'The pleasures of the Fens' countered the drainers' verses, with lines such as the following:

> The toiling Fisher here is tewing [i.e. preparing] of his Net:
> The Fowler is employed his limed twigs to set.
> One underneath his Horse, to get a shoot doth stalk;
> Another over Dykes upon his Stilts doth walk:
> There other with their Spades, the Peats are squaring out,
> And others from their Carrs, are busily about,
> To draw out Sedge and Reed, for Thatch and Stover fit,
> That whosoever would a Landskip [i.e. landscape] rightly hit,
> Beholding but my Fens, shall with more shapes be stored,
> Then Germany, or France, or Thuscan can afford.[15]

Common of pasture was the principal and most cherished right enjoyed by fenmen. Rich fenland pastures fed the commoners' dairy and beef cattle, maintained their sheep, oxen and swine, and, in some areas, enabled them to breed horses. Abundance of summer fodder fed their livestock through the winter months when most of their commons lay under water (although surplus stock was slaughtered at Michaelmas in the fens as elsewhere) and dung from the livestock in turn enriched both their pastures, and their arable land, which was

---

[14] *The Picklock*, p. 12.
[15] M. Drayton, *The second part, or a continuance of Polyolbion* (1622), p. 108. Cf., 'The powtes complaint' attacking fen drainage by undertakers in Cambridgeshire (B.L., Harleian 837, fols 73–5).

said to be 'the richest and certainest corn land in England, especially
for wheat and barley'.[16] These customary rights were vital to the
survival of the towns and villages that had grown up on the edges of
the fens or on higher grounds within them. The new drainage
schemes had, for example, a crucial effect upon the towns and
villages on the edges of the East and West Fens and of the adjacent
Wildmore Fen. According to one contemporary estimate, nearly 4000
families residing in the Skirbeck wapentake (in Holland) and the soke
of Bolingbroke (in Lindsey) were to some extent dependent upon these
fenland commons, where they enjoyed common of pasture, without
stint, for all kinds of livestock (with each town and village having its
own distinctive brand), and it was this availability of commons that
had attracted 'multitudes of people' to settle there. Pasture rights in
Wildmore Fen alone (an area of approximately 10 300 acres) were
enjoyed by about 930 families in twenty towns in the soke of Horncastle as well as by the inhabitants of the barony of Scrivelsby, a few
towns in the soke of Bolingbroke and at least one town, Fishtoft, in
Holland. Contemporary estimates of the number of commoners
varied between 2000 and 5000, although the latter figure is probably
a wild exaggeration if the total fenland acreage is recalled.[17] Eleven
villages in the wapentakes of Kirton and Skirbeck had common rights
in the neighbouring Holland Fen. The Holland division of Lincolnshire as a whole had long possessed a strong sense of community
which enabled the local inhabitants to co-operate together in the work
of drainage and reclamation from the early Middle Ages, and this
division was richer than either of the other two in the sixteenth century. Great stocks of cattle, sheep and horses were maintained by an
increasing population on these fens, which were by no means an area
of helpless destitution, and the large numbers of livestock supported
by them contradicts the drainers' claims that they were subject to

---

[16] *V.C.H., Huntingdonshire*, iii, 261; Lilburne, *Epworth*, p. 2; *The Anti-Projector*, p. 8;
B.L., Additional MS. 33466, f. 184. The commoners of Winterton (whose grounds
were included in the Ancholme Level scheme) claimed in 1665 that the manure from
their livestock fed in pastures faced with enclosure was vital to the successful tillage of
their arable land (P.R.O., E. 134/17 Chas. II/East. 14).

[17] Thirsk, *English peasant farming*, op. cit., p. 82; 'The case of the lords, owners, and
commoners, of 22 towns in the soke of Bolingbroke, and eight towns in East Holland'
in Thompson, *Collections*, p. 151; P.R.O., S.P. dom. 16/473, f. 50; E. 134/10 and 11
Chas. I/Hil. 27; ibid., 11 Chas. I/Mich. 39; ibid., 10 Chas. I/Mich. 66; ibid.,
1656/Mich. 26; B.L., Harleian 4127; H.L.R.O., Main Papers, 8 July 1663 petition of
the freeholders and owners of land within the soke of Horncastle.

frequent and extensive flooding.[18]

Although the fenland pastures were extensive, there was a limit to the demands that could be made upon them, and there were clear signs that that limit was being reached in some areas even before the drainers' enclosures. There were fears of a pasture shortage in the Isle of Axholme towards the end of the sixteenth century as a result of increased population and the erection of new cottages on the commons. Wildmore Fen by the early seventeenth century was apparently barely sufficient for the commoners' needs, and they were occasionally obliged to delegate two or three of their number to drive off cattle taken in by brovers because the commons were 'overcharged' and to take steps to prevent several wealthy commoners from keeping large flocks of sheep in the fen. In Holland Fen, some of the wealthier landowners (and perhaps some of the less substantial) had started to bring in cattle from other parts of the country giving rise to similar complaints of a pasture shortage.[19] Hence any schemes that further reduced the area of pasture were bound to be intensely unpopular and provoke resistance.

Commonable pasture was the most valuable of a number of exploitable fenland resources. Fish and wild fowl provided a convenient supplementary food supply which, in periods of dearth 'when greater commodities do fail', was vital 'for the relieving of hungry souls with food'. In a draft of arguments to be advanced in support of a Bill for the Great Level in 1641, it had originally been intended to make the point that fenmen lived a lazy and unproductive life 'exercising no trade nor industry but live by catching fish', but the reference to fishing was deleted after the realisation had presumably dawned that it could be turned against them. In the manor of Crowle, in the Isle of Axholme, some of the commoners had much prized copyhold fisheries, while in the adjacent Hatfield Chase the extensive rabbit population was thought crucial to the survival of the poor. The importance of fishing and fowling rights to the inhabitants of the Isle

---

[18] H. E. Hallam, *The new lands of Elloe: a study of early reclamation in Lincolnshire* (University of Leicester, occasional papers no. 6, 1954), pp. 41–2; Thirsk, *English peasant farming*, op. cit., pp. 27, 45, 78; *Agrarian History*, p. 39; Thirsk, *Fenland farming in the sixteenth century*, op. cit., pp. 11, 42, 44.

[19] Thirsk, 'The Isle of Axholme before Vermuyden' in *Agricultural History Review*, i, 1953, pp. 24–5; Thirsk, *English peasant farming*, op. cit., p. 37; P.R.O., E. 134/10 Chas. I/Mich. 66; ibid., 10 and 11 Chas. I/Hil. 27; ibid., 15 Chas. I/Trin. 6; E. 178/5433; S.P. dom. 18/37, f. 11III; Lincs. R.O., Monson 7/17/51.

of Axholme was recognised in the drainers' agreement to compensate for their loss, after drainage, by providing a grant of £400 to the parishes concerned for a provision of flax and hemp to employ the poor in making rope, netting and sackcloth.[20] The fenmen could also exploit another resource in the form of turf, sedge and dead wood which provided fuel not only for domestic purposes but also for brewing, baking, malting and similar pursuits. The fens of Cambridgeshire and the Isle of Ely furnished the neighbouring towns and countryside, including the royal court at Newmarket, with fuel, and thereby gave employment and a supplementary income to the poorer fenmen.[21] The commoners could, in addition, gather reeds to thatch their homes, dig clay and soil to manure their tenements, collect willows for weaving baskets or grow hemp and flax, for which the rich alluvial soil was particularly suitable. The latter stimulated the growth of a domestic industry of spinning and weaving and thus provided supplementary employment. However, the curing process, which involved soaking the hemp and flax in dammed sections of waterway, could prove incompatible with the maintenance of large-scale drainage and invite censure at sessions of sewers.[22] The exploitation of these varied resources was carefully regulated by fenland communities like that at Cottenham, in Cambridgeshire, where the commoners formed a village community which had purchased its freedom from manorial rights.[23]

Opponents of seventeenth-century drainage schemes categorically denied their necessity and claimed that their traditional works, dictated by local experience over the centuries, could not be improved upon and, if adequately maintained, were quite sufficient. The actual state of the fens in the early seventeenth century varied considerably from area to area, but the general picture would appear to have been that the areas drained by the Rivers Ouse and Witham were comparatively dry, while those drained by the Welland, Nene and

---

[20] *Agrarian History*, p. 405; Thirsk, 'The Isle of Axholme before Vermuyden', op. cit., pp. 22, 27; Hughes, pp. 20–1; Harris, *Vermuyden*, p. 50; Stonehouse, pp. 404–5; P.R.O., S.P. dom. 18/37, f. 11III; ibid., 16/480, f. 88; ibid., 16/362, f. 23; E. 134/1649/Mich. 11; Camb. U.L., Ely diocesan records, A/8/1, f. 80.

[21] Harris, *Vermuyden*, p. 50; Stonehouse, pp. 404–5; P.R.O., S.P. dom. 16/152, p. 84; B.L., Additional MS. 33466, f. 200; Camb. R.O., R. 59/31/9/9I, f. 9.

[22] *Agrarian History*, p. 13; Thirsk, 'The Isle of Axholme before Vermuyden', op cit., pp. 21–2; W. Camden, *Britain* (1637), p. 491; *The Anti-Projector*, p. 8; P.R.O., S.P. dom. 16/152, f. 84; E. 134/1649/Mich. 11; Notts. U.L., H.C.C. 9111, fols 103, 210.

[23] W. Cunningham (ed.), 'Common rights at Cottenham and Stretham in Cambridgeshire' in *Camden Miscellany*, xii, 1910, *passim*.

Steeping rivers were particularly liable to flooding, and were becoming progressively more so as the channels of these rivers silted up. Generally the fens were flooded during the winter months and could be 'hurtfully surrounded' at other times of the year in particularly wet seasons. The object of the new schemes was to make part of the fenland dry enough for tillage and to secure as much of the rest as possible from flooding at all times of the year so that it could be used as pasture.[24] Those who argued in favour of the traditional economy denied that their commons were often flooded in summer and welcomed seasonal flooding as a boon rather than a grievance. In the southern part of the Great Level, summer floods were allegedly a rare occurrence and the area remained flood-free the whole year round in moderate winters. Likewise, in the Hatfield Level, although floods did occasionally occur in summer, they rarely covered the ground for more than a fortnight and only affected a limited area, so that the southern part of Epworth common (an area of approximately 5000 acres) never experienced summer flooding, and in exceptionally dry summers water actually had to be let into the commons.[25] Far from being harmful, periodic flooding actually improved the quality of the pasture by enriching the land with silt. According to the commoners of Cottenham, 'unless the floods happen in summer (which is very seldom) we do find that the grounds receive more benefit than hurt thereby and are thereby much bettered and enriched, for those grounds which lie lowest and are oftenest and longest overflown in the winter season are the most fertile grounds and yield the best yearly value',[26] or, as the commoners of Lakenheath, in Suffolk, observed, 'when the fens are not overflown in winter, it causes them to be sterile and barren and to yield much less profit the year following'.[27] Similar claims of the sufficiency of traditional drainage works, and the beneficial effects of periodic flooding, were advanced in other areas.[28]

[24] Albright, p. 52.

[25] Thirsk, 'The Isle of Axholme before Vermuyden', op. cit., 25; Badeslade, pp. 78–82, 85; 'The 1636 Exchequer decree', pp. 36–7; P.R.O., S.P. dom. 14/18, f. 102; ibid., 18/37, f. 11III; E. 178/5412; E. 134/1649/Mich. 11; B.L., Harleian 6838, fols 186, 193; Camb. R.O., R. 59/31/4 no. 1, f. 28; Camb. U.L., Ely diocesan records, A/8/1, f. 49.

[26] B.L., Additional MS. 33466, f. 184.

[27] Ibid., f. 200.

[28] *Sir William Killigrew his answer*, p. 7; *The Picklock*, p. 11; *A Breviate of the Cause*, p. 2; 'The case of the lords, owners, and commoners, of 22 towns in the soke of Bolingbroke' in Thompson, *Collections*, p. 151; P.R.O., S.P. dom. 16/152, f. 84; ibid., 14/18, f. 102; E. 134/10 Chas. I/Mich. 66; ibid., 10 and 11 Chas. I/Hil. 27; B.L., Harleian 6838, f. 186; Additional MS. 33466, f. 198; Lincs. R.O., Monson 7/18/2.

The fenmen's denunciation of seventeenth-century works as at best ineffective, and at worst positively damaging, was not without foundation. *The Anti-Projector*, attacking the Earl of Bedford's works in the Great Level, complained that 'by the new drains there is very little good done, but by draining the barren North, and drowning the rich South for private ends; as will experimentally appear at the first floods which shall break out'.[29] Commoners within the Cambridgeshire manor of Over denounced works constructed by Sir Miles Sandys, junior, and others around 1630 which had resulted in the loss of 'their feeding of low grounds which are at every small rising of waters surrounded or drowned'. When, about six years later, Sir Miles and fellow sewers commissioners ordered the cutting of another new drain near the River Ouse, claiming that it would be an improvement on traditional works, the commoners were understandably sceptical and sixty-three of them journeyed to Bathing to present their case before the commissioners, yet Sir Miles 'would not permit them to speak but commanded them to be gone or else he would make a proclamation and commit them. By which means, they were compelled to part and were not heard.'[30] The chief drainage engineers squabbled among themselves as to the merits of their respective works. Andrew Burrell, a native of Wisbech, defended Bedford's scheme and denounced the work of his successor, the great Dutch engineer, Sir Cornelius Vermuyden. The former witnessed in 1642 that the level had been 'drowned, and made unfruitful for many years past', thereby confirming the accuracy of the commoners' denial of the effectiveness of Vermuyden's works, although he was convinced that the continuance of Bedford's works would have made the drainage effective.[31] Works later undertaken in the Great Level, under the 1649 Act, were also condemned as worsening, rather than improving, its drainage. Two inhabitants of Ramsey, in Huntingdonshire, complained in July 1652 that, since the works, every time the water level rose 'their grass is not only subjected to be destroyed and carried away with the floods but their cattle to be drowned which was not in former times'. Complaints of harm done to the commons by

29 *The Anti-Projector*, p. 7.

30 P.R.O., S.P. dom. 16/339, f. 45.

31 G. E. Aylmer, *The State's Servants: the Civil Service of the English Republic, 1649–60* (1973), p. 292; *Exceptions against Sir Cornelius Vermuyden's Discourse for the draining of the great Fens* (1642), *passim*; A. Burrell, *A brief relation discovering plainly the true causes why the great Level of Fens . . . have been drowned, and made unfruitful for many years past* (1642), *passim*.

new works were also voiced in other parts of the level.[32] An early eighteenth-century observer, Badeslade, judged that the southern part of the level had become in fact more liable to flooding in winter than previously, due to the erection of the Denver sluice as part of the 1630s and 1640s works. Furthermore, he concluded that 'in the Course of a very few Years, those very Works which were designed to drain the Fens (particularly the South Level) and to have made them good Winter Lands, did the Reverse, i.e. absolutely drowned the Level, now no longer Summer Land'.[33] The efficacy of works in the Hatfield Level was similarly open to doubt. A special commission awarded in 1630 to inquire into the state of the Isle of Axholme works resulted in two conflicting returns into the Exchequer and the commons were not certified as having been satisfactorily drained until Sir Thomas Wentworth and others had conducted further investigations in 1631.[34] Yet longer experience of the works led to the questioning of this judgement. Although John Lilburne, who had become involved in the commoners' cause in the early 1650s, admitted that the commons of Epworth were 'by accident . . . made somewhat drier', others protested that they had not been improved but were as subject to flooding as beforehand.[35]

A much graver charge levelled at Vermuyden in the Hatfield Level was that he had drained previously flooded, only to drown formerly dry, land. Work in Hatfield Chase did indeed produce severe flooding to the west and north-west, in an area stretching from Fishlake to Drax in the West Riding of Yorkshire. From 1629 to 1635 the privy council was bombarded with complaints from the inhabitants of Fishlake, Sykehouse, Pollington, Snaith and other adjacent places (confirmed by a certificate of West Riding justices from a quarter sessions held at Pontefract on 7 April 1630) of widespread flooding resulting in the loss of corn, hay and cattle, waterlogged arable and damaged homes and barns. Blame was laid upon a newly constructed bank which turned the waters of the Don and Aire into an inadequate channel, but drainers identified the decay and lowness of the old bank

---

[32] Camb. R.O., R. 59/31/9/9I, fols 24, 34–6, 38, 40; R. 59/31, 20–22 September [1653?] commissioners meeting at the Bear, Cambridge; R. 59/31, c. 1653–63 book of petitions to commissioners for draining the Great Level of the Fens.

[33] Badeslade, pp. 14, 22, 81–2.

[34] 'The 1636 Exchequer decree', pp. 38–9; P.R.O., E. 178/5412; ibid., 5430.

[35] Lilburne, *Epworth*, p. 6; *The declaration of Daniel Noddel*, p. 263; *A brief Remembrance When the Report concerning the pretended Riot in the Isle of Axholme shall be read* (1653); P.R.O., E. 134/1649/Mich. 11.

belonging to the flooded parishes as the culprit and urged that it be heightened and strengthened. On 12 May 1630 the board ordered everyone in the affected area to contribute £200 to Vermuyden towards the cost of strengthening the old bank which was afterwards to be maintained by yearly sewers rates assessed on the inhabitants. The problem was also referred in the following June to Wentworth, Lord Darcy and Mr Justice Hutton for local inquiry. Having twice met at Hatfield and viewed Vermuyden's works, they managed to bring both sides to an agreement in August 1630, which was to be confirmed by decree in the Exchequer and before the Council of the North. But Vermuyden subsequently refused to have the award decreed, neglected to perform the agreement and evaded attempts to sue him and his fellow drainers for damages.[36] The inhabitants estimated that they had sustained damages of at least £10 000 by 1634 from flooding so that 'the said Townships which heretofore for corn cattle and other provisions were a help to the Country, are now become so miserable poor themselves, that most of them stand in need of the Alms of others'.[37] In this area at least, the drainers' pledge to create plenty in place of poverty must have had a hollow ring. Similar desolation, with losses estimated at £5000, was reported in the vicinity of Drax, Newland and other towns to the north-west of the Chase in 1635, which was blamed on a new sluice constructed on the River Don.[38]

Flood damage as a direct consequence of new works was also reported in the north-eastern corner of Nottinghamshire, albeit on a less extensive scale than that experienced in the West Riding. Complaints emanating from Misterton could not be investigated, because of an epidemic in the town, until September 1633 when John, Earl of Clare, and Sir Gervase Clifton viewed the works and reported to the privy council that Vermuyden and his associates had done a great deal of harm, largely as a result of the blocking up of the River Idle and the diverting of its waters into Bycker's Dyke. Even the attorney-general's drainer-biased report on Misterton on 4 December 1633 frankly admitted that some previously dry cornfields had been

[36] P.R.O., P.C. 2/39, fols 183–4, 792–3; ibid., 40, fols 35, 527, 539; ibid., 41, fols 94–5; ibid., 42, fols 392–4, 584, ibid., 43, f. 152; ibid., 44, fols 561–2; S.P. dom. 16/196, f. 55.

[37] P.R.O., P.C. 2/43, fols 509–10; S.P. dom. 16/307, f. 37. The *Cal. S.P. dom., 1635–6* suggests 1635 as the date of the latter undated document but, on internal evidence, 1634 seems more likely.

[38] P.R.O., P.C. 2/45, fols 250–1; S.P. dom. 16/312, f. 87.

drowned. The inhabitants of Gringley, Everton and adjoining townships, in their November 1633 petition to the King, claimed that their meadows and commons had been drowned for five consecutive years owing to the works, with damages running at £1550 a year. Further north, the inhabitants of Misson alleged that the blocking of a traditional waterway had rendered the freeholds of Misson, and the adjacent towns, subject to drowning while their commons received no benefit from the works.[39]

Complaints about the ineffectiveness of new works, or the consequent flooding of formerly dry land, were voiced elsewhere. In the Lindsey Level, even parts of the uplands and corn lands were said to have been rendered flood-prone, 'so they drown us to drain us, but the remedy is worse then the disease'. Blame was apportioned between the new drains, which lacked the descent of the old, and the selfishness of the Earl of Lindsey in draining his own part at the cost of flooding the commoners' portion. No less a personage than Theophilus, Earl of Lincoln, petitioned the House of Lords, on 19 November 1640, bemoaning the fact that fens belonging to five of his manors within the level were, as a result of the bank made to safeguard Lindsey's grounds, upon every flood 'sooner and longer and deeper surrounded then it hath been heretofore within any man's memory' and that the town of Swaton was in danger of being overwhelmed. Admittedly the Earl of Lincoln may have been acting out of pique, having previously lost out to Lindsey in a struggle for the drainage contract, yet confirmation of the poor state of the level in the spring of 1640 is contained in a letter written by one of the drainers' own agents in which it was observed that 'there hath not been known such floods this 60 years as have been within this week'.[40] The inhabitants of Waddingham and Snitterby, whose fens were included in the Ancholme Level, raised similar protests, especially when the winter of 1639–40 brought deeper and more extensive flooding than anyone could recall.[41]

Both in the losses sustained during the actual construction of works, and in the frequent allegations of the inequitable, or even un-

[39] P.R.O., S.P. dom. 16/246, f. 65; ibid., 252, f. 17; ibid., 250, f. 55; P.C. 2/43, f. 374; Notts. R.O., P.R. 2313 and P.R. 2321.
[40] L. Stone, *The crisis of the aristocracy, 1558–1641* (Oxford, 1965), p. 356; *The Picklock*, pp. 11, 13–14; *Sir William Killigrew his answer*, p. 9; P.R.O., S.P. dom. 16/416, f. 5; ibid., 450, f. 97; H.L.R.O., Main Papers, 19 November 1640 petition of Theophilus, Earl of Lincoln.
[41] Lincs. R.O., Monson 7/18/2.

lawful, nature of the subsequent divisions and enclosures, the fenmen had ample additional grounds for grievance. Works and enclosures in the Ancholme Level, it was claimed, not only deprived the fenmen of a substantial part of their commons 'but also some of their several freehold and Lands of inheritance are digged away enclosed cut through spoiled and taken away from them without giving or allowing them any recompense for the same'.[42] The inhabitants of Misterton were compelled to allow the drainers to cut works through some of their several grounds, while in nearby Misson the drainers were accused of encroaching upon that part of the commons left to the inhabitants as they enclosed their own allotted grounds, and in neither case was there any compensation.[43] The drainers' enclosure of 'very many' several grounds belonging to a number of landowners near the West Fen prompted one, Robert Barkham, esquire, to challenge their action. He was proceeded against and imprisoned for his defiance until the Long Parliament, declaring the action taken against him and his imprisonment as illegal, found in his favour.[44]

The actual allocation of respective portions once drainage had been judged completed raised a storm of protest from commoners. Those of Epworth insisted that the drainers had taken the best land and left them the poorest, so that 1 acre of the drainers' land was of greater value than 3 acres of that allotted to the commoners.[45] This complaint was echoed in the nearby manor of Crowle where Vermuyden was reported to have left the commoners with the lower, more flood-prone, parts of the fens.[46] Superior land in the East Fen, conveniently adjacent to the towns, was allegedly enclosed by the drainers, leaving the poorer residue to the commoners. The lord of one of the manors on the edge of this fen, Thorpe near Wainfleet, claimed that the one-third enclosed by the drainers there was equal in value to the commoners' two-thirds.[47] Similar complaints emanated from the Great Level and on one occasion at least, in July 1652, adjudication commissioners, appointed under the 1649 Act, acknowledged the justice of the charge levelled by two Cambridgeshire towns of an

[42] Ibid.
[43] P.R.O., S.P. dom. 16/246, f. 65; P.C. 2/43, f. 375; Notts. R.O., P.R. 2321.
[44] P.R.O., S.P. dom. 16/473, f. 50.
[45] J.L., *A Discourse concerning the great benefit of Draining and embanking*, op cit., p. 9; Lilburne, *Epworth*, p. 2; P.R.O., E. 134/1649/Mich. 11.
[46] P.R.O., E. 134/9 Chas. I/Mich. 56; ibid., 1649/Mich. 11.
[47] P.R.O., S.P. dom. 16/375, f. 43; H.L.R.O., Main Papers [1640] petition of Edward Ironside, gentleman.

'unequal and undue setting out' of fenland and took steps to rectify the situation.[48] The Lindsey Level drainers strenuously denied such charges for they had taken their allotment 'in the very middle which was generally the lowest part and very sink of the Fens', farthest away from the towns and the inhabitants' several grounds. But they faced an added charge of having taken more land than they were entitled to; they were accused of enclosing at least 230 acres more than they had been allotted in Dunsby Fen and of putting pressure on the commoners to accept the equivalent acreage elsewhere. In the fens of Donington, Horbling and Billingborough, it was the officers responsible for the division of land who were criticised for mistakenly allotting the drainers more than 350 acres in excess of their entitlement there, while allotting commoners a lesser quantity in adjoining fens.[49]

The cumulative effect of the drainage schemes, and the subsequent enclosure of substantial portions of fenland commons, impaired the ability of the fenman to exploit successfully the resources of his local environment in the time-honoured manner and arguably left him considerably worse off. A pasture shortage, already in evidence before the advent of new schemes, was greatly exacerbated after drainage and enclosure. The commons of Epworth, barely meeting the demand for pasture prior to enclosure, were said to have maintained only half the previous stock after it, and commoners were frequently forced to joyst cattle outside the Isle of Axholme or convert their meadow into pasture, with some even selling their estates as a direct consequence of reduced pasturage.[50] Crowle commoners complained of a serious shortage of pasture after the allocation of Vermuyden's one-third, with many inhabitants constrained to hire joyst from Dutch settlers or local gentry, or to feed their cattle upon their several grounds. This complaint did not go unchallenged for one of the local gentry and a Crowle 'husbandman' asserted that, following successful drainage, formerly drowned land had become pasturable, and the commons supported over 200 additional cattle

---

[48] Camb. U.L., Additional MS. 22, f. 88; Camb. R.O., R. 59/31/9/9I, fols 13–15, 17, 20, 22–5, 29–31, 46; ibid., R. 59/31.

[49] *Sir William Killigrew his answer*, pp. 8–9, 13; *The Picklock*, p. 11; P.R.O., S.P. dom. 16/416, f. 71; ibid., 279, f. 99; H.L.R.O., Main Papers, 10 August 1641 petition of the governors of Charterhouse Hospital.

[50] *The declaration of Daniel Noddel*, p. 263; *A brief Remembrance When the Report concerning the pretended Riot in the Isle of Axholme shall be read*, op cit.; P.R.O., S.P. dom. 18/37, f. 11III; E. 134/1649/Mich. 11.

and produced a further 300 loads of hay.[51] This Crowle husbandman was one of those who had been guilty of over-burdening the commons with large flocks of sheep, and had been badly assaulted by a number of commoners on one occasion when he had tried to prevent the removal of his sheep. Had he been in the Lindsey Level, he would have been anti-, rather than pro-drainer, according to Sir William Killigrew's analysis, so that he could continue to over-burden the commons. Across the border in Nottinghamshire, the commoners of Misson were similarly driven to feed their cattle on their several grounds, and elsewhere, for lack of pasture after enclosure.[52] A slightly more complex situation obtained in Misterton, where the inhabitants were deprived of a valued area of common which had been the subject of litigation in the reign of Elizabeth I, with Misterton commoners claiming that it lay in Nottinghamshire and was called North Carr, while those of Epworth called it Haxey Carr and claimed it as Lincolnshire ground. The verdict had gone against Misterton, and yet part of this common continued to be inter-commoned by the inhabitants of both manors until it was allotted to Epworth by the drainers as part of the commoners' portion, with the resultant loss of vital pasturage to Misterton.[53]

Where new works were successful in draining the fens, the effects could be far from beneficial. Parts of the Lindsey Level were allegedly drained so dry that the commoners were forced to buy water for their cattle during the summer season and to drive them a considerable distance to water them, and the amount of fodder they could derive from the fens, on which to winter their cattle, was also reduced when they were deprived of the beneficial effects of periodic land floods.[54] The draining of meres and streams, and the rechannelling of water-ways, deprived some commoners of their fish and wildfowl and adversely affected local transport and communications. In the manor of Crowle, valuable 'fishings', said to be worth £300 a year to the copyhold fishermen, were lost by drainage, although 100 acres of common was set aside for them as compensation.[55] Cambridge and King's Lynn were particularly hostile to works in the Great Level that

[51] P.R.O., E. 134/9 Chas. I/Mich. 56; ibid., 1649/Mich. 11.
[52] Notts. R.O., P.R. 2313.
[53] P.R.O., S.P. dom. 16/246, f. 65; P.C. 2/43, f. 375; E. 178/5412; S.P. dom. 18/37, f. 11III.
[54] *The Picklock*, pp. 11, 13.
[55] P.R.O., E. 134/9 Chas. I/Mich. 56; ibid., 1649/Trin. 2; ibid., East. 5.

led to a deterioration of their navigation, and similar complaints, including even the total loss of navigable rivers, were voiced by the inhabitants of Brandon and Thetford, in Suffolk and Norfolk, of Fletton, in Huntingdonshire, and of Soham, in Cambridgeshire.[56] The blocking up of the River Idle, as part of the Hatfield Level scheme, meant the loss of an important navigable river for the Isle of Axholme and Misterton and its neighbourhood, with the latter area being forced to transport commodities by a longer, and hence more expensive, route.[57] Communications over shorter distances were also impeded as works and enclosures made access to neighbouring towns, or even several grounds and commons, difficult. The inhabitants of Belton in Axholme were cut off from the next market town to the north, as well as their turbary grounds, by the construction of a new river, and works in Misterton placed obstacles in the way of access to some several grounds. In the Ancholme Level, new works were reported to have made the commoners' access to their commons arduous, entailing long detours along routes that were 'so straight and deep with mire and dirt as they cannot drive their cattle to them and get their fodder therein without great danger of their cattle and great labour and trouble'.[58]

Finally, the contribution that drainage was said to have made to local employment, and the reduction of poverty, does not survive close scrutiny. Dutch and French workmen were imported at the very outset for the drainage of the Hatfield Level and subsequently settled there to engage in arable husbandry. Archbishop Neile of York, who was openly hostile to the introduction of the French Church into England, lamented in June 1636 the way in which the drainers exclusively employed Frenchmen and a few Dutchmen. He estimated that about 200 alien families had been planted in the Hatfield Level, and additional ship-loads of settlers were on their way to 'take the bread out of the mouths of English subjects by overbidding them in the rents of the land that they hold, and doing more work for a groat than an Englishman can do for 6d'. Immigrants planted a virtually

[56] C. H. Cooper, *Annals of Cambridge* (Cambridge, 1845), iii, 275; Badeslade, pp. 14, 53, 54–5, 55–7; B.L., Additional MS. 5813, f. 113; Camb. R.O., R. 59/31/9/9I, fols 9, 31, 42.
[57] Lilburne, *Epworth*, p. 6; P.R.O., E. 178/5412; S.P. dom. 16/246, f. 65; P.C. 2/43, f. 374.
[58] Notts. U.L., H.C.C. 6001, f. 9; P.R.O., S.P. dom. 16/246, f. 65; P.C. 2/43, f. 376; Lincs. R.O., Monson 7/18/2.

new settlement at Santoft where the French congregation in 1645 numbered over a thousand.[59] Although Archbishop Neile probably overstated his case, and the scale of the demand for labour inevitably necessitated the employment of local, as well as foreign, workmen, the benefits proved short-lived as wages soon fell into serious arrears. West Riding justices were inundated with complaints about unpaid wages from over a thousand drainage employees in 1633, and the arrears were reckoned to be in excess of £1500 by 1635. Failing to comply with a payment order from the Council of the North, Vermuyden and his associates were sued to a writ of rebellion and, on 8 May 1635, were ordered by the privy council to be proceeded against at York if they failed to satisfy wage arrears. Throughout the 1640s and 1650s complaints of sizeable arrears continued as craftsmen and officers, as well as ordinary labourers, were reduced to penury, with the officers facing the added burden of lawsuits commenced by their employees.[60]

Almost the same situation obtained in the Great Level where, following the first season of the Bedford works, a group of about 250 labourers complained of unpaid wages. Their arrears totalled just over £399 and the salary of the paymaster, who had set them on work, was over £27 in arrears. Towards the end of 1638, after the intervention of the privy council, the workmen received some of their back-pay plus a promise of payment in full once the arrears of drainage taxes had been paid in. Yet in the following March and May the board again received complaints of substantial wage arrears. Master-workmen appointed when the King superseded Bedford protested that, having engaged 800 labourers, they had received nothing from the expenditor general, John Latch (rumoured to have had £7000 of the King's money in his hands), and had been forced to provide for them while awaiting payment of £3500 in arrears. By 1641 the arrears had risen to about £5000, leaving many of the master-workmen, and others involved, facing ruin as they were either committed to prison for debt or forced to sell their homes and goods to meet the wage bills.[61]

---

[59] G. H. Overend, 'The first thirty years of the foreign settlement in Axholme, 1626–56' in *Proceedings of the Huguenot Society of London*, ii, 1889, p. 302; P.R.O., P.C. 2/40, f. 115; S.P. dom. 16/327, f. 47; H.L.R.O., Main Papers, 15 November 1645 petition of Peter Berchett, minister, and others.
[60] P.R.O., S.P. dom. 16/279, f. 97; P.C. 2/44, fols 561–2; Notts. U.L., H.C.C. 6001, fols 184, 357, 522; ibid., 6002, fols 81, 281.
[61] *Fenland notes and queries*, vi, 6–7; P.R.O., S.P. dom. 16/533, f. 122; P.C. 2/49, fols 563–5, 591; ibid., 50, fols 159–60, 341–2; Camb. R.O., R. 59/31/9/5, fols 75–7.

Workmen mutinied in October 1649 and seized their officers, threatening to 'carry them away, and cut them in pieces, in case they have not speedy payment'. But the meeting of wage bills in full had by then become impossible for drainage taxes were also well in arrears and purchasers for defaulters' lands were not forthcoming. Even when, in the summer of 1651, a pay day had taken place, the workmen's satisfaction soon turned to anger upon the discovery that they had been paid in clipped money. The company were obliged to dash off a letter to be read before them denying that it had ever been their intention to pay them in anything but good money in an attempt to assuage their anger. Wages continued to fall into arrears during the 1650s, and pay days were sufficiently irregular occurrences to merit a pleasing record by the company as when, in April 1652, they welcomed the news of a pay day at Sutton, in the Isle of Ely, because elsewhere wages had not been paid for fourteen, or perhaps as many as nineteen, consecutive weeks, leading men to desert the works. One of the agents responsible for recruiting workmen in Cambridgeshire implored the company in December 1655 to 'take off that danger that lies upon me by not paying the workmen their money which I cannot but acknowledge to be justly due unto them. I cannot be in any place but they are about me for their money and to speak the truth they are very much abused and more then hundreds of them ready to starve.' Yet in the following February it was still being reported that 'the workmen are in great want of money and thinks it very long a coming'.[62] The future progress of the Lindsey Level scheme was being imperilled in 1640 by unpaid wages as the drainers ran short of money.[63] Far from drainage bringing prosperity to the East and West Fens, the commoners moaned that they 'were never pestered with beggars and thieves, more than in the time of their undertaking'. They may have had in mind the large numbers of workmen whom the mayor and burgesses of Boston described, in 1640, as a 'multitude of dykers poor indigent fellows but of strong and able bodies' who could be expected to descend into 'riotous disorders' once the trained band had left for York.[64]

---

[62] Camb. R.O., R. 59/31/9, no. 1, f. 30; R. 59/31/9/2; R. 59/31/9/3, f. 5; R. 59/31/9/5, fols 99, 206, 239; R. 59/31/9/9I, f. 11; Records of Bedford Level: correspondence various, 1655–87; ibid., accounts 1656.

[63] P.R.O., S.P. dom. 16/450, f. 97; ibid., 453, f. 116.

[64] 'The case of the lords, owners, and commoners, of 22 towns in the soke of Bolingbroke' in Thompson, *Collections,* p. 151; P.R.O., S.P. dom. 16/461, f. 71.

The fens of eastern England in the early seventeenth century attracted the attention of enterprising men who saw in fenland drainage opportunities for a profitable return upon their investment of money and expertise. Denigrating the traditional fenland economy, and denouncing their local opponents as at best self-interested and at worst feckless and inert, they made extravagant claims of the advantages accruing from their various schemes, which were often difficult to sustain and were decidedly far from self-evident to fenland commoners. The latter had for centuries exploited the varied resources of their fens in a way that enabled them to sustain a livelihood which compared not unfavourably with the peasantry of other regions, and had engaged as a community in the maintenance of old, and construction of new, works to avert destructive flooding.

1   The Fenland Undertakings

THE seventeenth century fenland schemes may be divided into four main sections which take account of the composition of the original undertakers and the nature and chronology of each enterprise. The first section is devoted to the Hatfield Level, the earliest of the major schemes; the second to the Great Level alongside which has been added the Deeping Level which, although the subject of distinct schemes from the late Elizabethan period, was effectively linked by geography and undertakership with the massive enterprise to the south; the third, to the Ancholme Level, the smallest enterprise; and the fourth, to three schemes (the East, West and Wildmore Fens; the Lindsey Level; and the Holland Fen) where a courtier group played a key role.

The Hatfield Level

The Hatfield Level, on the borders of Yorkshire, Lincolnshire and Nottinghamshire, contained an area of approximately 70 000 acres of fenland. Charles I, as lord of the four principal manors of Hatfield, Epworth, Crowle and Misterton, and of thirteen other adjacent manors, originally contracted with the Dutch engineer, Cornelius Vermuyden, on 24 May 1626 to drain Hatfield Chase, in the western part of the level, but the Isle of Axholme to the east was later included in the scheme. The Crown's chief interest in drainage was undoubtedly finacial: Charles had been persuaded that he could increase his revenue from these estates while coincidentally serving 'the general good' of the commonwealth.[1]

In contracting with Vermuyden, the King had made choice of a man of great resolution who ruthlessly, and, when necessary, unscrupulously pursued his objectives with scant regard for criticism and apparent indifference to the unpopularity which he deservedly

---

[1] Albright, pp. 55–6, 62; Hunter, *South Yorkshire,* i, pp. 153, 160; J. Thirsk, 'The Isle of Axholme before Vermuyden', p. 25, note 2; J. Korthals-Altes, *Sir Cornelius Vermuyden* (1925), appendix II, pp. 5–10; P.R.O., P.C. 2/38, f. 514; Notts. U.L., H.C.C. 9111, f. 8.

earned in most of the enterprises with which he was associated. Vermuyden was able to conduct himself in this manner with impunity largely due to the patronage that he secured from both James I and Charles I and the presence of powerful supporters at Court. One particularly useful ally was Sir Robert Heath, the attorney-general from 1625 until his appointment as chief justice of Common Pleas in 1631. Vermuyden and Heath came to be associated together in a number of other enterprises, apart from fenland drainage, in which the latter did not always resist the temptation to use his official position to further their business alliance. Of immediate relevance is the fact that it was Heath who around 1625 drew up the document that explored ways of increasing the royal revenue and included fenland drainage as one of its proposals.[2]

In order to understand the varying response of the commoners in this level to drainage and enclosure, it is important to note that there were essential differences between the situation obtaining in Hatfield Chase and the manor of Crowle, in the northern part of the Isle of Axholme, and that in the rest of the Isle. In Hatfield Chase, where the inhabitants were predominantly copyholders, disafforestation had preceded drainage and common rights were not nearly so extensive as in the neighbouring Isle. A majority of the 'better sort' of inhabitants of the Chase were reported to have submitted to both disafforestation and drainage and to have acquiesced in the allocation of enclosures.[3] The manor of Crowle, annexed by the King after the dissolution of the monasteries to Hatfield Chase and placed under the control of its officers, was leased by Charles I to the corporation of the City of London from whom it was purchased by Sir Jervis Elwes, Jeremy Elwes and Nicholas Hamerton, esquires. Most of the inhabitants of Crowle were copyholders with turbary rights inherited from the dissolved abbey of Selby and a number of copyhold fisheries. The commoners apparently accepted the allotment of a third of their commons to Vermuyden (at least until the very changed circumstances of 1651) but only after they had been threatened by one of the lords of the manor with the withdrawal of his assistance and protection. Leadership of the Crowle commoners was assumed by Henry Rutter, gentleman, a former royal bailiff of the manor. Following a suit commenced in the

[2] Harris, *Vermuyden*, pp. 43, 55, 57–8, 117–18, 120, 140.
[3] J. W. Gough, *The rise of the entrepreneur* (1969), p. 255; Harris, *Vermuyden*, p. 50; J. Tomlinson, *The Level of Hatfield Chase and parts adjacent* (Doncaster, 1882), p. 90; P.R.O., S.P. dom. 14/180, f. 82; E. 178/5960.

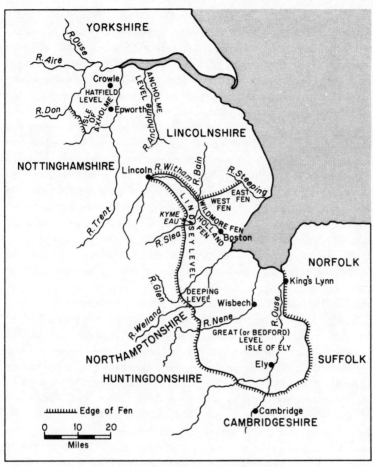

Map 1 The Fenland undertakings

Exchequer in 1629 by the attorney-general (on Vermuyden's behalf)
against Rutter and other commoners, commissioners were appointed
who, meeting at Crowle on 12 August 1629, set out 600 acres for
Vermuyden and left over 1000 acres to the commoners. Nicholas
Hamerton pressurised the commoners into accepting the division by
allegedly threatening those present with the words, 'Masters either
stand to the part and allotment and order that the Commissioners
make for you Else I will leave you to your selves and do what you
can.' When the commissioners' award was later decreed in the
Exchequer, Rutter attended and consented to the decree as the
commoners' representative. Yet initially the latter were by no means
unanimous that he should act in that capacity. According to
one report, when Rutter had urged the commoners in the parish
church to raise money for his expenses prior to his departure for London, they refused either to meet his expenses or consent to the decree.
However, most of the commoners did eventually agree to his acting
as their representative and a document was drawn up to that effect.
Although most of them did contribute to his expenses on his return,
there still remained a hard-core of commoners who refused.[4]

The position of commoners in the predominant manor in the Isle,
Epworth, was markedly different to those of Hatfield and Crowle.
Epworth had a large body of freeholders and its commoners had
rights with legally recognised safeguards originating in an agreement
of Sir John Mowbray, in the reign of Edward III, whereby Sir John, as
the then manorial lord, in return for their consent to his enclosure
of part of the commons, granted the commoners the remainder free
from any further improvements by the lord or his successors. This
agreement was enshrined in an indenture dated 31 May 1359, a
document treasured by the commoners and carefully preserved in the
parish church of Haxey in a specially prepared chest bound with iron.
The keys to the chest were entrusted to some of the chief freeholders,
and the whole parish were kept regularly aware of the document's
existence as the chest was placed under a window which depicted Sir
John Mowbray holding a document, commonly reputed to represent
the indenture. At least one of the local gentry had a copy of the deed
in his custody, and a local yeoman testified to having been shown the
original in his youth and instructed as to its substance, presumably

[4] Harris, *Vermuyden*, p. 50; Stonehouse, pp. 404–5; P.R.O., E. 134/9 Chas. I/Mich.
56; ibid., 10 Chas. I/Mich. 1; ibid., 1649/Trin. 2.

with the express intention of preparing him for such future testimony. Hence Epworth commoners were fully conscious of their unassailable legal position on the question of title, and they, and their legal advisers, were adamant that since the Mowbray agreement successive lords of the manor, including Charles I, had no right to encroach upon their commons and hence acted illegally when they attempted to do so without the full prior consent of the commoners. This conviction was voiced in the first major riot against drainers in the Isle by irate commoners exclaiming that 'they cared not for the king for their lands were their own and he had nothing to do with them'. For nearly a century successive Epworth spokesmen repeatedly insisted that the King had possessed no right of improvement in their commons; that the grant to Vermuyden had been illegal; and that the drainers who had first entered their commons had been the actual rioters.[5]

The consent of the commoners of Epworth would have given legality to the extension of the drainage scheme over their fens, and successive drainage supporters claimed that this consent had in fact been gained. The drainers' claim became the subject of a lengthy and bitter controversy between themselves and the commoners. Issue was joined over two related questions: how far consent had been freely given by, or extorted from the commoners; and how representative, if at all, were those commoners who had consented? In Charles I's original grant to Vermuyden authorising the enclosure and improvement of 7400 out of a total of 13 400 acres of Epworth commons, it was stipulated that agreement was to be reached with the commoners three months before work started. Yet no such agreement could at this stage be secured from commoners who valued their fens as they were and felt their position assured by virtue of the Mowbray deed. Impatient of delay, Vermuyden dispatched workmen into Haxey Carr in August 1628 and thereby provoked a series of riots, including

---

[5] Korthals-Altes, op. cit., pp. 14–17, 110–11, appendix I, pp. 1–4; Tomlinson, op. cit., p. 90; Stonehouse, pp. 77–8, 111; G. H. Overend, 'The first thirty years of the foreign settlement in Axholme, 1626–56' in *Proceedings of the Huguenot Society of London,* ii, p. 316; Lilburne, *Epworth,* pp. 1–2; *The declaration of Daniel Noddel,* pp. 258, 259–62; *The great complaint,* pp. 271–2, 275; P.R.O., E. 178/5412; ibid., 5960; E. 134/1649/Mich. 11; ibid., 1 and 2 Jas. II/Hil. 25; S.P. dom. 16/113, f. 38I; H.L.R.O., Main Papers, [11 November] 1647 petition of the inhabitants of the manor of Epworth to the House of Lords; Notts. U.L., H.C.C. 9111, fols 124, 210–11; ibid., 6002, f. 132; ibid., 8939, fols 1–2; Lincs. R.O., Monson 7/17/52.

one in which a commoner was shot dead by his agents.[6] In Michaelmas term of the same year, Vermuyden's friend, attorney-general
Heath, exhibited a Bill in the Exchequer against several Epworth
tenants in which the King's right, as lord of the manor, to enclose and
improve the 7400 acres was asserted. The defendants responded by
insisting on their title to the whole 13 400 acres under the Mowbray
agreement and denying the King's right of improvement. Shortly
afterwards, a special Exchequer commission was awarded for a
further attempt to secure the commoners' agreement and to allocate
Vermuyden's and the King's respective portions whether the
commoners consented or not. From their meeting at Gainsborough
on 9 September 1629, the commissioners reported that 'many of the
better sort' of commoner present consented to the King's proposals
and 'some others', who would also have publicly consented had they
not been afraid of their neighbours' wrath, were ready to subscribe to
any document testifying to their free consent, but 'the poorest and
meanest sort' of commoner was implacably opposed to any such
agreement. Having failed in their first task, the commissioners
proceeded, as instructed, to set out Vermuyden's third part (over
4000 acres) and suggested that of the remainder the commoners
should receive 6000, and the King 2620 acres.[7]

Renewed rioting greeted the attempt to enclose the allotted
grounds in Epworth, and it was at this point, according to the
commoners, that agreement under duress replaced earlier attempts at
agreement by free consent. A number of commoners involved in
riotous attack upon drainage works and enclosures in the Isle in 1628
and 1629 were the subject of Star Chamber proceedings, resulting in
massive fines being imposed upon fourteen convicted rioters (five
men and nine women) in Michaelmas term 1631. Four of the men
were fined £1000 each, and the fifth, 500 marks, while one of the
women was fined £500, and the rest, 500 marks each. Vermuyden
was also awarded 2000 marks in damages, and substantial penalties
were set upon Haxey and other towns in the manor of Epworth for

[6] 'The 1636 Exchequer decree', p. 40; *An answer to the Case of the Commoners of the Manor
Epworth . . . Published in Opposition to the Bill for making the Statutes of Edw. 1 and Edw. 6
against Destroying Improvements more Effectual* (undated); W. Dugdale, *The history of
imbanking and draining of divers fens and marshes* (2nd ed., 1772), pp. 144–5; Lilburne,
Epworth, pp. 1–2; Notts. U.L., H.C.C. 8939, f. 2; P.R.O., S.P. dom. 16/113, fols 38,
381–IV.
[7] 'The 1636 Exchequer decree', pp. 36–8; P.R.O., E. 178/5969; Notts, U.L., H.C.C.
8939, f. 2; Lincs, R.O., Monson 7/17/51.

destroying enclosures.[8] Although the charge was firmly denied, the commoners interpreted these fines as a deliberate tactic on Vermuyden's part to force some of them to consent to a decree confirming the enclosures, and acknowledging the benefits of drainage, in return for a remission of unendurable penalties. Faced with ruin, and urged on by one John Newland, 'who, though a Commoner, was underhand Solicitor for the Participants', four of the convicted commoners allegedly entered into a secret compact to appear to a new Exchequer Bill, to be exhibited by Vermuyden in Trinity term 1632, against themselves, Newland and other commoners (totalling twenty-two in all) and, on behalf of all the tenants of Haxey, confess the substance of the Bill to be true. By this means, Vermuyden managed to extract from the commoners concerned an acknowledgement that the draining had been effective and a form of consent to the subsequent enclosures. A Belton weaver was to recall much later how Star Chamber fines and imprisonment had forced some of the commoners to capitulate to the drainers out of concern for their wives and children.[9] The rest of the commoners strenuously denied that Newland and his associates had acted in a representative capacity and commenced Star Chamber proceedings against them for their presumption. For this, and other offences, committed on the inhabitants of Epworth, Newland and the others were sentenced to stand on the pillory, in the neighbouring market towns, displaying papers describing their offences, and one miscreant was fined £500 and sentenced to go before the Exchequer Bar, with a paper in his hat, and there acknowledge that he had given the court false answers to the prejudice of Epworth commoners. But these offenders 'escaped the shame and punishment due unto them (by tampering with and taking off the prosecutors) by reason whereof the Sentence was omitted to be entered'.[10]

As a counter to the Epworth commoners' denigration of the new works, the attorney-general, on reference from the Exchequer,

[8] Spittlehouse, *The Case and Appeal*, pp. 2–3; 'The 1636 Exchequer decree', pp. 42–3; J. Rushworth, *Historical Collections* (1721), iii, appendix, pp. 39–40; P.R.O., S.P. dom. 16/362, f. 103; Lincs. R.O., Monson 7/17/51; Notts. U.L., H.C.C. 8939, f. 2.

[9] 'The 1636 Exchequer decree', pp. 42–4; *The Case of the Manor of Epworth in the Isle of Axholme, in the County of Lincoln, concerned in the Bill for an Act for settling the Level of Hatfield Chase* (undated); P.R.O., E. 134/1649/Mich. 11; Lincs. R.O., Monson 7/17/51; Notts. U.L., H.C.C. 8939, fols 2–3.

[10] *The Case of the Manor of Epworth . . . concerned in the Bill for an Act for settling the Level of Hatfield Chase*; Lincs. R.O., Monson 7/17/51; Notts. U.L., H.C.C. 8939, f. 3.

recommended that the participants should be allowed to plough and sow the land in order to demonstrate the draining's effectiveness. But, with the approach of harvest, there was more violence resulting in another Star Chamber Bill.[11] Up to this point, Vermuyden and his allies had derided their opponents as men of low social standing, yet in Easter term 1633 propaganda surrendered to fact when Edmund, Lord Sheffield, and Ralph Eure of Washingbrough, in Lincolnshire, esquire, the greatest freeholders of Epworth manor, and two other esquires, Robert Ryther of Belton and William Gregory of Barmby upon Don, in Yorkshire, exhibited an Exchequer Bill on behalf of themselves and the rest of the Epworth commoners. The object of the Bill was to cross all the former Exchequer proceedings concerning the Epworth commons and to establish how Vermuyden had pressurised a few commoners into submitting to enclosure by threatening to implement the 1631 Star Chamber sentence. Vermuyden appeared and denied the charges but, as the plaintiffs were preparing to go to commission to examine witnesses, proceedings were stopped.[12]

Further attacks upon drainage works and enclosures in May 1634 led to the initiation of yet more legal proceedings. The participants portrayed the attacks as serious offences committed at night and in-volving large numbers of unidentifiable offenders, but they may in fact have been simply entries made by one commoner to try his title. Nevertheless, they resulted in an award of £2500 damages in King's Bench leviable by distress upon all villages within the manor of Epworth. Although some goods were distrained, the King's Bench action, like the Star Chamber proceedings, was another attempt at coercion. Those commoners who submitted to the attorney-general's award and the Exchequer decree confirming the enclosures were to be immune from the levying of distresses (an arrangement that received the Exchequer's approbation in their order of 13 February 1636 to the sheriff of Lincolnshire), and those who had already suffered distraints were to be reimbursed upon submission.[13] The commoners' solicitor was also said to have received a bribe of £80 to collect about 370 signatures in the locality to a document pledging acquiescence in the

[11] 'The 1636 Exchequer decree', pp. 41–2; Lincs. R.O., Monson 7/17/51.
[12] Hughes, p. 18; 'The 1636 Exchequer decree', pp. 42–4; P.R.O., E. 178/5430; Lincs. R.O., Monson 7/17/51.
[13]Lilburne, *Epworth*, p. 3; P.R.O., K.B. 29/284/152, 164, 187 dorso, 208, 215 dorso; ibid., 295/74–74 dorso, 76–76 dorso, 110; E. 134/24 Chas. I/East. 4; ibid., 1649/Mich. 11; Lincs. R.O., Monson 7/17/51.

attorney-general's award. Dismissing any notion of a free and voluntary subscription, the commoners insisted that some signatures had been obtained under threat of distraint for the damages awarded in King's Bench; others by their solicitor's duplicity in misinforming them that they were merely signing a note authorising action for removing their fines; and many more signatures had been forged or people had signed more than once. Two of the participants' agents and a few imprisoned commoners were said to have subscribed most of the names. When one of the latter, Hezekiah Browne, returned to the Isle and informed his neighbours that 'he had made bold with their names to the reference', they upbraided him that 'he was more bold than welcome and that they gave him no thanks for his pains'. The commoners were demonstrably on firm ground in their denial that the subscribers constituted a major part of their number. Assuming that all the signatories had common rights in Epworth (and it was protested that less than one-third actually did so and they were 'of the meanest sort'), they were said to have constituted less than one-seventh of the total commoners. Contemporary estimates of that total varied between 1200 and 2000, making the subscribers a minority of between 30.8 per cent and 18.5 per cent, which, although greater than the estimated one-seventh, still constituted a minority, with no mandate to commit the rest.[14]

The award of the attorney-general, Sir John Banks, of 7 June 1636 (decreed in the Exchequer on 18 June) broadly confirmed the previous division of the commons, with a few palliatives for the commoners: the addition of Epworth South Moor; the liberty to crave a royal pardon to remove the King's Bench distresses; and the allocation of £400 by the participants to provide a stock to employ the poor.[15] Hence by 1636 the participants had achieved their principal objectives: the commons of Epworth had been enclosed and respective portions allotted; the commoners had been prevented from obtaining a trial of title under the Mowbray agreement; and a form of 'consent' had been extracted from some of them. When Lilburne later

[14] Stonehouse, pp. 76–7; Lilburne, *Epworth*, pp. 3–4; *The Case of the Manor of Epworth . . . concerned in the Bill for an Act for settling the Level of Hatfield Chase*, op. cit.; *The declaration of Daniel Noddel*, p. 258; *A brief Remembrance When the Report concerning the pretended Riot in the Isle of Axholme shall be read* (1653); P.R.O., E. 134/1 and 2 Jas. II/Hil. 25; Lincs. R.O., Monson 7/17/51; Notts. U.L., H.C.C. 8939, fols 2–3.

[15] Hunter, *South Yorkshire,* i, 166; 'The 1636 Exchequer decree', pp. 44–5; Notts. U.L., H.C.C. 8939, f. 3; Lincs. R.O., Monson 7/17/51 in which the author claims that the money was never in fact set aside for the poor.

took up the Epworth cause, he explained, rather than justified, the riots against the drainers as acts of desperation committed by people deprived of legal remedy and subjected to violence and oppression.[16] One important way of testing the legality of recent enclosures was by use of writs of replevin. By this procedure, commoners drove cattle into enclosed grounds to be impounded for trespass whereupon writs of replevin were obtained by the commoners (requiring the redelivery of the cattle in return for a pledge to try the right of distraint) in order to have a legal trial of whether or not they were trespassers. Yet the likelihood of such a trial going against the participants led them to procure an Exchequer order of 21 November 1634 staying all commoner suits on present, and prohibiting future, writs of replevin in the Isle.[17] The confidence of the Epworth commoners in their legal position under the Mowbray agreement, coupled with their inability to establish their title by peaceful means owing to the drainers' evasive manoeuvres (as they themselves resorted to coercion), irresistibly pushed the commoners in a violent direction.

The inhabitants of two other manors within the level, Crowle and Misson, were also subjected to a certain amount of pressure to gain a form of consent to drainage and enclosure. It has already been noted how Crowle commoners were induced to agree to Vermuyden's enclosures by a virtual ultimatum by one of the manorial lords, and that even then they were by no means unanimous. An Exchequer commission awarded to John, Lord Savile, and others to reach agreement with the commoners preceded the drainage of Misson. The commissioners felt able to report on 10 September 1629 that 'some of the better sort' of inhabitants, negotiated with as though representative of the generality of Misson commoners, had agreed to abide by their award. However, the commencement of work produced commoner opposition, and the fens were not enclosed until Savile, acting on a second Exchequer commission of 20 September 1632, had again secured the consent of 'divers of the better sort' of commoners.[18] Yet simmering resentment at the enclosures among a large section of commoners surfaced in 1646 when those who had been parties to the Exchequer decree sanctioning enclosure took legal advice, disputing whether a simple majority of Misson commoners

[16] Lilburne, *Epworth, passim.*
[17] Ibid., p. 2; *The declaration of Daniel Noddel,* p. 258; Lincs. R.O., Monson 7/17/51; T. E. Tomlins, *The Law-dictionary* (1835), ii, replevins.
[18] P.R.O., E. 178/5421; Notts. R.O., P.R. 2323.

(non-subscribers having been outnumbered by no more than six) could in fact grant away their commons, and they were advised that they could not. Additional advice tendered in 1651 assured those who had neither consented to the decree, nor claimed under it, that they were not bound by its provisions and could drive their cattle on to the commons, with the caveat that they should 'take care that riots be avoided'.[19]

The Great Level and the Deeping Level

The most ambitious drainage project in the seventeenth century, the Great (or Bedford) Level, encompassed 300 000–400 000 acres of fenland and extended into six counties – Lincolnshire, Northamptonshire, Huntingdonshire, Cambridgeshire (and the Isle of Ely), Norfolk and Suffolk.[20] Immediately to the north lay the Deeping Level, comprising 30 000 acres of Lincolnshire fenland between the Rivers Glen and Welland, within which fifteen towns enjoyed common rights. Although the Deeping Level was later included in schemes for the Great Level, drainage works were apparently carried on in the former level on a separate basis.[21]

Both levels had been the subject of planning, or had actually experienced drainage schemes prior to the major operations of the 1630s. The Deeping Level was one of the earliest areas of fenland to be organised into a comprehensive scheme, perhaps because of its reputation as the most flood prone of all the Lincolnshire fens.[22] In 1598 captain Thomas Lovell, esquire, enjoying the favour of Lord Burghley, was appointed chief undertaker for its drainage with a recompense of 10 885 acres.[23] When Lovell attempted enclosure, he encountered riotous resistance from local commoners, resulting in two Star Chamber actions, one at the end of Elizabeth I's reign, and the other at the beginning of James I's reign.[24]

In the Jacobean action, Thomas Wells of St James Deeping, described as a day-labourer, was singled out as both instigator and

[19] Notts. R.O., P.R. 2321, 2322.
[20] Badeslade, appendices, pp. 119–20; *The state of the Adventurers' Case, in Answer to a Petition exhibited against them by the Inhabitants of the Soke of Peterborough* (undated); Sir Cornelius Vermuyden, *A Discourse touching the draining the great Fens* (1642), p. 2; Camb. R.O., R. 59/31/9/3, f. 5.
[21] Darby, *Draining*, p. 45; Albright, p. 62; B.L., Lansdowne 87, fols 13–14.
[22] W. Camden, *Britain* (1637), p. 534.
[23] B.L., Lansdowne 87, fols 13–14; Lincs. R.O., Spalding sewers 500, fols 303, 304–9.
[24] P.R.O., STAC. 8/7/3; Lincs. R.O., Spalding sewers 500, fols 306–7.

ringleader. Filled with a sense of injustice at the wrong done to the commoners by Lovell's works and enclosures, Wells harangued the parishioners in his local church at the end of the service on 1 April 1603 to fill in the enclosure ditches and kill anyone who stood in their way. A local justice, William Lacy, esquire, was present and may have guardedly sympathised with the aggrieved commoners. While duly committing Wells to the stocks for his outburst, and voicing opposition to direct action, Lacy apparently took no effective action to head-off the subsequent violence, and thus invited the accusation of having countenanced the riots. At least sixteen commoners entered the neighbouring fen on 5 April to level the ditches and beat off Lovell's workmen; they threatened to bury Lovell in one of his own ditches and cripple or kill returning workmen. The rioters gained reassurance from the belief that 'there was no danger to do more than that for until the King was crowned there was no law wherefore they might do what they would for that the Parliament would clear all'. These actions were repeated on 8 April and 9 May. The accused commoners tried to explain away their behaviour as simply making footways for their cattle over sections of ditch, when alternative routes risked losses by drowning, and emphasised that only two commoners had been involved on separate occasions, and four or five at the most on another occasion. They also cherished a paternal notion of the King that permitted them to discharge workmen in his name: Wells had previously petitioned the King not to allow the fens to be taken from him and his poor neighbours and assumed a sympathetic response. The existence of a locally raised fund to hire a guard against Lovell was lent some substance by Wells's confession that the wives of five inhabitants had hired him and another commoner for 18d each to make a footway for their cattle over an enclosure ditch. All the defendants denied the more serious charge of sending a messenger to a contact in Spalding, on a market day, to 'raise up the meaner sort of people' there for joint action in two days' time. The messenger was said to have disparaged Lord Burghley while assuring his Spalding contact that 'the best men of their side' countenanced their actions, although outwardly affecting disapproval (a further reference, perhaps, to William Lacy). A royal proclamation condemning the disturbances elicited a petitioned response against Lovell's scheme in the name of all commoners which was entrusted to a Market Deeping linen draper for delivery to James I.[25] Lovell tried, without success, to obtain parliamentary confirmation of his title to one-third of the Deeping Level.[26]

Lovell's scheme having finally proved defective, Thomas, Earl of Exeter, became the drainer of the Deeping Level in 1610 for the same recompense and, over the next five years, as he threw up embankments (principally on the River Welland) his enclosures went unmolested. However, the melting of winter snows in the spring of 1615 produced severe flooding to the east of the Welland, with towns and villages ringing their bells backwards to alert help, and inhabitants taking to boats as the efforts of hundreds of fenmen to stem the waters proved futile. Local gentry on the commission of sewers were entreated to sanction emergency action, more particularly to authorise the cutting of 'slakers', or breaches, in the Earl's Welland bank, to save their towns, and men from Moulton (including the dyke-reeves and a constable), Whaplode, Cowbit and thereabouts, assuming sewers' authorisation, cut three breaches in the bank on the afternoon of 20 March. Four more breaches were cut the following night by inhabitants of Gedney 'playing the Rogues that night', which was the only indication of any malicious designs on the Earl's works. Yet the Earl denounced the whole of this action as a calculated attack by more than a dozen commoners upon his works and enclosures under cover of darkness, and claimed that he had been forced to hire 400 men to work on defensive banks for six weeks to preserve the towns of Spalding and Pinchbeck from peril.[27] By 1631 Exeter's works had proved no more effective than his predecessor's, and Francis, Earl of Bedford, became the new undertaker.[28]

Under James I, repeated attempts had been made to secure parliamentary backing for drainage schemes that would have comprehended a large part, if not most, of the Great Level. In May and June 1604 efforts were made to rush an extensive drainage Bill through the Commons but it failed to attract much support. Its critics denigrated it as private gain parading as public good, and accused its local supporters of being simply out to evade their share of the cost of trusted, and effective, traditional works maintained by laws of

[25] P.R.O., STAC. 8/7/3, mm. 16, 18 and fols 2–4, 9–14.
[26] *Commons' jn.*, i, 250–2, 999, 1000–1; *Lords' jn.*, ii, 341; Lincs. R.O., Spalding sewers 500, fols 304–9.
[27] P.R.O., STAC. 8/111/25, mm. 1–3.
[28] Albright, p. 62; Lincs. R.O., Spalding sewers 463/2/6.
[25] P.R.O., STAC. 8/7/3, mm. 16, 18 and fols 2–4, 9–14.

sewers.[29] Two 1606 drainage Bills, one for over 40 000 acres of fenland in the Isle of Ely (with a comparatively modest eighth part as the undertakers' recompense)[30] and the other for the Great Level, [31] also proved abortive. And a similar fate attended a Bill introduced in February 1607, which sparked off a lively Commons debate, and was said to have moved several fenland towns to raise money for its defeat upon the supposition that it involved large-scale enclosure and mass impoverishment.[32] Yet in the same session, a Bill for the drainage of about 6000 privately owned acres near Wisbech completed all its stages in June 1607, and thus earned the distinction of being the only scheme sanctioned by an early Stuart Parliament.[33] With this sole exception, drainage advocates continued to be outnumbered by opponents and sceptics in Parliament: another Bill foundered in 1610[34]; and the denunciation of a 1621 Bill 'for the better improving commons' as a further attempt to win parliamentary backing for drainage, linked with the dangers of anti-enclosure riots and recollections of Ket's rebellion, helped guarantee its demise.[35] Fenland drainage may have become an election issue in 1614 in the choice of the Cambridgeshire knights of the shire. Some freeholders had allegedly been swayed by a deliberately engineered rumour that 'their Fens would be drained, and a third part be given away to the Undertakers' if two of the candidates were returned. However, the principal target of this rumour, Sir John Cutts, did in fact secure election.[36]

Jacobean landowners who favoured new drainage enterprises had another means of implementation at hand in courts of sewers – institutions of medieval origin whose function was to attend to the maintenance of traditional drainage works. These courts, endowed with wide powers by an Act of 1531, were composed of commissioners (appointed from among the more substantial local landowners), and

---

29 *Commons' jn.*, i, 202, 207, 232, 236, 237, 239; Camb. U.L., Ely diocesan records A/8/1, fols 50–86.

30 *Commons' jn.*, i, 270, 277; P.R.O., S.P. dom. 14/18, f. 100.

31 *Commons' jn.*, i. 296, 298, 305–6, 308; D. H. Willson (ed.), *The Parliamentary Diary of Robert Bowyer, 1606–7* (Minneapolis, 1931), pp. 149–50, 157.

32 *Commons' jn.*, i, 340, 357, 364, 371–2; P.R.O., S.P. dom. 14/26, f. 37; B. L., Harleian 6838, fols 179–80.

33 Albright, p. 54; *Commons' jn.*, i, 380, 382, 384, 387; *Lords' jn.*, ii, 528, 529–31.

34 *Commons' jn.*, i, 411, 414, 417, 420, 423.

35 Ibid., 611.

36 C. H. Cooper, *Annals of Cambridge* (Cambridge, 1845), iii, 62; T. Carew, *An historical account of the rights of elections of the several counties, etc. of Great Britain* (1755), p. 109; *Return of Members of Parliament,* pt I, appendix, p. xxxvii; *Commons' jn.*, i, 485.

sewers' juries (drawn from the lower ranks of fenland society), who assisted the commissioners in determining questions of fact. But these institutions proved inappropriate vehicles for innovation, as rivalry and disagreement rent the commissioners and the rulings of higher courts restricted their powers, and local financial backing was not forthcoming.[37] New works constructed in the Isle of Ely in 1609 under laws of sewers were questioned in the privy council by local commoners for procedural irregularities. Frustrated in their intentions by sewers' juries, the drainers were accused of securing a 'select jury' composed partly of men who had been retained on high wages as officers in overseeing the new works, and partly of 'men of small understanding' who had been led along in confusion by the others. The new jury duly approved the works, taxes were imposed and warrants were directed to the sheriff to distrain and sell tax-refusers' goods.[38] But commissioners of sewers could be confident of privy council support, as those commoners who resisted their decrees in Northamptonshire and three neighbouring counties discovered in 1616; they were forced to submit and drop their lawsuits against the commissioners and their officers, and one obdurate offender was kept in custody until he complied.[39]

Among the most enthusiastic advocates of new works in this period were Sir Miles Sandys, baronet, a substantial Cambridgeshire landowner, and his son, Sir Miles, junior. The elder Sir Miles of Wilburton, in the Isle of Ely (the third son of Edwin Sandys, Archbishop of York 1578–88), had acquired considerable experience of litigation over common rights in properties where he had an interest from the end of Elizabeth's reign. Armed with a petition purporting to voice local support, Sir Miles's allies at court succeeded in persuading James I at the start of his reign that a scheme he had in hand for drainage works in the Isle of Ely was for the public good. James was, however, subsequently enlightened by four leading landowners while hunting in the area as to the scheme's basically fraudulent nature, and he proceeded to condemn it before Parliament which promptly threw it out as 'a base cheating monopoly'.[40] This rebuff did not deter

---

[37] Albright, pp. 54–5; Darby, *Draining,* pp. 1–5.
[38] Camb. U.L., Ely diocesan records A/8/1, fols 122–3, 127–8, 131–3.
[39] *A.P.C., James I,* iii, 59.
[40] *V.C.H., Cambridgeshire,* iv, 98, 149, 153–4, 159; *Harleian Society,* 1897, xli, 6; *Complete Baronetage* (ed. G. E. C., Exeter, 1902), i, 89–90; *The Picklock,* pp. 7–8; *The Anti-Projector,* p. 2.

Sir Miles from continuing to support new works as an energetic commissioner of sewers, with privy council backing when some commoners questioned the legality of the commissioners' proceedings.[41] As manorial lord of Willingham, he welcomed the decision of a Wisbech sessions of sewers in May 1618 to construct a new drain through the fens of Willingham and Cottenham and improve an existing drain in the Haddenham and Wilburton fens. Despite protests that the work was unnecessary, and expressions of anxiety emanating from the townspeople of Haddenham and eight other centres within the Isle that their fens might very well become flooded, the work went ahead. Opposition was rallied by Thomas Castle, a Haddenham gentleman who, on Sunday, 25 April 1619, stayed behind in Haddenham church after the morning service to discuss with several parishioners their general antipathy towards the Wisbech decree. Castle's detractors claimed that he had harangued the parishioners from the minister's seat, urging them all to prevent the planned opening of the old Haddenham drain, but he placed it in the content of a customary discussion of parish affairs, with careful consideration being given as to how they might best 'most safely without offence' seek relief from the decree. The outcome was a decision, with only two dissenting voices, to argue their case at the next sessions of sewers. Shortly afterwards, about £10 was said to have been collected locally and handed over to Castle (presumably to help meet expenses) who addressed similar gatherings elsewhere, accompanied by four other 'ringleaders'. The end result was a huge popular demonstration at Ely against the commissioners' proceedings one evening in June 1619, in which about 2000 'of the common sort of people' rang bells, banged drums and discharged muskets around bonfires for much of the night. The sheriff and two justices were accused (wrongly, according to Cambridgeshire assize judges) of courting popularity, and gathering money, from local commoners by posing as the saviours of their commons and navigation on the court of sewers. The same assize judges urged a peaceful accord upon Sir Miles Sandys and Thomas Castle and his neighbours, but the former took matters into Star Chamber. Sir Miles and his son later became principal undertakers with the Earl of Bedford.[42]

Other pre-Bedford schemes within the Great Level met with

---

[41] Camb. R.O., law of sewers made at Huntingdon, 24 February 1618.
[42] Albright, p. 57; *A.P.C., James I,* iv, 475–6; ibid., v, 73; P.R.O., STAC. 8/27/8.

similar hostility. Commissioners of sewers presented drainage proposals for the soke of Peterborough to a specially convened assembly of 'the better sort' of commoners at Peterborough in December 1619 who judged them 'unreasonable' but, after lengthy persuasion, agreed to give the undertakers a derisory one-fortieth of the Great Fen, terms that were predictably rejected. When the poorer commoners heard of these discussions, they pleaded with the commissioners 'not to give away their Common' until the scheme was abandoned.[43] The granting of a commission to drain fens in the vicinity of Littleport, in the Isle of Ely, was followed by disturbances there in the summer of 1619. The fee farmer of the royal manor of Littleport was Sir Thomas Josselyn who had been made a commissioner of sewers in order to forward drainage. Yet the disturbances of August 1619 arose primarily from a dispute, which had been in agitation for a number of years, over the respective boundaries of the Littleport and Upwell fens rather than the new drainage proposals, although the dispute may have been reactivated by Sir Thomas's attempt to establish title to part of the Upwell fens with a view to increasing the acreage he would receive as improvement. When his bailiff and assistants made a drift of Littleport fens as a prelude to improvement on 23 and 24 August, they encountered the combined resistance of the inhabitants of Upwell and Welney: on the 23rd, they were assaulted by seven men and relieved of cattle due for the pound; and on the 24th, they were chased away by at least forty commoners. Since then, according to Sir Thomas, daily gatherings of commoners excluded his bailiff, and a common fund had been organised to hire guards and meet other expenses in keeping the bailiff, or any Littleport freeholders, out of the fens. Moreover, no officer dared serve legal process upon offenders because they kept themselves 'so close together within their town, houses and holds in the day time', so that others could be expected to follow suit 'whereunto the mutinous people in those parts are but too prone and ready'.[44] By 1622 Sir Thomas had fallen so deeply into debt that he was forced to hand over the manor of Littleport to his creditors, Sir Miles Sandys, senior and junior, who thereby acquired an interest in one more fenland manor.[45]

James I took personal control of the drainage of the Great Level in

---

[43] P.R.O., S.P. dom. 14/111, f. 85.
[44] Ibid., STAC. 8/189/9, mm. 1-2; K.B. 9/4 or 5 James I/East.
[45] *V.C.H.*, *Cambridgeshire*, iv. 98.

1621 and instructed sewers commissioners to make drainage contracts in their respective counties. The King, who was to receive a total of 120 000 acres as undertaker, placed the burden of reconciling the commoners on the commissioners as experience had shown that

> the common sort of people are apt to be jealous of anything that is new, though never so much for their better, we therefore expect from you, upon whose judgement the commoner sort of people rely, that you make such good impression in them of this work, as the clearness of our intent and the general benefit which will ensue unto them, doth deserve.

If a voluntary agreement were not forthcoming, the commissioners were to proceed against anyone who opposed or disturbed the work, but the extent of commoner resistance was never put to the test as drainage was deferred. Shortly after the King's assumption of undertakership, Cornelius Liens (Vermuyden's brother-in-law and a later shareholder in the Hatfield Level) placed proposals before him for draining the level with Vermuyden as co-undertaker, but they were rejected.[46]

The piecemeal enclosure of fenland within the Great Level, usually with drainage in mind, continued from the closing years of James's reign up to the introduction of more systematic enclosure under Bedford's scheme. In 1624 about 4000 acres of fen in the Isle of Ely parish of Sutton was enclosed by 'some rich men' of the parish who had secured the agreement of the dean and chapter of Ely by granting them a share in the enclosures. Sir Miles Sandys, senior, as a tenant of the manor of Sutton, was probably involved in the whole business. The poorer inhabitants protested at such a severe blow to their livelihood and when, in 1645, some of them prepared a petition to the Commons about this longstanding grievance, seven of them (all parliamentarian soldiers) were committed to gaol at Ely by Sir Miles, junior.[47] An attempt to survey and partition Cambridgeshire fens at Soham in 1629 led to serious disorder. Exchequer commissioners attended the manor court in Whitsunweek to read out the order dividing the commons and met with a mixed reception. 'The better sort' of commoners seemed satisfied with the order, but the more

---

[46] Harris, *Vermuyden,* pp. 27, 33, 60; Vermuyden, *A Discourse touching the draining the great Fens,* op. cit., p. 1; *The Anti-Projector,* pp. 2–3; B.L., Additional MS. 34217, f. 7; ibid., 33466, f. 196.

[47] *V.C.H., Cambridgeshire,* iv, 159; H.L.R.O., Main Papers, [1649] petition of divers poor inhabitants of the parish of Sutton.

humble remainder greeted it with 'mutinous words' and had to be restrained by the commissioners and the steward of the manor. The aggrieved faction subsequently sent along their wives and other women, in a crowd of 200 or 300, to throw stones at and assault the commissioners who were forced to take refuge in a nearby house. The women laid siege to the house, vowing that they 'would Tear the Commissioners and whomsoever else had any hand in the business', until justices arrived whereupon the commissioners wisely withdrew.[48] Cambridgeshire experienced two more outbreaks of violence aimed directly at new works in the following year. In January 1630 a group of commoners broke up sluices in an unspecified Isle of Ely fen and, later that year, works in Chippenham came under attack. In the latter instance, not only did commoners try to interrupt work on a new river but, as work neared completion, some of the men actually employed on its construction attempted 'to fill up the said River again, by flinging in the earth which they were paid for to fling out'.[49]

A general drainage of the level was finally embarked upon in the 1630s after more than a quarter of a century of abortive projects. Charles I initially proposed Sir Anthony Thomas as undertaker but commissioners of sewers, led by Francis, Earl of Bedford, raised objections to the scheme. Bending, perhaps, under pressure from Charles, who threatened to revive his own claim to the undertakership derived from his father, the commissioners agreed to make Vermuyden undertaker, with an award of 90 000 acres (10 000 acres more than Sir Anthony Thomas had been prepared to do the work for). The King was to receive 30 000 acres out of the award and Bedford and other local landowners were expected to involve themselves. The contract was fiercely opposed by the commoners who expressed 'much unwillingness that any contract should be made with an Alien born or any other stranger'. In the event, it fell through – perhaps partly because of the strength of commoner opposition, but possibly more directly as a result of Vermuyden's inability to raise capital in Holland, or elsewhere, after his Hatfield Level experiences. The Earl of Bedford was subsequently nominated undertaker at a court of sewers held at King's Lynn on 13 January 1631 with an award of 95 000 acres, of which the King was to receive only 12 000. The whittling down of the Crown's share may have been recalled to

Bedford's cost in 1638 when the effectiveness of his scheme was challenged and Charles supplanted him as undertaker with a greatly increased award. In the short term, however, the King's Lynn contract received royal assent on 26 July 1631 by letters patent as a matter of State which was not to be altered or impeded in any way.[50] In the following August and September, the Deeping Level was judged to be 'hurtfully surrounded' by a court of sewers and a tax of 10s per acre was imposed, ostensibly to finance drainage. When the tax was not paid, a meeting of sewers commissioners at Spalding, on 4 October 1631, contracted with the Earl of Bedford, and other undertakers, to drain the level in return for an award of 12 500 acres, and this contract also received royal assent.[51]

Francis Russell, Earl of Bedford, the dominant figure in both levels, had an estate of about 20 000 acres at Thorney and Whittlesey, in the Isle of Ely. The Russells were not unfamiliar with fenland drainage for in 1590 Francis's father, Sir William Russell, had brought over three Dutch experts with a view to draining the Thorney estate. Under the 1630s enterprise the same estate was to be planted with French and Dutch settlers by 1640. Francis had apparently been a drainage advocate in 1621 and, according to Sir Edward Peyton's recollections, had been prepared to forward the work by base means if necessary. As a Member of the 1621 Parliament, Sir Edward recalled how the Earls of Bedford and Westmorland, and Sir Francis Vane, had attempted to bribe him with the offer of either £10 000 outright or £500 a year, as he preferred, not to oppose the bill of the Fens', but he had conscientiously refused to betray his 'country'. Although patriotic motives were attributed to the Earl of Bedford's participation in fenland improvement, there is every reason to believe that it was profit, rather than patriotism, that primarily dictated his involvement. The earlier denunciation of undertakers as pursuing private advantage under the guise of public good could, therefore, be applied with equal justice to Bedford and his associates. The Earl actively engaged in both enterprises, holding three of the twenty shares in the Great Level, and the resultant financial commitment partly explains the heavy debts he had accumulated by the time of his

[50] Albright, pp. 60, 62; S. Wells, *The History of the Drainage of the Great Level of the Fens called Bedford Level* (1830), i, 106 and ii, appendices, pp. 98–110; Badeslade, p. 37; *The state of the Adventurers' Case, in Answer to a Petition exhibited against them by the Inhabitants of the Soke of Peterborough*; P.R.O., S.P. dom. 16/231, f. 27; P.C. 2/41, f. 110.
[51] Albright, p. 62; Lincs. R.O., Spalding sewers 463/2/6.

death in 1641. Numbered among the other shareholders in the Great Level were the ubiquitous Sir Robert Heath and Sir Miles Sandys, junior.[52]

The Earl of Bedford and his fellow undertakers were accused of having 'packed' the commissioners of sewers so that they behaved in a most partial manner, forcing the undertaking upon the commoners without the necessary majority consent. Substantial local figures could generally expect to be listed as commissioners, and thus local landowners like Sir Miles Sandys, and other Bedford supporters, were inevitably included. But for extensive areas, like the Great Level, the list was a long one, totalling 194 commissioners in June 1635.[53] Drainage was declared completed according to contract on 13 June 1636 at a Peterborough sessions of sewers, and the undertakers were allotted their lands in the following autumn.[54] Yet the consequent commoner violence, and their insistent petitions to the King at Newmarket denouncing the scheme and denying its efficacy, enabled Charles to call an investigatory sessions of sewers at Huntingdon. On 12 April 1638, after six days of examination, the commissioners declared that drainage had not been perfected within the agreed six-year period and, at a further session held on 18 July, the King superseded Bedford as undertaker with an increased award of 152 000 acres. Charles, who had agreed to provide the necessary capital, engaged Vermuyden's expertise. The Huntingdon decision was not as severe on Bedford as might at first glance appear. Under the original contract, Bedford and his associates had been granted 95 000 acres but, when allowance is made for the King's 12 000 acres and the 40 000 acres earmarked to provide an income for the maintenance of the works, only 43 000 acres had been theirs absolutely – which was not far short of the 40 000 acres left to them, free of all liabilities for the works, when the King became undertaker.[55] Charles also took over Bedford's works in the Deeping Level,

[52] L. Stone, *The crisis of the aristocracy, 1558–1641* (Oxford, 1965), pp. 355, 357; Harris, *Vermuyden*, pp. 63–4, 67–8; Sir Edward Peyton, *The Divine Catastrophe of the Kingly Family of the House of Stuarts* (1652), p. 118; *An Answer to a Printed Paper dispersed by Sir John Maynard entitled The humble Petition of the Owners and Commoners of the Town of Isleham* (1653), p. 5; P.R.O., S.P. dom. 14/128, f. 105.

[53] Wells, *Bedford Level*, op. cit., i, 105; *The state of the Adventurers' Case*, op. cit.; *The Anti-Projector*, p. 3; P.R.O., C. 181/5, fols 18–22; B.L., Harleian 5011, f. 7; Camb. R.O., R. 59/31/9/3, fols 3–4.

[54] Albright, p. 64, note 47; Camb. R.O., R. 59/31/9, n. 1A, f. 179.

[55] Albright, pp. 61–2; Harris, *Vermuyden*, pp. 68–9; Vermuyden, *A Discourse touching the draining the great Fens*, op. cit., *passim*; B.L., Harleian 5011, pt II, fols 622–5; Additional MS. 5821, f. 101; Camb. R.O., R. 59/31/9, no. 1A, fols 180–5.

after they too had been judged defective in July 1638, with an award of 12 000 acres. A new syndicate of local landowners, headed by the second Earl of Exeter (following in his father's footsteps), was given the task of finishing the works within a year. The undertaker's portion of the Deeping Level was later settled by Chancery decree upon Elizabeth, countess dowager of Exeter, who engaged with other undertakers in further works.[56]

The Ancholme Level

On either side of the River Ancholme, running through the central lowlands of the Lindsey division of Lincolnshire, lay about 18 000 acres of fenland which also attracted the attention of drainers in the 1630s. Following the procedure usually adopted to initiate new schemes in this decade, commissioners of sewers found the land subject to flooding and imposed a drainage tax upon all parishes bordering upon the river. The tax, initially set at 8s an acre in 1634, and increased to 13s 4d in 1635, was not paid – thus allowing the commissioners to draw upon their legal powers to confiscate land for the financing of works.[57] The undertaker was Sir John Monson, a local landowner, who went to great pains to stress the altruistic nature of his motives, becoming involved, he emphasised, 'upon the request of the Country, and as a servant to them, without any private reflection or self-end' after he had decided that the demands of some 'foreign' undertakers were excessive and had offered to do the work himself for a fourth part less.[58] Commissioners of sewers contracted with Monson on 24 August 1635, settling 5827 acres (or just under a third) upon him as undertaker, and the procedure was completed by gaining the King's assent. But works on the scale envisaged involved heavy expenditure and, presumably hoping to draw upon local capital, Monson gave neighbouring landowners one month in which to decide if they wished to participate in the project. Fourteen out of a total of twenty-six manorial lords responded positively and invested in the venture on a joint stock basis, with terms modelled upon the

[56] Stone, *The crisis of the aristocracy*, op. cit., p. 356; Albright, p. 62; B.L., Harleian 5011, pt II, fols 622–5; Lincs. R.O., Spalding sewers 463/2/6.
[57] Albright, pp. 56, 62; J. Thirsk, *English peasant farming: the agrarian history of Lincolnshire from Tudor to recent times* (1957), pp. 189–90.
[58] Lincs. R.O., Monson 19/7/1/10; ibid., 7/17/18. For similar protestations of altruism see Monson 7/18/3 and H.L.R.O., Main Papers, 15 December 1654 petition of Sir John Monson to the House of Commons.

agreement between Bedford and his participants in the Great Level. At the allocation of the respective portions of the 5827 acres at Brigg on 8 April 1636, 977 acres (or just over one-sixth) were reserved for Monson. A further ten manorial lords, according to Monson, gave their consent to the scheme, even though they had personally declined his invitation to participate, and he was confident of virtually unanimous local approval.[59]

Sir John's boast that he had been primarily moved by considerations of local and national good, rather than personal profit, elicited a sardonic riposte from those who saw their livelihood adversely affected by his project. Such benevolence was unfamiliar for they knew him 'to be a gentleman of so good judgement and understanding in the world that he will not bestow his labour and charge altogether for the country without some regard and respect to himself in the first place' – an assessment more in accord with the Sir John who was fined £300 in 1637 by commissioners for depopulating enclosures on his lands in Yorkshire and Lincolnshire. But the brunt of the commoners' criticism was reserved for the commissioners of sewers who had allegedly imposed drainage taxes, without public notification and explanation, upon the commons in general with no mechanism for calculating the commoners' individual contributions. Furthermore, some sewers' juries, composed of 'men of mean and weak understanding and small estates', were manipulated by Monson and his associates to secure favourable verdicts, while less compliant juries were dismissed and replaced until an acceptable verdict was obtained. Three juries were empanelled before the necessary verdict as to the extent of flooding in the level was obtained on 31 March 1635 and, even then, one juror, Thomas Place of Winterton, refused to add his own signature to the verdict and was fined for his non-compliance. The commissioners were denounced, with good reason, as 'both Commissioners, and undertakers, judges and parties': seven of the eight who contracted with Monson in 1635 became fellow shareholders shortly afterwards.[60]

The precise attitude of commoners to the new scheme was a bone of contention, with Monson laying claim to the express consent of the most substantial inhabitants, and silent acquiescence of the rest, while

---

[59] Lincs. R.O., Monson 7/18/6; ibid., 19/7/1/10; 7/17/19; 7/18/1.
[60] Ibid., 7/18/2; 7/18/6; 19/7/1/8; P.R.O., E. 134/17 Chas. II/East. 14; *The Anti-Projector*, p. 3.

his critics objected that scarcely one man in a hundred had signified approval, and 'many hundred owners and commoners . . . whom the said draining doth concern, never gave their consent thereunto but are grieved thereat or thereby'. When the scheme's critics appeared to put their case to the commissioners, they were allegedly silenced whereas Monson was allowed to speak at length in its favour. Ranked against the scheme were men of substance, like Sir Michael Wharton, and his eldest son, and Edward Moseley, esquire, and men of social standing, like the parson of Waddingham, Lancelot Harrison, who led the commoners of Waddingham and adjacent Snitterby in their opposition.[61]

Courtier-dominated undertakings: the East, West and Wildmore Fens; the Lindsey Level; and the Holland Fen

An opportunistic group of courtiers, headed by Sir Robert Killigrew and his son and heir, Sir William, were quick to see scope for profitable investment in fenland improvement and came to play a leading role in three schemes in the 1630s. The Killigrews were an archetypal courtier family: Sir Robert was an agile courtier–businessman who, following the path set by his father, used courtly influence to build up the family's fortunes. He had been one of the original shareholders in the New River Company (21 June 1619) before he was drawn into fenland drainage, and his court career culminated in his being appointed vice-chamberlain to the Queen on 2 January 1630. After his death in 1633, his heir, Sir William, continued the family's courtier tradition and enjoyed enough royal confidence to be made gentleman-usher to Charles I, and to be entrusted with the command of one of the troops of horse that guarded his person during the Civil War. Sir William also possessed literary skills as a dramatist which were drawn upon for propagandist purposes when his fenland enterprises came under attack. The Lindsey Level scheme alone was estimated in 1646 to have cost him over £30000, of which he still owed more than £11000. His younger brother, Thomas, was to earn notoriety as a licentious favourite of Charles II.[62] Associated with the Killigrews were two other court figures, Robert Long and George Kirke, esquires. Long enjoyed the Queen's favour and was appointed

---

[61] Lincs. R.O., Monson 7/18/2, 3.
[62] *D.N.B.*, xi, 110–11, 116–17; T. Birch (ed.), *The court and times of Charles I* (1848), i, 461; P.R.O., S.P. dom. 23/97, f. 431.

her surveyor-general in June 1641. After the King's execution, he was appointed secretary to the exiled Charles Stuart and gained a reputation for avarice in his management of the prince's financial affairs. Commenting on the corruption charge levelled against Long in 1648, an admittedly biased Clarendon opined that he 'was so notoriously inclined to that way of husbandry, that he was always thought guilty of more than he was charged with'.[63] George Kirke, who held the influential court offices of master of the King's robes and groom of the bedchamber, was also a beneficiary of another of the Crown's revenue-raising schemes exploited by courtiers, disafforestation, as lessee of part of Gillingham Forest in Dorset.[64]

In denouncing this courtier group after the Civil War, one of the commoners' spokesmen placed their enterprises in the context of the period of the personal rule, with its extension of the royal prerogative to the endangering of the subjects' property rights and the undermining of fundamental law. Thus enterprises begun in a long interval between Parliaments were maintained by prerogative power through privy council orders and Star Chamber actions, for the benefit of undertakers who subsequently fought for the King in the Civil War. The latter were 'the Old Court-Levellers, or Propriety-Destroyers, the Prerogative Undertakers', and analogies were drawn between their 'illegal' proceedings and the threats to property posed by the decisions of judges in the ship money and forest laws disputes. The forest laws analogy was particularly apposite for whereas some of the judges would have made out the whole of England to be a forest, 'so this generation of Undertakers would have incorporated, and got a standing Commission in all Counties, and so made England the Level, and England to be surrounded, and in short time would have taken all we had'. If the courtiers had been successful, they 'would have commanded all the Land in England to have been at the King's disposing; Then all had been their own, for the King was little the better by such Projects, the Courtiers gained all.' In the subversion of fundamental law, their offences were more heinous than the Earl of

---

[63] *D.N.B.*, xii, 107–8; Edward Hyde, Earl of Clarendon, *History of the Rebellion and Civil Wars in England* (ed. W. D. Macray, Oxford, 1888), iv, 341, 372–3; Bodl., *Two Petitions . . . from Thousands of the Lords, Owners, and Commoners of Lincolnshire; against the Old Court-Levellers, or Propriety-Destroyers, the Prerogative Undertakers* (1650), p. 3; P.R.O., C. 181/5, fols 391–4.

[64] P.R.O., C. 181/5, fols 84, 392; Sharp, p. 87.

Strafford's in that they had introduced 'an arbitrary and tyrannical government' and had 'imprisoned our persons, and destroyed juries, and put out the two eyes of the Law, Liberty and Property', in direct contravention of freedoms enshrined in Magna Carta.[65]

Courtier participation in drainage began with the project for the East, West and Wildmore Fens, in the south of the Lindsey division of Lincolnshire between the Witham and Steeping rivers, which extended over an area of approximately 45 000 acres (the East and West Fens combined totalling 34 700 acres, and the Wildmore Fen accounting for a further 10 300 acres). The King was lord of the soil of the East and West Fens as part of the Duchy of Lancaster and, as such, had right of improvement and of brovage in both fens, while Henry, Earl of Stamford, was lord of the soil of the Wildmore (or Armtree) Fen. As a first step, Sir Robert Killigrew acquired a grant from Charles to himself and other patentees (including Robert Long and George Kirke) of his right of improvement in the East and West Fens. Advocating drainage in order to profit from the grant, Sir Robert then reached a satisfactory arrangement with Sir Anthony Thomas before recommending him to the King as undertaker for the drainage of the East, West and Wildmore Fens. After the return of a verdict that the fens in question were 'hurtfully surrounded', a Boston court of sewers in April 1630 imposed drainage taxes, which were not paid, and at a further sessions on 15 May commissioners contracted with Sir Anthony Thomas. The contract (ratified at Boston on 15 April 1631) stipulated that the fens were, within four years, to be drained so dry that not more than 3000 acres remained covered with water, and as recompense Sir Anthony and his associates would receive 10 000 acres in the East Fen, 5000 in the West Fen, and 1300 in the Wildmore Fen. It was later asserted that Sir Anthony had been at the time a man of 'a mean estate' who had previously been a prisoner in the Fleet for debt and that he had been seeking 'to repair his ruined fortunes' by this enterprise.[66]

Commoner opposition to the contract was somewhat assuaged by creating the initial impression that Killigrew, and his fellow paten-

[65] *Sir William Killigrew his answer,* p. 5; *The Picklock,* pp. 3–6, 8–10, 16; *A Breviate of the Cause,* pp. 5, 13–16; Bodl., *Two Petitions,* op. cit., pp. 3–4 and title page.
[66] Albright, pp. 58–9; Thompson, *Collections,* pp. 148–9, 151–2, 154–5; *The Title of Sir Thomas Dawes Kt [and others] to certain Improved Lands in the West and North Fens in the County of Lincoln* (1654); P.R.O., D.L. 44/1134; E. 178/5433; E. 134/10 Chas. I/Mich. 66.

tees, would not be demanding further enclosures under their right of improvement, but, once work had been completed, they proceeded to enclose an additional 1000 acres in the East Fen, 6700 in the West Fen and 4000 in the Wildmore Fen under that right. Out of the 45 000 acres of fenland, therefore, a grand total of 28 000 acres, or 62.2 per cent, was eventually enclosed. In percentage terms the impact was greater in the East and West Fens, where the commoners' loss approached two-thirds, than in the Wildmore Fen, where it was just over a half, and this probably helps to explain why anti-enclosure violence began in the first two fens. Work commenced in August 1631, and was judged completed on 16 July 1634 when Boston sewers commissioners certified that not more than about 1600 acres remained drowned (well within the 3000 acres stipulated in the contract). The first steps had been taken towards securing a further division of the fens, for the benefit of Killigrew and his associates, in the previous summer when a Duchy commission had issued forth to settle the respective shares of commoners and patentees under the latter's right of improvement. The commissioners, meeting at Horncastle on 22 September 1633, were urged by the commoners' representatives to disallow further enclosures on the grounds that the patentees had promised to surrender the right of improvement and brovage in 1630 once the undertakers' portion had been allotted (and they produced court records to substantiate this). But the commoners were no match for this powerful courtier group with royal backing, and they were coerced into agreeing to further enclosures as improvement in August 1635. The increased profit to the King from this enterprise was, in relative terms, dramatic (his revenue from the West Fen jumped from £18 to about £600 a year), yet the chief beneficiaries were those of his courtiers who had grasped the exploitative potential in fenland drainage.[67]

Allegations of chicanery and consent under duress abounded in these, as in other, drained fens. Royal instructions to commissioners of sewers to assemble a jury of forty-nine 'able persons of good estates' to view the fens failed to provide the drainage pretext as only the East Fen, and some adjacent severals, were found 'hurtfully surrounded'. Sir Anthony Thomas and his fellow undertakers refused

---

[67] Albright, pp. 53, 59–60; P.R.O., D.L. 44/1134; S.P. dom. 16/473, f. 50; ibid., 257, f. 25; ibid., 330, f. 48; ibid., 479, f. 44; E. 178/5433; P.C. 2/44, fols 195–6; ibid., 46, f. 340; *Lords' jn.*, iv, 220.

to accept a verdict that excluded them from the richer lands of the West Fen and, presumably through their courtier allies, procured a new commission of sewers which substituted undertakers and drainage apologists for some of the old commissioners. Sir Robert Killigrew and Robert Long were nominated commissioners for the East, West and Wildmore Fens in March 1630 to serve alongside Robert, Earl of Lindsey, and at least three other future Lindsey Level shareholders, and Sir Robert was one of the commissioners who originally contracted with Sir Anthony Thomas. Dispensing with a jury, the new commissioners found both the East and West Fens in need of draining and went through the procedure of imposing taxes, 'which they knew beforehand could not possibly be paid as the same was taxed', and decreeing substantial areas of fenland to the undertakers when they were not paid. Numerous Duchy privy seals were then served upon bewildered West Fen commoners for no other purpose but to coerce them into reaching agreement with the patentees over further enclosure as improvement, and some of them, fearful of legal proceedings, forsook the dissident 'very many of the most Considerable' commoners and capitulated. The additional enclosure was confirmed in the Duchy Court and lands were settled on the patentees by injunctions 'unduly and illegally obtained'. The commoners were reportedly left with 'such narrow screeds and bits' of fenland as resembled 'but highways to the said participants' great enclosures than a common for so many thousands of people as have right of common therein', while none of the agreement's beneficial articles were performed.[68]

Patentees and purchasers of land in the West Fen naturally put an entirely different construction on events. The additional enclosure compensated them for the surrender of all right of common or brovage in the remaining commons, and a written agreement to that effect had secured between 1500 and 1700 signatures (more, in fact, than those entitled to common rights). The Duchy privy seals were in accord with the commoners' own request that the agreement be confirmed in that court which entailed process being served upon mandated commoner representatives. All those with 'any shadow of right' to common in the fen had given their consent while the

---

[68] Thompson, *Collections,* pp. 151–3; P.R.O., D.L. 44/1134; S.P. dom. 16/473, f. 50; C. 181/4, f. 46; H.L.R.O., Main Papers, [1640] petition of Edward Ironside, gentleman.

allegedly two or three hundred dissenters were dismissed as cottagers or recent squatters possessing no legally recognised common rights. But even the latter were said to have eventually joined with the others in signing the former agreement in December 1635, after further negotiations with Duchy commissioners, and early in 1636 the Duchy court entrusted the task of dividing the fen to eight commissioners, four chosen by the King and four by the commoners. The commissioners had completed their work by 2 May, following which a Duchy injunction established possession, and the whole arrangement was subsequently decreed in the presence of the attorney-general and the commoners' counsel. The commoners' remaining fenland was from thence freed of any royal claims of common or brovage, and they themselves were castigated for the nonperformance of a vital part of the agreement owing to their failure, despite repeated reminders, to decide on their nominees to receive the grant of the soil of their portion of the fen.[69] Nevertheless, the credibility of this account is somewhat undermined by the fact that it hardly squares with the commoners' opposition to any such agreement in September 1633 and their later riotous attacks upon those very enclosures.

A courtier group, headed by Sir William Killigrew, also secured a large share in the Lindsey Level, an area of about 70 000 acres of fenland in the southern half of Lincolnshire extending from the River Glen up as far as the city of Lincoln (but excluding the Holland Fen which became a separate undertaking). There had originally been a struggle for the contract between the Earls of Lincoln and Lindsey, but the latter, helped by his partner, Sir William Killigrew, won the contract on 2 June 1635. Although Robert, Earl of Lindsey, was a leading Lincolnshire landowner, opportunities for local participation in his enterprise (on an Ancholme Level scale) were severely restricted because of the extent of the courtier group's share in the undertaking.[70] According to the terms of the contract, Lindsey and his associates were to receive 24 000 acres after completion of the work but priority was, in fact, accorded to the southern section of the level, an area of 40 210 acres of fenland lying between the Rivers Glen and Kyme Eau. Work was judged to have been completed here on 14

---

[69] *The Title of Sir Thomas Dawes*, op. cit.; H.L.R.O., Main Papers, [January] 1641/42 application for further order for quieting the King's possessions in Lincolnshire; P.R.O., P.C. 2/46, f. 340.

[70] Stone, *The crisis of the aristocracy*, op. cit., p. 356; Albright, pp. 59, 62.

March 1639 and the undertakers were accordingly awarded 14000 acres, while work on the level north of Kyme Eau to Lincoln was never completed.[71]

Undertakers and commoners presented conflicting accounts of the way in which approval was secured for the Lindsey scheme. According to the former, 'the Country's kind compliance and joyful invitations did encourage the Drainers to adventure on the work': taxes were laid upon the level once drainage had been judged necessary and, in the absence of a local initiative (an option that had been open for three years), thirty-two commissioners, including many local landowners, contracted with the Earl of Lindsey at a public sessions at Sleaford attended by thousands of commoners. Crowds estimated at 6000 – or 7000 – strong thronged around the church where the contract was debated because the sessions hall could not accommodate the numbers, and everyone threw their hats into the air on the Earl's acceptance, 'hollowing loudly Acclamations of joy in his Honour', and accompanied him back to his lodgings to eat and drink at his expense. There were emphatically no dissenting voices, 'for if any words of Dislike had been from the Country, the Earl and his Participants would never have laid out their Estates on this work'.[72] Lindsey's opponents, in contrast, justifiably accused the Earl and his court allies of persuading the King (with whom, through the Lord Keeper, the nomination of commissioners of sewers rested) to purge the commission of their critics and replace them with 'strangers' and future undertakers. The exclusion of local landowners who 'would hinder a public good for private ends', and the substitution of 'the chief of the drainers . . . who were become a part of the Country by that interest', was perfectly defensible, in Sir William Killigrew's opinion, when over 200 county gentry remained on the commission to safeguard the county's best interests. The continuing support of the King, and of powerful government figures, was ensured with handsome grants of fenland: the King received 3000, and the Queen 500 acres, and there were further grants to the Lord Keeper, the

[71] *Sir William Killigrew his answer*, pp. 12–13; *A Breviate of the Cause*, p. 5; P.R.O., S.P. dom. 16/416, f. 53.

[72] *Certain papers concerning the Earl of Lindsey his Fens* (1649), p. 6; *Sir William Killigrew his answer*, p. 8; *A short State of the Case for the Earl of Lindsey's Fens* (1652); *The late Earl of Lindsey his Title, by which participants, do claim 24000 Acres of Lands in the Fens in Lincolnshire* (1661); P.R.O., S.P. dom. 29/72/46, p. 5; B.L., Additional MS. 21427, f. 141.

Chancellor of the Exchequer, and the two secretaries of state.[73]

As an earlier view by a jury of part of the land had provided no justification for drainage, the remodelled commissioners, claiming that the 1531 statute gave them discretion to dispense with jurors, proceeded to view it themselves and hence, as 'judges and parties', with 'their covetous corrupt eyes...took land for water'. The non-payment of the subsequent drainage tax of 13s 4d an acre (replacing a previous 5s rate) was allegedly guaranteed by its imposition of the level in general, rather than on particular towns and individuals, thereby enabling the commissioners to contract with Lindsey. The scheme's opponents claimed to outnumber its supporters by ten to one, with the latter composed mainly of cottagers whose signatures had been procured for the Earl by two local alehousekeepers. Lindsey's opponents were then subjected to fines and imprisonment, and the impounding of their cattle until excessive sums had been paid.[74]

The experience of a number of Bourne commoners in 1640 confirms that some coercive pressure was exerted upon recalcitrant commoners. On Michaelmas day the livestock of a number of commoners were rounded up by the undertakers' agents in fens near Bourne and impounded at Pinchbeck. Sir Edward Heron (one of the participants) and Sir William Killigrew later proffered different explanations for these distraints; they were upon a sewers' warrant for nonpayment of a drainage tax, according to Sir Edward, while they were a consequence of riots against works in Bourne Fen in Sir William's recollection. Several commoners, including one Thomas Kirke, approached Sir Edward Heron to redeem their livestock and all, save Kirke, were required to pay 2s a beast, but he was asked for 10s and told that he 'could not have them there without he would subscribe to the granting away of the said common'. Armed with a replevin, Kirke tried to recover his livestock, but they were moved from Pinchbeck to an enclosure of Sir William Killigrew's in Donington Fen and, when he tracked them down, he was assaulted

---

[73] Albright, pp. 58, 60; *Sir William Killigrew his answer*, pp. 5–6; *The Picklock*, pp. 2–3; *A Breviate of the Cause*, p. 5; Bodl., *Two Petitions*, op. cit., p. 3; P.R.O., S.P. dom. 16/431, f. 16.
[74] *The Picklock*, pp. 1–4, 8–9, 12; *A Breviate of the Cause*, pp. 3–4, 14; *The Anti-Projector*, p. 6; *A Reply to Sir William Killigrew's dispersed Papers, by the Owners and Commoners in Lincoln-shire* (undated); Bodl., *Two Petitions*, op. cit., pp. 2–3; H.L.R.O., Main Papers, 10 August 1641 petition of the governors of Charterhouse Hospital.

by the undertakers' servants as he tried to serve the writ. Sir William, Robert Long and Sir Edward Heron were said to have deliberately encouraged defiance of the writ 'as they had done many others', warning Kirke 'that if he got a replevin and came with the sheriff they would shoot him', and his livestock were sold after three weeks of futile legal action. He was also forced to hide from pursuivants sent into Bourne by Long and his associates with the express purpose of cowing the commoners into submission, for 'all such as would subscribe to a deed for the granting away of our commons were set free, but others who refused were pursuivanted and served with Star Chamber process to their excessive charge, trouble, and molestation'. Although contemptuously dismissive of Kirke's charges, Sir William did recall 'some poor men', who had cut drains and driven cattle into the undertakers' corn, having their cattle returned 'upon their submission and tears', and thought perhaps 'the like favour was offered to Thomas Kirke, which he rejected, and by persevering in his riots did compell the drainers to distrain his cattle and sell them'.[75]

The same group of undertakers who had engaged themselves in the Lindsey Level later took over the drainage of the adjacent Holland (or Eight Hundred, or Swinehead) Fen which lay in the Kirton wapentake of the Holland division of Lincolnshire, between the Lindsey Level and the River Witham. The King claimed the lordship of the soil of this fen, which covered an area of about 21 500 acres, but his title was disputed by the commoners.[76] Drainage had first been proposed around 1635 by one of the King's advisers (perhaps George Kirke) who put forward suggestions as to how the commoners might be coerced into agreeing to a drainage scheme. These suggestions provide a valuable insight into some of the thinking current in court circles which lay behind the intervention of some courtiers into fenland drainage. The commoners should be deprived from the outset, it was urged, of their authority to govern the fen or raise money to defend suits and oppose the King in the work of drainage. A

[75] H.L.R.O., Main Papers, 14 December 1640 petition of Thomas Kirke of Bourne; ibid., 31 January 1648 petition of Thomas Kirke; ibid., 22 February 1648 petition of Sir Edward Heron, K.B.; ibid., petition of Sir William Killigrew. A further allegation that the commoners' consent was gained by force was made in *A Reply to Sir William Killigrew's dispersed Papers.*

[76] J. Thirsk, *Fenland farming in the sixteenth century* (University of Leicester, occasional papers no. 3, 1953), p. 24; Albright, pp. 60–2; *A Paper delivered qnd dispersed by Sir William Killigrew* (1651); Bodl., *Two Petitions*, op. cit., p. 9.

commission should then be issued to inquire into 'certain particulars' which were not spelt out but were apparently 'such as will much conduce to make the commoners desire a composition'. This was to be followed by 'a legal prosecution of some principal opposers, who have combined and levied monies in an under course against his Majesty'. After these preliminaries, the way would then be open for

> The Country being thus perplexed, and their leaders taken off, and all the fen taxed, whereby they see a great quantity thereof ready to be decreed (which is the thing they most fear) there are certain gentlemen of the Country who will make them sensible of their case, and will sound them to know what they will give for a composition, and if they be then willing to give such a proportion as his Majesty shall think fit to accept (which I conceive will be at least 10000 acres) a commission may be issued to fit persons to treat and compound as formerly there hath been.[77]

Commissioners of sewers went through the familiar procedure of finding the fen 'surrounded', imposing a tax upon 16000 acres, which was not paid, and then contracted with the King on 1 June 1637 to undertake the drainage in return for an award of 8000 acres. The King, in turn, subcontracted with the Earl of Lindsey, and the rest of the Lindsey Level undertakers, on 31 May 1638 to undertake the work for 1500 acres, thus benefiting substantially from this last scheme.[78] The commissioners involved in these transactions were later denounced, with considerable justification, as interested parties inserted into the commission for their own ends. Among the eighteen commissioners of sewers nominated for Holland Fen on 16 March 1637 were the Earl of Lindsey, Sir William Killigrew, Robert Long and two other future undertakers. Thus undertakers in Holland Fen, 'pretending the King's Title to the said Fens, when as in truth no such ever was or could be made appear', acting as 'new Commissioners of Sewers, illegally procured, and as illegally executed, without inquisition, verdict of Jurors, or other legal means', declared a great part of the fen to be 'hurtfully surrounded' and granted away 8000 acres at the very time when a shortage of water, rather than flooding, was the chief problem.[79]

Royal favour or initiative and courtly or goverment influence, combined with a keen eye for profit, set in motion drainage schemes

[77] P.R.O., S.P. dom. 16/307, f. 31.
[78] Stone, *The crisis of the aristocracy*, op. cit., p. 356; Albright, pp. 60–2.
[79] Bodl., *Two Petitions*, op. cit., pp. 9–10; P.R.O., C. 181/5, fols 131–2.

that promised to transform the traditional fenland economy. Nothing that stood in the way of an undertaker's ambitions deflected him from his course, whether it were a long-standing legal title, traditional procedure, recalcitrant commissioners (or juries) of sewers, or the requirement of commoner consent. Ultimately, he could rely upon the King's support, and with it the powerful resources of privy council, Star Chamber, the Duchy court or court of Exchequer to surmount these obstacles by extracting conformity or crushing opposition.

2 Commoners, Undertakers and the Privy Council

THE fenland disturbances, which constitute one of the two central themes of this book, are examined in a chronological narrative subdivided, where appropriate, into respective undertakings. However, in order to signpost the reader through the descriptive detail, and place the riots in a coherent framework, some prefatory discussion of their character, the composition of activists, the reaction of the authorities and other important features is essential. As a starting point, it has to be appreciated that these disturbances were essentially defensive, conservative and restrained in character; the fenmen were defending their traditional economy against innovation and, despite the efforts of their detractors to impute wider motives, were not striving to turn the world upside-down. When they resorted to force, it was only after appeals to custom or the law had been ignored or obstructed, whereupon action was directed at specific targets of immediate concern – enclosure ditches and fences, new drainage works, farming implements (symbols of the new agrarian economy), crops growing upon former commons, the houses and property of tenants and foreign settlers planted in their midst, or the contents and fabric of the settlers' church (while the building itself was left standing).

Violence directed against persons, like property, was far from indiscriminate. Murder, mayhem and other spine-chilling threats in store for the commoners' enemies, should they come within reach, abounded but were rarely put into practice. Their chief purpose was to terrify and deter workmen, tenants and settlers, collectors of sewers' taxes and the like, and actual assaults upon the person were normally unpremeditated incidents, arising from attempts to restrain or repress riotous commoners or distrain their goods. In most cases the physical assault probably took the form of a thorough beating, a crack over the head with a stave, a prod with a pitchfork, or a ducking in an adjacent waterway, but in a few instances serious injury was done, including gunshot wounds, a sword wound on the head and broken ribs, or other injuries severe enough to require a surgeon's attention, and there was the odd fatality. There were two specific cases of men killed by rioters (from the Isle of Axholme), but in both cases, as will be seen, there were questionable circumstances, and the inexplicable lack of precision surrounding two further allegations of men slain by rioters (also from the Hatfield Level) suggests that they were part of a deliberately dramatic presentation of fenland violence to alert help. Yet viewed as a whole, commoner violence was directed principally at property rather than persons, with assaults on the latter incidental and, only in exceptional cases, grave.

Not only were the fenmen generally restrained and discriminating in their actions, but they were often anxious to legitimise them by claiming the sympathy, or support, of the King (or, in the early 1640s, the House of Commons) or local aristocrats, like the Earls of Lincoln and Exeter, or by appealing to custom and law. The fiction that the King had been ignorant of the fenmen's plight, and even wept at the news of it, allowed them to take direct action confident of royal approval, and protestations of absolute obedience to royal authority helped minimise their own perception of the gravity of their offences. But such reverence could not be sustained when, as in the Isle of Axholme, it was Charles I who had launched the enterprise and rioters were more inclined to direct abuse at the King's person. When they drove cattle into the undertakers' crops, cut turf in their enclosures, or mowed and carted off their hay, the fenmen were reasserting customary rights in former fenland commons, and when they distrained goods, or made token entries into enclosures, their object was to secure a trial of title. Awareness of their legal position, and the irregular or unjust way in which fenland had been wrested from them, informed their actions. Thus in Epworth, where the Mowbray charter was treasured like an object of veneration, the drainers were viewed by the commoners as the riotous intruders, while they themselves were the defenders of legality. The inhabitants of Winterton considered themselves exempt from the Ancholme scheme because the Winterton juror had refused to append his signature to the verdict of 1635 returning the fens as hurtfully surrounded. Elsewhere, commoners expressed a readiness to pay the rents accruing from grounds they had occupied pending a trial of title, or agreed to abide by the judgement of the King or Commons (tacitly assuming throughout that it would be in their favour), and orders forbidding the destruction of the undertakers' crops were observed by commoners simply harvesting and appropriating them.

Circumspection as to the law governing riots also helped to mould the precise form of some disturbances. Commoners intent upon using force sometimes carefully divided themselves into groups of two so as to technically avoid a riot charge. At other times, offenders had recourse to constitutional and legal pretexts that seemed to promise them impunity. Rioters in the Deeping Level in 1603 comforted themselves with the ancient popular belief that there was a legal hiatus until the new monarch was crowned,[1] and they would benefit from a parliamentary pardon at the beginning of the new reign, while in the Lindsey Level they anticipated the usual general parliamentary pardon at the end of the Short Parliament. Furthermore, when taking action, fenmen usually carried nothing more than staves or clubs, pitchforks or scythes, shovels, spades and other instruments required for such specific purposes as filling in drainage and enclosure ditches, harvesting crops, rounding up livestock and the like, and seldom sported guns, swords or daggers, weapons that might betoken a far more violent, or even murderous, intent.

With a few exceptions, the authorities were not inclined to recognise the restrained and self-disciplined features of many of the fenmen's actions, or their anxiety to repudiate rebellion and keep within the law, but were encouraged in their predisposition to exaggerate both the scale of violence, and motives behind it, by the undertakers. This point must always be borne in mind when examining the extent to which fenland disturbances were premeditated events possessing some form of organisation, or the level of local support which they attracted, since these details almost invariably appear in hostile official reports or the testimonies of witnesses procured to damn the rioters. The authorities were tempted, perhaps too readily, to ascribe a military formation to larger disturbances with rioters organised into companies or troops (commanded by captains or lieutenants), and marching to the sound of a drum or carrying improvised flags. Other organisational features drew contemporary comment: crowds were assembled by the ringing of bells or beating of drums; notice of a fictional football match might serve as an invitation to riot (with the ball itself acting as a signal to gather); and at the end of the century, printed papers were posted or verses

---

[1] Holmes, *Lincolnshire*, p. 91.

distributed urging action upon fenmen. Towns and villages sharing a common interest in a particular fen passed intelligence back and forth to help co-ordinate an anti-drainer offensive, and the existence of a 'common purse' or fighting fund was noted fairly frequently, with Oliver Cromwell himself allegedly implicated in one such arrangement in 1637. The money raised was intended to meet the legal and other costs incurred in challenging the drainers and defending commoners faced with prosecution, or it was drawn upon to hire men to watch over goods threatened with distraint or even engage in acts of violence at the behest of local leaders.

Fenland communities themselves provided an obvious framework around which some semblance of co-ordinated and ordered action might be built. Communities that had for generations regulated the common exploitation of fenland resources could be expected to draw together for concerted action when the resources themselves were under threat, and local networks of social and family relationships can be traced among the personnel involved in many disturbances, with the gentry or substantial peasantry often providing leadership or direction, and servants accompanying their masters, sons their fathers, and wives their husbands, as neighbour stood by neighbour in defence of their commons. Towns and villages stood on alert ready to resist arrests in the aftermath of a riot; heaps of stones were gathered and the inhabitants poured forth on to the streets when arrests were attempted. Similar organised resistance met attempts to collect sewers' taxes or distrain goods, and communities closed ranks and protected offenders with a wall of silence against attempts to gather information. In some series of disturbances (and especially in the Isle of Axholme) a distinct continuity of personnel from one incident to the next can be discerned, providing a hard core of experienced activists to guide and temper the rest. Planning was also evident in the timing of some actions after dark so as to take opponents unawares and reduce the possibility of an open confrontation. In addition, the cover of darkness helped offenders escape detection and prosecution, as too did the wearing of vizards or caps which concealed much of the face, or men disguising themselves in women's clothes.[2]

It would be easy, nevertheless, to rely too heavily upon the opinion of authorities who tended to think in conspiratorial terms and over-

---

[2] The wearing of disguises by rioters was regarded in Star Chamber as an offence deserving severe punishment (B.L., Harley MS. 1226, f. 27).

emphasise the fenmen's solidarity and unity of purpose, or exaggerate the degree to which their actions followed a preconceived plan, and ignore the fortuitous or spontaneous element in them. Disagreements over the merits of particular improvement schemes, or the advisability of compromise when pressure was exerted, may have sometimes divided the 'better', or more substantial, commoner from the 'meaner' type. Many of the former sort in Epworth were believed ready to consent to the King's proposals in 1629 but the 'poorest and meanest sort' set their faces against them, and there are indications of a similar dichotomy in Misson, Sutton and Soham, while the reverse position may have been initially true in the Lindsey Level where most of the 10 per cent procured to consent to the Earl's scheme were cottagers. The situation in Crowle was more complex with commoners, for example, dividing into rival factions over the issue of the grounds awarded to the fishermen as compensation for their loss of livelihood. Further examples of division may be added: a compromise agreement proffered to the Lindsey undertakers in 1649 by no means had the backing of all commoners, and the 1691 Epworth agreement may only have had the support of a small minority of strife-weary commoners. Individual fenmen were occasionally prepared to break ranks and either lease land from the undertakers or enter their service, and there were a few spectacular acts of treachery as commoners informed upon their neighbours, or deserted the cause they had earlier affected to champion to join forces with the enemy.

The commoners' leaders certainly did not always enjoy the extensive local following they boasted: Henry Rutter experienced difficulties in rallying Crowle commoners behind him in 1629 and there were later doubts about the extent of his popular following; Hezekiah Browne lost any influence he may have had in the Isle of Axholme after submitting to the 1636 award; and the Quarles brothers, and their two fellow gentry, may not in fact have spoken for the majority of inhabitants in the soke of Peterborough as they pretended in 1650-1. The portrayal of fenmen as prone to insurrection does not readily square with the occasional instances when local support for a move against the drainers fell short of expectations, or leaders felt obliged to use coercion to raise a following. Even in the notoriously militant town of Belton in Axholme there were times when local leaders apparently deemed it necessary to spur the townspeople on with threats and intimidation. The willingness of commoners to contribute towards a common purse was not always constant, and such co-operation may sometimes have been a figment of their opponents' imagination. The organisers of a fund in the soke of Peterborough in 1650 encountered a generally disappointing response; the commoners of Mildenhall Fen in 1684 met only part of the legal costs incurred in defending their interests; some Belton townspeople in 1682 may have contributed towards legal costs only under duress; and some doubt surrounds the actual existence of a common fund in Wildmore Fen in 1663. The effectiveness of a leader's authority also varied considerably, and those who disappointed their followers were swiftly repudiated. Leading figures in the Isle of Axholme experienced some difficulty in trying to check the commoners' excesses in 1650 and 1651, and later representatives who gave their consent to the 1691 agreement were accused of treachery and corruption, upon their return into the Isle, for making concessions and thus lost the commoners' confidence. Finally, the prime responsibility for an outbreak of disorder did not always rest with the fenmen themselves who may occasionally have risen to the bait of deliberate provocation.

Fenland riots rank among the larger-scale disturbances of the century, drawing forth crowds of a hundred or more on at least thirty-two occasions. Contemporary estimates of crowd size must obviously be treated with caution; they sometimes varied by as much as 200, or were imprecisely recorded as 'many hundreds' (with some of the imprecision arising from the way in which numbers might grow during the course of an incident). In almost 60 per cent of these large-scale incidents, the rioters numbered at least 200 and in eight instances crowds numbered 400 or more. The largest crowds recorded were of approximately 2000 and 1100 people, at Ely and in the Deeping Level respectively, but these numbers were exceptional and the nearest to them was a crowd of 500 or 600 rioters in the Lindsey Level. Each level witnessed at least one major riot, but over 40 per cent of them took place in the Isle of Axholme, 25 per cent in the Great Level and the same percentage in the East, West and Wildmore Fens plus the Lindsey Level.

Any social analysis of those implicated in fenland disturbances has to take account of a broad spectrum of local society from poorest peasant to substantial gentry. There were incidents involving only the poorer social element but they were invariably small-scale, and very much the exception, and sometimes aroused suspicions that the poor were being manipulated by their superiors. Three alleged instigators or ringleaders were described as labourers, but there are good grounds for doubting the accuracy of such social placing in at least one case. However, so far as social composition is concerned, one of the most significant points that will emerge from the following narrative is how frequently members of the local gentry became involved in organising opposition to the drainers and encouraging direct action, either by open participation, or covert instigation and direction. Thus members of the gentry are to be found penning petitions against new works, and eulogising the traditional fenland economy; masterminding local resistance; providing a continuity of leadership (with three successive generations of one gentry family, the Rythers, championing the commoners' cause in Epworth); directing rioters from their midst, or animating them from a safe distance and sending along servants and material aid; and persisting in challenging the undertakers in the law courts despite injunctions to the contrary. At least two fenland clergymen also helped foster opposition to the drainers. Where the support or connivance of the local governing elite was lacking, or where the drainers had succeeded in winning over many of the chief landowners (as in the Ancholme Level), opposition was decidedly more muted, and less violent, than elsewhere. But where fenland gentry assumed leadership in the struggle against the undertakers, and promoted, condoned or did little to prevent violence, there was nothing to restrain the peasantry, both of the 'better' and 'meaner' sort, from forcibly recovering their commons.

An analysis of the sex of offenders shows that women were involved in a significant proportion of fenland riots, but only on relatively rare occasions did they constitute the predominant element in a disturbance, or were classified as initiators or ringleaders. In fact the overriding impression is that women participated in these disturbances at the dictate, and under the direction, of their menfolk. Hence wives were dispatched by their husbands to engage in riotous activities, and husbands and wives not uncommonly appeared alongside one another on riot indictments, occasionally joined by daughters and maidservants. Women also performed auxiliary functions such as bringing rioters food and drink, or preparing a celebratory supper on their return. Moreover, they may sometimes have been deliberately pushed to the forefront by their menfolk in the belief that the law would treat them more leniently than male offenders.

So far as the geographical distribution of rioters is concerned, it seems clear that they were normally drawn from the immediate neighbourhood in which the offence took place – from adjacent towns and villages sharing a common interest in a particular fen. Despite the undertakers' grim forebodings, riots never assumed the proportions of a general insurrection, and violence did not generally spill over from one area into another. Hatfield Chase, for example, after some initial violent protests, remained calm for the rest of the century while the adjacent Isle of Axholme was continually rocked by tumult. On the other hand, news of a successful offensive in one fenland area could stimulate disorder in another without any direct links in terms of personnel or geography, or any conscious co-ordination.

Any attempt to investigate whether something resembling a 'political consciousness' developed among the fenmen, and informed their actions, is fraught with difficulties mainly because of the eagerness of their enemies to impute radical or insurrectionary sentiments to them. Words uttered by rioters in the course of a disturbance could be quoted out of context and distorted, or hostile witnesses could simply invent seditious dialogue to bring fenmen into total disrepute. Nevertheless, the general picture to emerge from those occasions on which rioters expressed themselves is that their sentiments were almost invariably related to specific grievances arising from new works and enclosures, and particular individuals associated with them, with little to suggest a generalised political stance. A few articulate leading spokesmen did relate the fenmen's experiences to more general issues like the defence of property against arbitrary intrusions, basic justice, the whole issue of enclosure without the commoners' consent, or the exploitation of the weak by the strong and the poor by the rich. Yet such issues were rarely taken up and articulated by the commoners themselves – with the notable exception of the inhabitants of Sutton, in the Isle of Ely, who in 1649 evidently saw their own struggle as part of a general one against rich oppressors, and appealed to the House of Commons as the protector of the poor and weak from the rich and powerful. In the manor of Epworth, verbal hostility was first directed at the King, as the enclosing landlord, but elsewhere rioters heaped abuse upon undertakers and their agents, commissioners of sewers, Exchequer decrees, justices of the peace and other local officials and the orders or warrants they sought to execute, while simultaneously protesting their loyalty and obedience to God and the King. Fairly regular expressions of contempt for orders of the House of Lords (establishing possession with the undertakers and condemning riotous intrusions), sometimes combined with declarations of reverence and obedience to the House of Commons or even, on occasions, to the King, were a feature of the immediate pre-Civil War period examined in Chapter 3. An awareness of the privileges issue raised in the Commons by the fenland intervention of the Upper House may in fact have percolated down to the commoners, thus lending a convenient air of legitimacy to their contemptuous defiance of the latter's orders. During the Civil War the commoners' allegiances and expressions of party sentiment were distinctly pro-Parliament in most levels (although in the Great Level the situation was more complex), but Chapter 4 provides ammunition for the argument that so far as most fenmen were concerned the chief significance of that period was the opportunity it afforded them to level enclosures, and regain common lands, whatever their ostensible party affiliation. When some of the schemes were revived, and the undertakers' interests defended, during the Interregnum, Parliament, and later the Protector, became the butt of the fenmen's abuse. After the Restoration, Epworth commoners reverted to the more familiar invection against a King, Lords and laws responsible for such injustice. Rioters occasionally drew attention to major national events, such as Felton's assassination of Buckingham (to illustrate the fate in store for a justice/undertaker), or Charles I's trial and execution (as a most untimely warning to the newly restored monarch), but recollections of this nature were very much the exception. Enormous energies were expended at the time in the task of projecting the involvement of Lilburne and Wildman in the fens in the early 1650s as the precursor to a Leveller-inspired peasant uprising, but, as Chapter 6 seeks to establish, such a conspiracy-theory was based upon slight and tainted evidence, and was totally at variance with contemporary political realities. On the whole, therefore, fenland rioters in the seventeenth century did not give expression to political feelings, but contented themselves with drawing attention to specific grievances of immediate concern while in most other respects observing their traditional place and obedience.

Given the degree of active or tacit support fenmen received from sections of the local governing elite, it follows that the latter did not always prove reliable when called upon to prevent or suppress riots. The key local official obliged to act when informed of a riot was the justice of the peace whose powers and duties had originally been specified in the riot statute of 13 Henry IV c. 7. Fenland justices, however, often shared the local resentment against disruptive new schemes, or sympathised with the plight of dispossessed commoners struggling to defend a traditional way of life, and consequently placed local loyalty before national duty. Some justices were unashamedly partisan and did not shrink from using their office to advance the commoners' cause, while others were only slightly less blatant in their mobilisation of opposition to the drainers. On occasion, justices may have signified their tacit support for the commoners by turning a blind eye to acts of violence in their vicinity, as complaints about their neglect and inactivity suggest, but generally they did not openly defy or ignore higher authority and the law when faced with a riot, preferring more circumspect and subtle ways of showing favour. A token display of action might be made by visiting the scene of a riot, and perhaps even requiring the rioters to disperse, but taking no more positive steps to protect a hated enclosure or new works. Some duties might also be performed in the aftermath of a disturbance to give at least a semblance of retribution, such as persuading a couple of rioters to yield themselves up as prisoners (on the assurance that they would be provided for and released shortly), or having offenders brought before them at quarter sessions where legal technicalities were exploited in their favour, trifling fines imposed and no attempt was made to bind them over to keep the peace prior to their discharge. In the Lindsey Level at least, undertakers were sufficiently aware of the shortcomings of fenland justices when it came to protecting their interests to seek parliamentary approval for a measure to make those who neglected, or refused, to move against rioters liable to a penalty of treble damages. Two recalcitrant justices were eventually put out of the commission of the peace but normally their superiors stopped short of such drastic action and contented themselves with a strongly worded reprimand. Not all fenland justices, of course, failed in their duty and there were occasions when they made a genuine effort to prevent or suppress a riot, or had earlier charges of bias and neglect removed. But even the most conscientious justice could be overwhelmed, and rendered powerless, by superior numbers when there was extensive local support for the rioters' objectives. The sheriff, or an undersheriff, was also expected to assist in the restoration of order, and a Lincolnshire friend of the undertakers like Sir Edward Heron could be relied upon to take vigorous action even when this entailed placing himself in considerable physical danger. However, some of Sir Edward's predecessors and successors showed less enthusiasm, and earned censure from the privy council, or House of Lords, for their failure to take the necessary prompt action, and an undersheriff positively obstructed proceedings against rioters in the West Fen in 1636. The performance of other officials gave similar cause for concern: the mayor of Boston in 1642 ignored repeated calls for assistance and finally appeared on the scene after the rioters had achieved their objective; and the coroner who presided over the inquest into a man slain by rioters in 1660 was allegedly corrupted by some of the accused. On the other hand, the peace-keeping role adopted by the steward of Epworth in 1647 shows how a man of influence could at least temporarily defuse a potentially explosive situation.

If justices who recognised the validity of the commoners' grievances sometimes proved uncooperative, the same applies with even greater force to constables summoned to give assistance and make arrests whose parishes had witnessed the depletion of their commonable fens. Constables not only repeatedly failed to perform their duties against neighbours engaged in the forcible recovery of their commons, but were also sometimes to be found in the ranks of the rioters themselves. The parish of Belton in Axholme appointed a whole succession of constables who made no secret of where their primary allegiance lay. Belton constables refused to execute warrants for the arrest of offenders; actively incited violence by recruiting townspeople for attacks on enclosures or by organising guards to resist attempts to impound the commoners' cattle; and engaged in, and helped to direct, the riots themselves. And constables at Upwell, in Norfolk, and at Soham and in the Swaffham neighbourhood, in Cambridgeshire, could show similar priorities when occasion demanded. Having finally surmounted these difficulties, and secured presentments for riot at quarter sessions, the undertakers' troubles were far from over as jurors recruited from a community in broad agreement with the rioters' objectives could be exasperatingly partial and obstructive. Inquisitions into riots in the Isle of Axholme, therefore, were occasionally held away from the area in order to avoid sympathetic local juries and secure verdicts. But the partiality of jurors could sometimes operate in the opposite direction if they fell victim to intimidation and bribery, as the adventurers' agents in the Great Level probably appreciated in 1653.

Large-scale and persistent rioting, or the failure of local agencies to take effective action, often resulted in the intervention of the privy council (or council of state during the Interregnum) or the House of

Lords. It became a regular procedure for the privy council to send for ringleaders and men of substance believed implicated, while leaving the lesser and poorer offender to local justice. The task of ensuring that they appeared before the board was either entrusted to local justices, or to messengers specifically dispatched into the area to make arrests or accept bonds for their appearance. Once in London, they were interrogated and kept in custody until they had made a submission and pledge of future conformity (occasionally guaranteed by a bond), or in some cases prior to 1641 the accused were forced to answer charges in Star Chamber. The board also intervened to remind local officials of their duty to preserve the peace and proceed against rioters, or investigated the behaviour of those officials who defaulted. In the early days of the Long Parliament, the House of Lords took over from the privy council the role of protector of the undertakers' works and enclosures. Prominent offenders, and especially those who had denigrated the Lords' orders establishing possession with the undertakers, were sent for, forced to enter bonds and sometimes committed to the Fleet pending their submission and payment of the messengers' fees. After the Restoration the privy council resumed much of its previous role in the suppression of the more serious fenland disturbances and punishment of principal offenders.

When civil authorities proved incapable of restoring order, military forces might be called upon, and this was especially true during the Interregnum when fenland disorders increased government anxiety over the maintenance of law and order, and military support was readily available. The Isle of Axholme was temporarily pacified in 1628 by the sheriff and thirty horsemen riding into the centre of Haxey and issuing dire threats about the consequences of further disorders. In the midst of the first Civil War, civil authorities found themselves unable to control a severe outbreak of disorder in the fens of Whittlesey without the assistance of a contingent of parliamentarian soldiers from Wisbech. Yet military assistance inevitably entailed the temporary quartering of soldiers in the disturbed area to ensure that rioting did not recommence once the soldiers had retired to their garrisons. Soldiers were thus billeted in Whittlesey for about a month in 1643, and in other fenland towns in the Isle of Ely and Cambridgeshire in the early 1650s, to preserve order and punish a recalcitrant neighbourhood simultaneously, or they were hired by the adventurers to mount guard over their works and enclosures. Military help was also enlisted to restore order at various times in

Norfolk and Suffolk fens comprised within the Great Level, and people in the Isle of Axholme were reportedly terrorised by a contingent of horse and foot for about five weeks at the beginning of 1652 while rents were extracted from them. Although military assistance enabled the adventurers to regain control of the situation in the Great Level by the end of 1653, as Chapter 5 demonstrates, it did have some serious drawbacks. There were complaints that soldiers lacked clear direction from their superiors, and protests over the quartering of soldiers in private houses (which resulted in their restriction to inns and alehouses). Hiring military help for any length of time was expensive and, when that assistance was finally dispensed with, civil authorities inherited an unwelcome legacy of local resentment. An appreciation of these drawbacks by the civil authorities probably helped to make the resort to military assistance a rare occurrence in the fens after the Restoration.

Punishments meted out by the courts to convicted fenland rioters varied markedly in their severity and did not always accord with a readily discernible logic. As misdemeanants, rioters were usually punished by fines but those involved in particularly serious disturbances might also render themselves liable to a term of imprisonment as well. The massive Star Chamber fines imposed upon fourteen Epworth rioters in 1631 were most exceptional and were almost certainly designed to force their capitulation to the drainers' demands. Some account may have been taken of the degree of active involvement of rioters in assessing fines, with heavier penalties being imposed on leaders and instigators, while the poverty of offenders might have had a moderating influence on their fines. Minor offenders who confessed, or placed themselves at the King's mercy, could also expect to escape with a small fine, normally not in excess of 1s. An additional burden was placed upon suspected ringleaders by the frequent practice of requiring bonds as a guarantee of future conformity and these could be quite substantial, bonds of £500 and £400 being demanded in two cases. When individual rioters could not be identified, damages were levied upon towns and villages bordering the scene of the riot on the assumption that local inhabitants were responsible for the violence, and were deliberately withholding information to protect offenders.

Some of the more serious incidents resulted in terms of imprisonment – in addition to substantial fines – being imposed on prominent offenders. An Ely man held responsible for the 1638 riots was fined

£200 and imprisoned at Ely until local justices, fearful of riots to secure his release, had him transferred to Newgate where he remained incarcerated, refusing to reveal his confederates, for nine months. Two indomitable opponents of the undertakers in the West Fen, Nehemiah Rawson and Robert Barkham, were each subjected, at different times during 1637–40, to two terms of imprisonment in the Fleet. Imprisonment in the Fleet became a favoured way of punishing notorious offenders in the early 1640s when the House of Lords took over the burden of restoring order in the fens. After disturbances in the Lindsey Level in 1641, the Lords committed seven rioters to the Fleet as part of their punishment, and ordered another to be confined in Lincoln castle pending his appearance at the assizes. Four West Fen offenders, who had the audacity to refuse to acknowledge their offences at the Bar of the House in February 1642, endured nearly four months' confinement in the Fleet until the Lords showed clemency. On the whole, terms of imprisonment for offences of this nature were relatively brief and were probably designed as a sharp lesson to extract a full confession and pledge of future conformity. Prison conditions were usually appalling and confinement had a psychological impact by isolating the offender from his fellow fenmen and leaving his family unprovided for in his absence.

The fees and other costs involved in an appearance before the Lords and subsequent imprisonment could constitute a formidable added burden. Seven Lindsey Level offenders committed in 1641 incurred a bill of nearly £80 in fees and legal expenses, while thirteen Whittlesey rioters faced a demand of £265 for messengers' fees in 1643, without taking into account the fees due to the warden of the Fleet and the cost of their maintenance in prison. In the long term, a man like Thomas Vavasour of Belton may have been impoverished by the cumulative burden of these and other expenses. Further penalties were sometimes imposed upon offenders before their final discharge, such as the requirement that they make a public acknowledgement of their offences before a justice, on a busy market day, in a town or village close to the scene of the riot, or that they stand in the pillory at Westminster, and in a local town, wearing a paper on their heads desribing their offence of disparaging an order of the House of Lords (a penalty incidentally removed upon a plea for mercy).

Special provision for the punishment of fenland rioters was occasionally laid down by Parliament. All those implicated in the Isle of Axholme disturbances of 1650–1 were explicitly excluded from the

Act of Oblivion, and the Great Level Act of 1663 stipulated stiffer penalties for future violators of enclosures. Sir William Killigrew made an abortive attempt in 1641 to secure parliamentary approval for a Private Bill to make the destruction of drainage works in the Lindsey Level a felony and to lay down a mandatory sentence of three months in gaol for those convicted of levelling enclosures or destroying crops. For a brief period during the Interregnum, the malicious destruction of works in the Great Level was classified as felonious by an ordinance of 1654, provided that prosecution took place within four months of the offence. There is, however, no record of a fenland rioter having been executed for offences committed in the Great Level or elsewhere. Only in the Isle of Axholme were there instances of rioters sustaining fatal injuries in the course of a violent confrontation: two commoners died from gunshot wounds inflicted by the drainers' agents in 1628 and 1660 respectively, thus neatly counterbalancing the two precisely documented fatalities sustained by the other side.

Local reaction to the implementation of fenland schemes in the seventeenth century can be divided into a number of distinct phases. The first phase covers the period 1627–40, including, as it does, the personal rule of Charles I. It is followed in turn by a period of heightened expectations in the lead up to, and outbreak of, the Civil War; of choosing parties, or seizing the opportunity the divisions afforded, in the war itself; of renewed interest in fenland drainage during the Interregnum; of Leveller intervention and renewed optimism; and, finally, of Restoration and partial revival of pre-war schemes, giving rise to struggles that lasted beyond the end of the century. The present chapter is concerned with the first phase when new drainage works and enclosures first came under attack, and the undertakers looked to the privy council for assistance in suppressing, and preventing, riots and safeguarding their works and enclosures.

The Hatfield Level, 1627–40

As the earliest scheme, the Hatfield Level was the first to experience a full-scale riot in opposition to drainage. In early summer 1627 an unspecified number of inhabitants from the vicinity of Hatfield Chase marched to the sound of a drum into the Chase where they assaulted workmen and set fire to carts and timber being used in the works. The King and his council responded to news of the riot with expedition and firmness. The nearest deputy lieutenants were ordered to the works with a detachment of the trained band to protect the commissioners and their workmen and punish offenders, while four principal rioters (including the drummer) were sent for by council warrant following the King's insistence that the leaders be punished.[3]

The Hatfield riot proved a modest affair compared with the Isle of Axholme riots of 13 and 15 August 1628 which were 'accompanied with such extraordinary Circumstances both of Number and of violence'. On the eve of work commencing in Haxey Carr, in the south of the Isle, the townspeople of Haxey were preparing their resistance and, as a foretaste, laid about a drainage worker recognised on the street. Offers of outside help were said to have been received by the people of Haxey: a Gainsborough man had reportedly written two or three times offering eighty men and financial aid, and the bailiff of Owston Ferry was accredited with the resolution that 'if Mr Vermuyden came to the work, he would desire but to have one Blow, if he lost his life for the same'. Resistance was not mounted until the afternoon of 13 August, as the commoners perhaps took time to assess the situation. At about 2 p.m. a group of Haxey women (stage-managed no doubt by their menfolk, as they had been in an earlier stoning of a workman) took the lead by distracting the workmen with threats while Haxey men came up from behind and started stoning them. The rioters had apparently decided to strike terror into their hearts so that they would never return. Some were thrown into a dyke and held under for a time with long poles, and the point was reinforced with threats of broken limbs or burnings, and the spectacle of improvised gallows. When the overseer and his men retreated, attention was transferred to the works themselves, which were overturned, and the abandoned wheelbarrows, planks and assorted implements and materials, which were broken up or burned. The workmen were overwhelmed by the rioters' numbers, estimated at between 300 and 500, rather than arms, which went no further than stones, pitchforks and poles. A semblance of organisation and precise objectives guided the rioters' actions that afternoon. There is also evidence of the presence and leadership of men of some social standing: the townspeople were allegedly assembled by the knelling of a bell and divided into companies led by three men, two of whom (Vincent

[3] P.R.O., P.C. 2/36, fols 8–9.

Tankersley and Hezekiah Browne) were of sufficient substance to appear on subsidy rolls, and some of the rioters came on horseback. The King came in for some verbal abuse, with some rioters protesting that he had no right to their lands, and others that they 'neither cared for god nor the King' or that 'if the King was there they would kill him'.[4]

The workmen did not venture into Haxey Carr the next day but spent the time recovering in Nottinghamshire while awaiting further instructions from an absent Vermuyden. The latter's brother-in-law, Cornelius Liens, who with his brother, Joachim, had invested heavily in the level,[5] had been left in charge and, on the morning of 15 August, received directions from Vermuyden which presumably laid down the strategy for that day. Liens instructed an overseer to take a contingent of workmen and begin blocking the section of the River Idle which separated Haxey Carr from Misson Carr, and this action predictably drew forth a crowd from Haxey. But the drainers were now fully prepared for action, having brought up a boatload of muskets from Thorne earlier in the day to add to the swords and other weapons with which they had equipped a guard. Under the command of a captain Mylanas, the men crossed over in two boats into Haxey Carr from adjacent fens to answer Liens's call for protection. Before disembarking, they were approached by a delegation of four commoners, including Hezekiah Browne, and John Newland, who later allied himself with the drainers.[6] How subsequent events unfolded becomes more conjectural, as drainers and commoners furnished conflicting accounts, but the end result was the death of a Haxey commoner called Robert Coggan. According to the commoners, Coggan's death was a direct consequence of the guard's belligerence; they refused to negotiate and, promising to 'send them home singing with Bullets in their tails', they killed Coggan by firing indiscriminately into the crowd. The drainers admitted firing one warning shot into the air from the boats but claimed a willingness to enter negotiations, which had been disrupted by fighting between guards and commoners in which the former had fired two or three shots and Coggan had been killed. The overseer and a guard called George Booth had been set upon by commoners armed with clubs and pitch-

[4] J. Rushworth, *Historical Collections* (1721), iii, appendix, pp. 39–40; P.R.O., P.C. 2/38, f. 418; S.P. dom. 16/113, fols 38I and III; E. 179/139/724.
[5] Harris, *Vermuyden*, pp. 25, 27, 33, 39; P.R.O., S.P. dom. 16/113, f. 38.
[6] P.R.O., E. 179/139/724.

forks and Booth, although initially believed slain, was later found to have been detained in Lincoln gaol (on Sir Willoughby Hickman's warrant) upon suspicion of Coggan's murder. On 16 August, Booth, described as a Haxey labourer, was charged with felonious assault upon Coggan at a coroner's inquest. Although he had certainly fired his musket on 15 August, and was indicted of murder at a Lincoln gaol delivery, Booth entered a plea of not guilty and placed himself on the country; his indictment, and that of two named accessories, was removed into King's Bench and he was ultimately released, without anyone else being convicted of Coggan's murder or manslaughter. This was an excellent time for Vermuyden's enemies for all the guards present could theoretically be charged as accessories, as too could Vermuyden himself if the order to go armed were ever traced back to him.[7]

Coggan may not have been the only commoner fatality that day, for many years later a Belton weaver recalled that another had died 'standing in defence of his common', and a local clergyman also remembered having attended two burials. According to the same weaver, a justice's warrant had been issued for the arrest of a Dutch-man, who had given the order to shoot, but a serjeant-at-arms sent down to arrest rioters had relieved the constable of the warrant. Several commoners were also wounded that day in what was clearly intended as a display of ruthless determination to overcome com-moner opposition. The commoners were certainly stunned by the violence, and probably did not believe at first that the guards would actually open fire, but they remained determined that 'if the King did send 1000 men he should have no common there And if the King himself came thither he should have nothing to do there'.[8] Not sur-prisingly, the privy council did not see the commoners' deeds as a defence of legitimate title but as a particularly serious riot upsetting commendable work. While the drainers remained virtually immune from legal action for their strictly illegal armed guard and strong-armed methods, the board instructed five local justices to proceed against eighteen of 'the chief actors' in the Haxey riots, and impos-sibly onerous Star Chamber fines were imposed on some to serve as an example – fines that were later waived in return for their

[7] Ibid., S.P. dom. 16/113, fols 38, 38I-IV, 40; E. 134/1649/East 5; K.B. 9/788/50; K.B. 29/278/45 dorso.
[8] Ibid., E. 134/1649/Mich. 11; S.P. dom. 18/37, f. 11III; ibid., 16/113, fols 38 I-II.

submission to enclosure.[9]

Haxey Carr was the scene of renewed rioting on 20 September 1628, when about 300 commoners (mainly 'women boys servants and poor people whose names cannot be learned', according to Vermuyden's informant) cast down a recently constructed bank across the Idle, drove off the workmen and smashed wheelbarrows and planks. The rioters were allegedly supported and manipulated by 'all the better sort', who were reluctant to be 'seen actors in the Riots but . . . those which be of ability hide and conceal themselves and animate the baser sort'. Identifiable offenders were indicted at a sessions held two days later and two gaoled without bail to serve as an example to the rest. Work recommenced in Haxey Carr on 22 September, but was followed by three consecutive days of rioting in which works were extensively damaged, two workmen abducted, and a boat and some draining implements taken away. A Misterton justice, Francis Thornhill, accompanied by a constable and others, came to Liens's assistance on 25 September and demanded commoner obedience to the privy council's directive that work should proceed without hindrance. However, when the rioters 'scornfully refused' obedience, Thornhill and his company (who were keeping their distance as they 'durst not come within their reach') had no option but to retreat home and advise the board that only a 'strict and severe' course of action would prevent the reoccurrence of disorder.[10] The advice was well taken and acted upon: a serjeant-at-arms and two messengers were dispatched to return with nine named rioters; the sheriff and six local justices were ordered to recruit local help in apprehending both rioters and 'the principal animators and ringleaders of others'; all indicted offenders were to be confined pending substantial sureties, and 'chief offenders' reserved for Star Chamber proceedings; and the attorney-general drafted a proclamation for the King's signature forbidding any hindrance of Vermuyden's work in the Isle. Thus the privy council placed its repressive powers at the drainers' disposal, enabling them to overwhelm their Haxey opponents. The proclamation was read in the centre of Haxey by a serjeant-at-arms, accompanied by the sheriff and other officers, and thirty horsemen, and was reinforced by threats to sack and burn the town if there were further disturbances.

[9] Ibid., P.C. 2/38, fols 418–19.
[10] Ibid., S.P. dom. 16/117, f. 67.

The commoners totally capitulated and even helped restore works they had repeatedly destroyed, hoping to earn forgiveness for past offences and be relieved of possible prosecutions.[11]

With one part of the level temporarily pacified, trouble arose in another in the winter of 1628 when the inhabitants of Fishlake and Syke-house cut gaps in a new bank, which had turned the flood waters of the River Don on to previously dry land, and were proceeded against as rioters for endangering newly drained lands in the Chase. Robert Portington of Hatfield, esquire, who as magistrate, steward of Hatfield manor and deputy master of game in the Chase 'ought in his duty to have been a principal furtherer of the King's service', was suspected of being 'a great encourager of these disorders'. Although he had dutifully taken sworn statements from witnesses in the previous August concerning the Haxey riots, on this occasion he proved reluctant to proceed against neighbours struggling to relieve their lands from flooding and was sent for by the board, along with three rioters, on 29 December. Six others were either bound over, or imprisoned in default of surety, for their appearance at the next Yorkshire assizes. The privy council discussed the charges formulated by the attorney-general (on behalf of the King and Vermuyden) against Portington and the others on 10 April at the same time as charges raised against a Haxey yeoman, William Torksey, relating to the riots of the previous September. The charges included a new and surprising accusation that some workmen had been killed by rioters (a charge made only once and lacking surviving evidence of any criminal proceedings) as well as attacks on those seeking to serve Star Chamber process. Nevertheless, Portington and the other Yorkshiremen were immediately discharged upon entering sureties to answer any future charges raised by the attorney-general and Vermuyden, and the suggestion that he be put out of the commission of the peace was rejected on the understanding that he would henceforward facilitate drainage.[12] Torksey had to wait until 31 May for his formal discharge and faced a stunning Star Chamber fine of £1000.[13]

The renewal of drainage work in the following summer, after the winter floods had subsided, was followed by exaggerated complaints of attacks upon works in both the Hatfield and Axholme parts of the level

[11] Ibid., P.C. 2/38, fols 479–80, 482, 485, 491; S.P. dom. 16/117, f. 75; ibid., 119, f. 73.
[12] Ibid., P.C. 2/39, fols 27–9, 51, 183–4.
[13] Ibid., f. 287; S.P. dom. 16/362, f. 103.

at the beginning of July 1629. The board again placed its coercive powers at the drainers' disposal but Wentworth, as president of the Council of the North, replied to the call for action with an indignant denial of Vermuyden's charges in Yorkshire, 'this not being the first of his causeless complaints'.[14] The disturbances had in fact been confined to the Isle of Axholme which descended into serious disorder towards the end of July. On the 22nd, over a hundred Belton commoners (including a local gentleman, Nathaniel Browneley) drove off men constructing a dyke across their common and levelled part of it. Meanwhile, in nearby Haxey North Carr, over 350 commoners (mainly, if not entirely, women) drawn from Haxey and its neighbourhood similarly destroyed a dyke, returning upon three consecutive days to finish their task. On the 30th, the trouble spread to Epworth common where about forty-four Belton commoners assaulted a workman. The earlier July disturbances had resulted in the issuing of Chancery writs grounded upon the statute of Northampton, which forbade the armed intimidation of any royal officer going about his duty upon pain of imprisonment at the King's pleasure. As the sheriff had made the necessary public proclamation at Haxey, Belton and Epworth, the rioters of late July were proceeded against for acting in defiance of the statute, even though they had merely carried implements for filling in dykes, such as shovels, spades and forks, and two were imprisoned in Lincoln Castle.[15] Nine of the women rioters were eventually proceeded against in Star Chamber and were among the fourteen Lincolnshire rioters subjected to crushing fines in 1631.[16] But in the shorter term, the Isle apparently remained turbulent until the privy council, on 27 August, empowered the sheriff to raise the power of the county to suppress attacks on Vermuyden's works and imprison offenders.[17]

Suppressive measures taken in the summer of 1629 in the Isle of Axholme succeeded in restoring order for a few years. There were no reports of violent disturbances directed at drainage works in the Isle in 1630, 1631 or 1632 (the Crowle disturbances of 1632 being of a different nature) and the enclosure and conversion of fenland commons appears to have progressed unhindered. Not until 12 July 1633 did reports again emanate from the Isle that commoners had

[14] Ibid., P.C. 2/39, fols 337, 351; S.P. dom. 16/148, f. 42.
[15] Ibid., K.B. 9/789/5; P.C. 2/39, f. 422; *Statutes of the Realm,* i, 258.
[16] P.R.O., S.P. dom. 16/362, f. 103.
[17] Ibid., P.C. 2/39, fols 422–3.

'risen in troops and cut and thrash their rape: trod the writs under their feet: threatened to kill the servants of the Dutch, rip up their bellies and throw their hearts in their faces'.[18] The sheriff was again instructed to raise the power of the county and a serjeant-at-arms was dispatched into the Isle to arrest some offenders. The continuance of disorder obliged the privy council to send additional instructions to the sheriff, deputy lieutenant and justices of Lincolnshire on 17 July, requiring their assistance in executing a Star Chamber order against the riots with as much military support as was judged necessary. A number of rioters were apprehended and imprisoned (including 'some of the chief' rioters) with a view to making an example of them at the next assizes.[19] One of the agents employed in tracking down and arresting these rioters was John Newland, who must by now have been enjoying a well-earned local notoriety. Newland in turn employed a Haxey labourer with an unsavoury reputation called John Browne who, as he openly confessed at a 1634 Lindsey quarter sessions, made additions and alterations to the warrant he had received from Newland and arrested and imprisoned several respectable persons whose names had not appeared on the original warrant.[20]

The July riots were probably the last major disturbance of the decade in the Isle. In the following summer the inhabitants of Epworth, Belton and Haxey were accused of having destroyed a considerable part of the drainers' fences and ditches under cover of night to evade detection. The drainers assessed the damages at over £2000 resulting from destruction on various nights from 1 May to 1 June 1634.[21] The inhabitants, on the other hand, protested that there had been no such widespread destruction and only a tiny amount of damage had been done in the course of some entries made by a commoner called Barnard to try his, and presumably all his fellow commoners' title.[22] At an inquisition held at Lincoln on 3 October 1635 (deliberately held, the commoners alleged, 20 miles from the Isle at the request of some of the drainers without due notice being given to the commoners), the jury found the destruction to have been done by 'a multitude of unknown persons' and the levying of damages by distress upon adjoining towns and villages was subsequently ordered in King's

---

[18] Ibid., S.P. dom. 16/242, f. 62.
[19] Ibid., P.C. 2/43, fols 159, 187–8.
[20] Lincs. R.O., Lindsey quarter sessions file, 1633–7, nos. 40, 45.
[21] P.R.O., K.B. 29/284/152, 187 dorso, 215 dorso; ibid., 295/74–74 dorso.
[22] Lincs. R.O., Monson 7/17/51; P.R.O., E. 134/1649/Mich. 11.

Bench.[23] Some distresses were later taken and the damages award was said to have been used to pressurise some commoners into an agreement. For the remainder of the decade the level was relatively peaceful and the participants and their tenants were able to consolidate their position. There is one rather imprecise reference to the laying waste of 500 acres of Haxey Carr in, or about, 1639 and 1640 and of similar destruction there beginning in 1641.[24] But the next major disturbance in the level for which there is clearly discernible evidence occurred on the eve of the Civil War.

Reaction in the Isle of Axholme to the drainage scheme in this pre-Civil War period was not uniform for, although the commoners of the manor of Crowle, in the northern part of the Isle, clearly felt themselves to have been seriously disadvantaged by the scheme, they did not emulate their Epworth neighbours and violently oppose the drainage and division of their commons. Crowle commoners reluctantly agreed to Vermuyden's enclosure of a third of their fens and conflict was confined to the remaining two-thirds and the rival claims, initially, of the lords of the manor and the commoners, and later, of two opposing factions of commoners.

The commissioners who allotted Vermuyden his one-third in 1629 left the remaining two-thirds as commons without any agreement having been reached as to its disposal by the lords of the manor and the commoners (who were almost exclusively copyholders). Crowle had only recently acquired three new manorial lords: Sir Jervis Elwes, Jeremy Elwes and Nicholas Hamerton, esquires. The latter was present at the commissioners' deliberations but refused to give his consent on behalf of his fellow lords to any further disposal of the two-thirds. When Hamerton was later approached by a group of commoners with an offer of pasture for the lords' enclosure in return for their freedom to order the remaining commons as they pleased, he was reported to have turned it down on the grounds that 'the tenants and commoners would be lords themselves and adding further that he . . . and other lords would not have any wastes but such as by the law they might have'. Yet he did appear more amenable when asked to consent to the commoners taking some remedial action to meet a serious pasture shortage following Vermuyden's enclosures, responding with genteel hauteur 'Let the tenants and inhabitants make what

[23] P.R.O., K.B. 29/284/152, 164, 187 dorso, 208, 215 dorso.
[24] Ibid., E. 134/1657/Mich. 2.

good orders they will for the good ordering of the commons for their own good, and he would give way and consent thereunto, for he would not endure the clamour of the poor people, for that they wearied him.' The commoners were instructed to inform his bailiff of their proposals and, if they met with his agreement, they would also be acceptable to Hamerton who would help procure an order at the assizes giving effect to them. As yet unaware of Hamerton's resolve to take part of the commons for himself and the other lords, the commoners proceeded to enter upon the remaining two-thirds of the commons, as their freehold and inheritance, and enclosed part of it to be used in severalty for digging turves, on the understanding that 'the Common was their own and they would dyke it for the lords had nothing to do therewith but only to receive their Rents'. But the purchasers of Crowle, anxious to maximise their profit, did not accept their exclusion and hired men to level the commoners' recent enclosures. The commoners reacted by driving off livestock belonging to the lords and their tenants and hiring men to renew the enclosures, believing that the lords should have been satisfied with their manorial rents, fines and sales of wood and been content to leave the remaining commons to commoners, short of pasture, and fishermen, deprived of their livelihood. The lords, on the other hand, also expected to benefit from the remaining two-thirds and were firmly opposed to any new arrangements that threatened to produce an expansion of freehold tenures in Crowle.[25]

The demarcation of areas in Crowle where commoners could dig turves was part of a comprehensive reorganisation of the remaining commons by a group of commoners led by Thomas Margrave, with the alleged encouragement of Henry Rutter, the Crowle gentleman who had represented the commoners when Vermuyden's enclosure award was decreed in the Exchequer. The commons were divided into two sections, one exclusively for sheep, and the other for cattle, and the new arrangement was enforced by groups of commoners who periodically drove sheep out of the cattle section. On one such occasion, one of the lords' tenants was warned that 'they would not be rescued or hindered by anybody in their purposes' when he confronted about twenty-two commoners rounding up his sheep. On another occasion, commoners led by Margrave drove off the sheep of William Dunlyn and Richard Mowld (two wealthy inhabitants accused of overcharging the commons with large flocks) and severely assaulted

---

[25] Ibid., E. 134/9 Chas. I/Mich. 56.

the former, 'they having sworn and vowed that they would kill him because he did resist them from driving his sheep off from the said Common'. Rutter was identified as the instigator of such actions but, as in his earlier assumption of leadership, by no means all commoners were prepared to follow him for it was said that 'a great part of the said Copyholders did condescend unto the said Rutter and divers others did not'.[26] William Dunlyn's sheep continued to cause offence and resulted in further incidents, like those of 27 and 28 March 1634, arising from efforts to exclude them by digging a ditch, in which both Dunlyn and his servant were assaulted and the latter very nearly buried alive in the ditch.[27]

With a pasture shortage after Vermuyden's enclosures, Crowle commoners were unlikely to tolerate further losses and even set about recovering one enclosure of many years' standing. Nuttlewood (or Nethall), enclosed by Thomas Tyldesley, a Crowle gentleman, about fifty years previously, was forcibly resumed as common, and efforts to re-enclose it in the winter of 1632 were resisted by commoners again allegedly prompted by Henry Rutter. Two men, 'hired and sent (as they said) by the inhabitants of Crowle', halted the work after about seven or eight days and violently assaulted Tyldesley's son, Edward.[28] The latter faced further violence on 16 April 1634 when he and his sister tried to retrieve three of his father's cattle which had been impounded by a Crowle commoner for straying on to his land. When the commoner was reminded of the fact that he stood bound to the peace following an attack on William Dunlyn the previous month, he reportedly answered 'what cared he for the peace for Mr Rutter would bear him out'.[29] Trouble was also provoked by the enclosure of the Lincolnshire section of an area of common pasture called Rainesbut in March 1633 by the new lords of Crowle. Some commoners sought the advice of Rutter and Margrave and were supposedly urged by the former to level the enclosure 'if thee will have me to do anything for you'. A large part of the ditch was accordingly filled in by two commoners in the following May, but the reversal was only temporary and the lords later secured an Exchequer order confirming the enclosure.[30] Rutter and Margrave were also involved in a dispute with

[26] Ibid.
[27] Lincs. R.O., Lindsey quarter sessions file, 1634, nos. 26, 33, 65.
[28] P.R.O., E. 134/9 Chas. I/Mich. 56.
[29] Lincs. R.O., Lindsey quarter sessions file, 1634, no. 33.
[30] P.R.O., E. 134/9 Chas. I/Mich. 56.

Robert, Earl of Kingston upon Hull, from about 1633 over part of a pasture called Acham Carr claimed by the Earl. Boundary staves were removed by several commoners led by Rutter, who was later indicted at Lincoln assizes for an assault and battery upon one of the Earl's tenants.[31]

The 100 acres granted to the fishermen of Crowle as compensation caused particular problems. The lords of Crowle challenged the supposition that the fisheries were the fishermen's freehold and inheritance and pushed a rival claim of ownership. But the grounds were enclosed by the fishermen in May 1632, causing bitter local resentment at the further depletion of commons. Henry Rutter and a Crowle yeoman, John Dunlyn, had purchased part of the awarded grounds and encouraged the enclosure of land in excess of 100 acres to the commoners' loss on the basis that the award had been 'the great hundred' (and hence was 120 acres). Rutter's role in this brought earlier resentments to the surface; he was accused of having retained possession of the Exchequer decree, after it had been read in Crowle parish church, instead of handing it over to the commoners who had paid him lavishly for his services in obtaining it. Dunlyn tried to silence protest by threatening to sell his part to the Dutch drainers, but the enclosure did not survive for much more than a year. A group of Crowle commoners, headed by Thomas Brewer and Thomas Scott, apparently hired men to level it and retain possession, and for fifteen or sixteen years their pasture rights went undisturbed until Rutter and his associates brought an Exchequer action against them in 1649.[32]

When the activities of the commoners of Crowle are compared with those of the rest of the Isle of Axholme in this period, Crowle emerges as the least disturbed part of the Isle, with what violence there was concentrated in a relatively brief period of three years (from 1632–4) and further strife absent until 1651. Remarkably, there were no attacks upon the undertakers' works and enclosures until that year. This was probably due partly to the different legal positions in the manors of Crowle and Epworth, as regards the commoners' title to their fens; partly to the predominance of copyhold tenures in one, and freehold tenures in the other; and partly to the fact that a leading figure, like Henry Rutter, was apparently not prepared to challenge the undertakers but submitted to the Exchequer decree on the

---

[31] Ibid.; E. 134/13 and 14 Chas. I/Hil. 22; ibid., 14 Chas. I/East. 3.
[32] Ibid., 9 Chas. I/Mich. 56; ibid., 1649/Trin. 2; ibid., East. 5.

commoners' behalf. Yet the latter were to demonstrate in 1651 that, with outside help and the encouragement of a successful offensive to the south, opposition to the drainers and their tenants could be mobilised.

The Great Level: the first phase, 1632–3

As the commoners in the Hatfield Level were being successfully forced to submit to the will of the drainers, commoners in the Cambridgeshire part of the Great Level were engaged in their first violent confrontations as Bedford's works got underway. In early May 1632 the manor of Soham witnessed a serious outbreak of disorder which, although immediately concerned with the interests of the lord of the manor, was recognised by the drainers of the Great Level as having momentous consequences for themselves. The lord of Soham was Vermuyden's friend and business associate, Sir Robert Heath, who had recently been appointed lord chief justice of Common Pleas. The manor was composed of about 800 acres of demesne, 2000 acres of freehold and copyhold land and between 9000 and 10 000 acres of fenland commons. An attempt three years earlier to survey and partition the latter had been abandoned in the face of violent commoner reaction, but in 1632 Sir Robert managed to secure an Exchequer award of 2000 acres of fenland for improvement, leaving the rest to the commoners to manage as they wished. A commission to divide the fens was subsequently directed to Sir Miles Sandys and other principal Cambridgeshire gentry who, Sir Robert claimed, gave the commoners every consideration and included 1500 acres of the poorest and most remote land in his allocation. After the division had been decreed in the Exchequer, Sir Robert enclosed 500 acres, but the enclosure was short-lived; it was levelled during the night by thirty or forty commoners, and other attempts at enclosure in May were similarly overturned.[33]

The adventurers for the Great Level, sensitive to the implications posed by such challenges to enclosures sanctioned by Exchequer decree, brought these riots to the privy council's attention on 11 May, calling for the severe punishment of all concerned as a deterrent to further outrages. A messenger was dispatched with a warrant commanding the constables and headboroughs of Soham, with the assistance of its principal inhabitants, to arrest four rioters – along with

---

[33] Ibid., S.P. dom. 16/225, f. 35; P.C. 2/42, fols 32, 49.

any other ringleaders they might discover – and pursue and arrest, either inside or outside the county, any who escaped. Those apprehended were to be brought before local justices and committed to the county gaol to await legal proceedings. Anticipating retribution, the townspeople of Soham were said to have banded together whenever strangers came into the town 'for fear they should be apprehended'. On one such occasion, two or three days before the warrant's arrival, the assembled inhabitants forced the sheriff and his bailiffs (who were in town to execute some legal process) 'privately to convey themselves forth of the town about 2 o'clock in the morning'. The warrant finally arrived on 1 or 2 June, and in the evening of Saturday, 2 June, three or four of those charged with its execution conferred together as to how they might effect the arrests without inviting tumult. It was eventually decided to call a meeting in Soham church for the following Monday morning and, through a constable, invite the attendance of everyone else charged with the warrant's execution. The Monday meeting duly took place, with only five or six absentees (who probably had not been informed), but news of the meeting had no doubt also reached the rioters, who had the whole of Sunday to plan their response. As discussion proceeded in Soham church on how best to execute the warrant, word was brought of crowds of townsmen milling about the streets with the four rioters named in the warrant in their midst. In these circumstances, those charged with the warrant's execution dared do no more than warn the townspeople of the gravity of disobedience, but the few waverers in the crowd were soon persuaded to keep ranks, and no further action was taken until 7 June. The reason for the delay is unclear yet it did contribute to the case later made before the attorney-general against three Soham men charged with the warrant's execution (Richard Peachy and Thomas Clarke, yeomen, and Thomas Hinson, gentleman) of having deliberately dragged their feet.

On 7 June, Peachy and his fellows met once again to discuss tactics, and inevitably men, women and children poured into the streets carrying forks, staves and stones. Faced by a crowd of about 200, Peachy and the rest simply exhorted the rioters to surrender and then retired to draw up instructions for the constable to summon the assistance of forty or fifty leading Soham men by 8 a.m. on the following day. Most obeyed the summons, with the effect that about sixty men were charged with the warrant's execution on the 8th, but they came unarmed, or at most carried staves or walking sticks, on the grounds that the warrant had not required the bearing of arms. Between 100 and 200 townspeople stood out in defiance, warning 'that if any laid hands of any of them, they would kill or be killed'. Two of Heath's men did manage to attach one rioter, but they were violently set upon by four or five townsmen and several were hurt coming to their rescue. When later questioned as to why they had not looked beyond Soham for help, Clarke, Hinson and Peachy gave the rather feeble reply that they had assumed the Soham men would have been sufficient. They most certainly had a case to answer in their failure to recruit more general assistance, or to arm themselves, on 8 June, bearing in mind that they had encountered about 200 crudely armed rioters on the previous day. However, on 9 June Peachy and his fellows finally managed to corner one of the four rioters in a nearby fen who was promptly committed to the county gaol by a local justice, Sir Edward Peyton. The latter had also directed warrants requiring assistance from four adjacent towns, which brought between 120 and 140 men to Soham on the morning of 11 June. These men were somewhat bemused at their reception because 'the Soham men did get them to come in aid of them, and when they came, they would neither show them a delinquent, nor lay hold of any of them themselves, so that it seemed to them, that they were unwilling to have them taken.' A neighbouring constable, with two or three helpers, arrested one rioter but they 'were beaten off, the rest never offering to aid them'. In fact Peachy and the others appear to have placed the most restrictive interpretation upon the authority vested in them by privy council warrant, seeing in it no justification for either weapons or the use of force to effect arrests. Hinson, Clarke and Peachy were interrogated by the attorney-general as to their shortcomings and, although given the benefit of the doubt and discharged, their apparent lack of urgency or enthusiasm, and inadequate state of preparedness (which the attorney-general charitably suggested might be 'some improvidence and no more') were clear grounds for suspicion as to where their sympathies lay.[34]

Opposition in Soham to the enclosure of any part of their fens had been, and was to remain, strong as subsequent events demonstrated. Apart from the rioter arrested on 9 June, another principal May rioter, Ann Dobbs, was also eventually caught and imprisoned in

[34] Ibid., P.C. 2/42, fols 32, 49–50, 99–100, 135; S.P. dom. 16/218, f. 40; 219, fols 1, 11; 220, fols 22, 221–III.

Cambridge Castle where, according to Sir Edward Peyton's recollections, she was kept on a diet of bread and water by a justice (a creature of Sir Robert Heath's) until she agreed to incriminate Peyton as a riot instigator. Peyton saw it as part of a Machiavellian plot by his neighbour, Heath, to acquire his manor on its forfeiture to the King for rebellion, but, although animosity between them continued into the Civil War and a 1632 Star Chamber action against Peyton and others for riotous assembly may have been related, if such a plot existed it was patently unsuccessful.[35]

Sutton South Fen, in the Isle of Ely, was the scene of a rather modest disturbance in May 1632 which, although possibly un-connected with the new undertaking, can certainly be seen as an assertion of the value of fens to commoners. On 15 May, eleven in-habitants of Sutton made a riotous entry into a 2-acre enclosure and proceeded to uproot willow trees and dig out turves. Six of them were skepmakers, and hence free access to willows was essential to their trade, and turbary was a cherished right for all commoners. The rioters were convicted at a Haddenham sessions before Sir Miles Sandys and another justice on 31 May and were fined 1s 6d for their offence.[36] On 14 June 1633, there was renewed rioting in Soham where about seventy rioters filled in six division ditches in an enclosure of Sir Robert Heath's eldest son, Edward, between 11 and 12 a.m. Fourteen of the twenty identified offenders were women, and one of the men (who was accompanied by his wife) had the same name as one of the four principal Soham rioters of May 1632. They were all indicted at a Newmarket sessions on 29 June.[37] This was the last serious incident in the level until the spring of 1637. There were three or four minor incidents within the Isle of Ely in the interval, at Mepal and Sutton, in September and November 1634, and at March, in March and April 1636 [38] (which may possibly have been related to opposition to drainage) but the next extensive riots occurred in the wake of enclosure once Bedford's works had been judged completed.

The East and West Fens, 1635–9

While the undertakers in the Hatfield and Great Levels were enjoying

[35] *D.N.B.*, xv, 1020–1; *Fenland notes and queries,* iii, 13–14 and vi, 186, note; Sir Edward Peyton, *The Divine Catastrophe of the Kingly Family of the House of Stuarts* (1652), pp. 62–3.
[36] Camb. U.L., Ely diocesan records, Ely 44 quarter sessions files, 1632.
[37] P.R.O., K.B. 9/801/31.
[38] Camb. U.L., Ely diocesan records, Ely 2/2 and 8.

a period of calm, their counterparts in the East and West Fens were experiencing their first confrontations with hostile commoners. Within about a year of the completion of work here, the privy council began receiving reports of riots on the undertakers' lands and legal challenges to their title. Lincolnshire justices were alerted to their duties after Sir Anthony Thomas had complained, on 15 June 1635, that great damage had been done to his lands, 'by the assemblies of divers riotous and unruly persons'.[39] In May 1636 the work of the surveyor-general in setting out the undertakers' portion of the West Fen was interrupted, not by force, but by allegedly vexatious lawsuits commenced by Nehemiah Rawson of Birkwood, in the parish of Reasby, gentleman. Rawson was to prove himself one of the drainers' most persistent opponents, and was to suffer several terms of imprisonment and considerable financial loss as a consequence. Having resolved to sue every workman who set foot on his lands, and spend £500 in lawsuits rather than part with any of it, he commenced suits against the surveyor-general and his men, arrested them for trespassing and had at least one imprisoned in Lincoln gaol. Rawson also made reproachful remarks about the court of sewers, earning him a fine of 100 marks, and his defiance encouraged others to mutiny against the undertakers. Arrested with five others (two more having evaded capture) upon a privy council warrant, Rawson appeared before the board in June, but Sir Anthony Thomas sent word that he was unable to attend and prefer charges because he was 'forced to stay and solicit the Justices of the country for the qualification of a seditious people that are like to rebel if order be not taken against them'. Rawson and a Thimbleby labourer were both forced to enter bonds to obey all future sewers' directives and cease all prejudicial actions concerning the undertakers' lands before their discharge on 24 June.[40]

Towards the end of June 1636, the privy council were receiving reports of 'divers insolencies' committed, and others threatened, on the undertakers' lands by the inhabitants of East and West Keale, High and Low Toynton, and adjacent towns. A list of seventeen offenders was compiled for interrogation, with other offenders and abettors, by five Lincolnshire justices who were instructed to bind

[39] P.R.O., P.C. 2/44, f. 606.
[40] Ibid., S.P. dom. 16/321, fols 59, 59I-III; 325, fols 71, 76; 327, fols 36, 78; P.C. 2/46, f. 289.

over, or commit to prison if recalcitrant, some of the 'principal delinquents' to appear before the board on the following 2 September.[41] The most serious rioting in 1636, however, did not take place on the undertakers' lands but on the patentees' enclosures in the West Fen as improvement. The first of these riots in the West Fen on 6 August was supposedly led by two men: Edmond Clipsham of Freiston, Lincolnshire, labourer, and William Richardson, whose abode and status are not revealed.[42] Two days later, 400 or 500 rioters, marching in a warlike manner to the sound of a drum under the leadership of Clipsham and Richardson, who 'termed themselves the Captain and Lieutenant', entered the West Fen and proceeded to fill in several of the patentees' enclosure ditches. The levelling occupied the whole day with passers-by being dragooned into assistance, or having money demanded from them, while the un-cooperative were threatened with burial in the ditches. When urged to disperse or forces would be raised to suppress them, the rioters were said to have replied that 'they feared no suppressing, for the next day they could have 500 come to them, and the next day after more'. On the following day, 9 August, four justices appeared on the scene, in response to the Earl of Lindsey's information, but could only arrest two or three 'poor labourers' as most of their fellow rioters had returned home. A private sessions on 2 September indicted eighteen rioters upon evidence provided by the arrested labourers who surrendered to promises of favour. Special attention was also drawn to a Boston man, Christopher Clarke of Long Hedges, who had been informed against on 16 August for saying 'that the Country would not rest thus, but make all as plain, as ever it was, before they had done'; he was imprisoned without bail. Although hampered by an outbreak of the plague near the scene of the riot, the justices succeeded in arresting most of the indicted offenders who were bound over to the next quarter sessions. But Clipsham and Richardson, 'two of the ablest sort and the principal Ringleaders', and four more prominent offenders were ordered to be committed to Lincoln gaol from whence they were not to be released without privy council authorisation.[43]

At the next quarter sessions, held at Horncastle on 3 October, the undersheriff charged with assisting the justices proved obstructive

[41] Ibid., P.C. 2/46, f. 297; S.P. dom. 16/327, f. 108.
[42] Ibid., S.P. dom. 16/490, f. 82; 356, f. 139.
[43] Ibid., 330, fols 48–9; 333, f. 11; 487, f. 37II; P.C. 2/46, f. 340.

and seemingly reluctant to be involved in anti-rioter proceedings. He was insolent to the justice who had ordered him to convey Clipsham and Richardson to Lincoln gaol without delay, and left for Lincoln the next morning with another prisoner, regarded by him as of greater consequence, leaving the two rioters to be brought at leisure by a bailiff. The undersheriff was no more co-operative when required to arrest the other four ringleaders and his dilatoriness caused apprehension that their followers would be encouraged 'to do more mischief which they daily threaten'. Consequently, on 10 October, the privy council was obliged to vest responsibility for the arrest on the sheriff (and notify him that his undersheriff would be 'called to account in due time' for his behaviour), but he too fell down in his duty and was strongly rebuked by the board on 28 November. In the meantime, the sheriff's inaction had allegedly so encouraged former rioters that they had threatened to indict workmen for renewing the enclosure ditches.[44] The sheriff's behaviour may have arisen from some temporary administrative confusion due to a recent changeover in the office, but the board's orders had been directed to both the old and new sheriff. On the other hand, perhaps he, and his undersheriff, sympathised with local commoners struggling against avaricious courtiers, or feared violence (especially a riotous rescue *en route* for Lincoln), or were simply reluctant to approach a plague-infected area.

Clipsham and Richardson were eventually incarcerated at Lincoln where George Kirke (a patentee) urged that they remain 'by which means the rest of the rioters will be found out these being the ringleaders of all the rest'. Clipsham and two other prisoners did in fact go on to reveal the identities of many rioters, and hence showed how authorities, faced with a local wall of silence, could extract information from a few early identified offenders by isolating them from their fellows, forcing them to endure the harsh, disease-ridden atmosphere of a prison, and presumably subjecting them to rigorous interrogation. The privy council decided on 22 March 1637 to make an example of Clipsham and Richardson; they were ordered to be confined in Newgate prison, from whence Clipsham was not released until 17 May on a £200 bond to guarantee his future conformity.[45]

[44] Ibid., S.P. dom. 16/536, fols 64, 73; P.C. 2/46, fols 424–5, 457.
[45] Ibid., P.C. 2/46, f. 457; 47, fols 258, 302, 422; 48, fols 67–8; S.P. dom. 16/536, f. 73; 348, f. 69; 351, f. 45; 356, f. 139.

While the patentees were enjoying a respite, the undertakers were facing renewed challenges to their possession. In a minor incident on 20 September 1636, a rioter of the previous June brought along his wife and another woman to cart two loads of hay out of one of Sir Anthony Thomas's enclosures (for which he and his wife were given a month's imprisonment).[46] But Sir Anthony was disturbed in a much more serious, albeit non-violent, way in late 1636 or early 1637 by two local gentry – Nehemiah Rawson and John Jessop of Cunesby, esquire. Both men sought the recovery of lands decreed to Sir Anthony: Rawson commenced further lawsuits against Sir Anthony's surveyor and workmen (in violation of his bond), and Jessop procured the indictment of some of his servants and workmen for trespass. Both were sent for by messenger on 10 February 1637, and subsequently entered bonds of £500 each to cease questioning Sir Anthony's possession. For his contempt of the board's earlier order, Rawson was committed to the Fleet were he remained until 4 March. While Jessop apparently caused no further trouble, Rawson, in contrast, recommenced his harassment of the undertakers that summer.[47] By then, orders from the King and council aimed at quieting the undertakers' possession were not being fully executed 'through the obstinacy and disobedience of divers persons ill affected to Government'. Rawson became embroiled with a local gentleman, William Boswell (alias Bossevile) of West Keale, a lessee of the Earl of Lindsey; in late August and September, he was said to have repeatedly driven cattle and horses to graze on Boswell's land and to have threatened to cart away his goods. Boswell's labourers also deserted his service due to physical intimidation and legal harassment (several being indicted at quarter sessions), and he was forced to recruit further labour out of the county, in Yorkshire. All these charges were denied by Rawson who, until the summer of 1639, apparently knuckled under an order of the privy council against further troublesome suits.[48]

Another notable recalcitrant, Robert Barkham, came to the board's notice in November 1637 for disturbing Sir William Killigrew's possession. He was committed to the Fleet, pending his con-

---

[46] Lincs. R.O., Lindsey quarter sessions file, 1637.
[47] P.R.O., P.C. 2/47, fols 140, 209–11, 217; Lincs. R.O., Lindsey quarter sessions file, 1637.
[48] P.R.O., P.C. 2/48, fols 145–6, 439–40; K.B. 9/822/52.

formity, for contravening council and sewers' directives, and his plea in January 1638 for liberty, and freedom to go to law over disputed lands, was rejected. A free man by the summer, Barkham returned to his constant harassment of Sir William's tenants and servants. Again committed to the Fleet on 23 January 1639, he risked being placed in close confinement by continuing to incite his tenants and servants to disturb Sir William's possession in the following summer. The board also intervened to stay King's Bench suits brought by him against Sir William, allowing the latter, or his solicitor, to accompany the attorney-general while he conferred with the judges for that purpose.[49] Barkham's imprisonment was later declared illegal by the Long Parliament and Sir William Killigrew and Sir Anthony Thomas were ordered to contribute towards his compensation.

There is a distinct similarity in the tactics employed by Barkham and Rawson in their defiance of the undertakers and insistence on a legal trial of title. Although their respective terms of imprisonment in the Fleet did not overlap, it is possible that they had reached agreement in Lincolnshire on how best to counter the undertakers' rapacity. Rawson showed no inclination to give up the fight: released on a writ of habeas corpus, he recommenced actions of trespass against both undertakers and tenants in the summer of 1639 (and secured £250 in damages); his cattle were driven into the undertakers' corn and grass; and several under-tenants were forced to pay him rent for lands decreed to the undertakers. He later claimed to have largely been the victim of Boswell's false accusations, but the board did not accept this explanation and issued a warrant for his arrest on 11 October 1639. The attorney-general was also instructed to recover the penalty of the £500 bond (entered into in March 1637) if its condition had been violated, as Rawson was believed to be on the point of selling his estate and leaving the kingdom to avoid payment, and due legal process was again halted by a request to the lord chief justice to stay all Rawson's suits pending their own investigation. Persisting in his contumacious ways even after his board appearance on 28 November, Rawson refused to yield obedience, or give any satisfaction for the wrongs committed on undertakers and tenants, and would not pay the messenger's fees, 'giving out he will have another habeas corpus so soon as he is Committed by your

[49] Ibid., P.C. 2/48, fols 349, 540; ibid., 50, fols 39, 526; S.P. dom. 16/409, f. 201; K.B. 29/287/217.

Lordships and be tried by magna carta, and that he will never yield'. This recalcitrance brought him another period in the Fleet, where he remained from 23 December 1639 until 13 February 1640. The warden had been given special instructions that his release was contingent upon an absolute submission and pledge of future conformity, but on 13 February he was permitted to return into Lincolnshire to attend to a calamitous blow to his fortunes (an accidental fire having destroyed most of his home and outbuildings) after entering a bond to return on 27 March, which a no doubt dispirited Rawson duly honoured.[50]

The Great Level: the second phase, 1637–8

Work on the drainage of the Great Level proceeded for almost four years without interruption until the early spring of 1637 when the commoners of Upwell, in Norfolk, rose in tumult and 'mutinously disturbed' works in their fens. Two messengers were sent into Norfolk by the privy council on 31 March to arrest rioters, nineteen of whom were identified, including Mr Sheppard Brewer and his wife, and the two constables of Upwell. The board had originally intended to have all named offenders brought before them but on 23 June, having been informed that several rioters were 'of so inferior and mean condition as are not fit to be brought up hither', they ordered two Norfolk justices to make a local example of them.[51] Drainage works in Cambridgeshire also came under attack in May 1637. Dr William Sammes, the civil lawyer, who had himself invested in fenland drainage (and was in some form of amicable association with Sir Miles Sandys, junior) was given the task of rounding up and in-terrogating rioters. On 25 May Sammes reported that those appre-hended were 'so miserable poor and base' that they were beneath the board's consideration. If they mainly were, as he claimed, dependent upon parish alms for their survival, their reluctance to relinquish any common land was all the more understandable. One of the rioters, a woman described as 'the first mover of this mutiny', was committed to prison at Wisbech. She had the local reputation of being a witch and was believed to have used magic as a weapon against the under-takers' helpers. Two other rioters, 'gross offenders, and presidents of

50 Ibid., P.C. 2/50, f. 700; ibid., 51, fols 41–2, 91, 214, 309, 407; S.P. dom. 16/435, fols 69, 69I; ibid., 443, f. 81.
51 Ibid., S.P. dom. 16/351, f. 80; P.C. 2/48, f. 45.

disorder to many others', were required to enter bonds for their appearance before the board, but the rest were dealt with locally.[52]

Norfolk fens inter-commoned by the inhabitants of Wretton, Stoke Ferry and Dereham, were the scene of a clash between commoners and workmen in May 1637 which was classified as tumultuous despite denials that force had been used. The commoners claimed to have been engaged in their customary procession around the bounds of the fens, on 16 May, when they came across workmen digging on the very spot where they usually caught wildfowl, and the men had obligingly left with their tools when asked to do so. Such a peaceful gloss on events failed to convince the privy council and, on 31 May, at the King's particular insistence, two local justices were ordered to proceed against offenders under the statute of Northampton. The nine Wretton commoners singled out as ringleaders (and hence required to enter £200 bonds for their future conformity on 20 June) seem to have come from the lower ranks of society; eight are described as labourers and the remaining one as a widow, and five subscribed to bonds with their mark. The frightening prospect of being brought before the board led a few commoners to beg the undertakers' mercy and mediation, which Bedford conceded by asking Secretary Windebank to spare those with bonds from the necessity of an appearance.[53]

Protest and opposition spread over the Great Level during the summer months of 1637 as the undertakers enclosed their awarded lands. The King decisively backed the undertakers at a council meeting on 11 July when complaints about the drainage scheme were debated, declaring that the judgements of commissioners as to the effectiveness of the drainage were final, and promising the undertakers immediate assistance if any disturbances ensued from their enclosures. Complaints emanated not only from the commoners of Over, Willingham and Cottenham, in Cambridgeshire, but also from the bishop and dean and chapter of Ely and from some Norfolk, Suffolk and Cambridgeshire justices. Yet the only concession Charles could contemplate was to refer complaints about the inequality of allotments made at Wisbech, especially those concerning Ely church, and Cambridge college lands, to the surveyor-general and com-

[52] B.P. Levack, *The civil lawyers in England 1603–41* (Oxford, 1973), pp. 267–8; P.R.O., S.P. dom. 16/357, f. 74.
[53] P.R.O., P.C. 2/47, f. 475; S.P. dom. 16/357, f. 152; 362, fols 10, 23, 231.

missioners responsible. The petitioners were reprehended by Charles
for having voiced complaints in the first place and, underlining the
significance of protest raised by such important local officials, he
expressed himself 'very sensible if any of those who are trusted with
the government of the country by him shall be found, for any
interests, or by respects, to be stirrers or inciters of complaints,
whereby the peace of the country may be disturbed and good work
put in danger, or shall sciently forbear to do their duties and
endeavours to prevent the same'.[54]

The board had already received intelligence of one such offender –
John Castle of Glatton, esquire, a Huntingdonshire justice. Castle
prevented any of his cattle from being driven out of Holme Fen, as a
preliminary to enclosure, by an overseer of division dykes on 26 June
1637 by ordering two servants to block the way. Shortly afterwards,
'a great many women and men' hurried into the fen brandishing
scythes and pitchforks to 'let out the guts of any one that should drive
their fens', and, with Castle looking on passively, they turned their
cattle back into the fen. Local commoners subsequently mowed most
of the grass there and drove in a flock of sheep. The high constable of
Yaxley (2 miles north of Holme) claimed that Castle had sent him an
urgent message suggesting that he rally the people of Yaxley, and the
neighbouring towns of Stilton, Farcet and Shand, to contribute to a
fighting fund, as other fenland commoners had already raised money
to petition the King to some good effect and 'if they would adventure
their money as they did they should fare as they fared'. Norfolk,
Suffolk and Cambridgeshire were quoted as counties where such
funds had been raised, and Castle allegedly hoped to extend the
arrangement to the whole of Huntingdonshire, where a start had
been made at Glatton by asking each household for a two shilling
contribution. Although some men subsequently visited Castle, there
is no conclusive proof that his proposal was put into operation.
Nevertheless, the abiding impression left by these events is that local
law enforcement officers either failed in their duty to maintain order
during the enclosure of Holme Fen, or actively organised opposition
to it. There is no record of the constables of Holme responding to the
overseer's call for assistance on 26 June, and the high constable of
Yaxley, although later testifying against Castle, apparently obeyed his
call to publicise the fighting fund proposal. Castle was as circumspect

[54] Ibid., P.C. 2/48, fols 128–9.

as possible in opposing enclosure; he was careful to order only two servants to block the overseer's way (thereby avoiding an incitement to riot charge), and 'stood by' without either actively encouraging or discouraging the subsequent rioters. But his very passivity could only have been read as tacit approval by a crowd that was, after all, following his example, and the point was not lost upon the privy council which removed Castle from the commission of the peace and sent for him by messenger. He was not finally discharged until 3 November, by which time an undisclosed agreement had been reached between the parties, yet he may have resumed something of his earlier role in May 1651 when, as chief spokesman for the towns of Glatton and Holme, he questioned the way in which fens had been allocated rather than opposing enclosure as such.[55]

Of even greater moment, in the light of subsequent English history, was the allegation that Oliver Cromwell had become a spokesman for, and organiser of, the commoners in Ely and adjacent fens by the summer of 1637. A final paragraph in the report detailing Castle's misdemeanours noted that it was 'commonly reported' by those commoners that 'Mr Cromwell of Ely hath undertaken they paying him a groat for every cow they have upon the common to hold the drainers in suit of law for five years and that in the meantime they should enjoy every foot of their common'. There is no confirmatory evidence to sustain this report of Cromwell's involvement, except that it is consistent with his supposedly being appointed to act as the commoners' spokesman at Huntingdon in April 1638 and his later assumption of the role of adviser and spokesman for a number of commoners in May and June 1641, but the motives for his intervention are not readily discernible. Cromwell was definitely not opposed to drainage as such for after the Civil Wars, true to family tradition, he actively encouraged fenland drainage. There is also a possibility that he had become acquainted with Vermuyden at Ely and St Ives, and that a friendship had developed between them (although this is largely conjectural) that formed the basis of a later close relationship.[56] But Cromwell may have been opposed to some of the more glaring injustices associated with the undertakers' award

[55] Ibid., fols 128-9, 338; S.P. dom. 16/230, fols 50-1 (wrongly dated in *Cal. S.P. dom.* as 1632; the correct date is 1637); Camb. U.L., Additional MS. 22, f. 88; Camb. R.O., R. 59/31/9/5, f. 49.
[56] Harris, *Vermuyden,* pp. 74, 85, 115-17.

and have had his social conscience stirred by the plight of the poorer commoners after enclosure. It is equally possible that Cromwell's ambition and shrewd political judgement may have dictated his intervention, for his stand in criticising a drainage scheme which was generally unpopular could only have served to increase his influence in the fens. According to Dugdale's admittedly contemptuous assessment, Cromwell acted as the commoners' spokesman in April 1638 before the commissioners of sewers at Huntingdon, 'in which adventure, his boldness and elocution gained him so much credit', that he was accordingly chosen as one of the MPs for Cambridge in the Long Parliament. The author of a major pro-drainage work published in 1641 may perhaps have had Cromwell in mind when, in the course of speculation about the motives of the drainers' opponents, he included 'such, who maintain and prosecute the rude and ignorant peoples begun malice, only out of a popular ambition'. The notion that Cromwell earned himself the title of 'Lord of the Fens' among the commoners at this time is, in fact, erroneous as the title was first applied by royalist propagandists in November 1643 to ridicule him.[57]

As the summer of 1637 faded into autumn, rioting broke out in the fens of Cottenham and there were disturbances of an undisclosed nature on the undertakers' lands in the Isle of Ely. Two Cottenham rioters (a weaver and a cordwainer) were tracked down by messengers and bound over to appear before the privy council, and two of the Isle of Ely offenders were brought before the board on 1 November and forced to enter bonds for their future obedience. Bedford interceded on behalf of several other 'poor men' in the Isle to spare them the burden of attendance before the board as they had apologised for their offences and were prepared to be bound to conformity.[58] A quiet winter was followed by fresh outbreaks of disorder in the Great Level beginning in the spring, and reaching a crescendo in the summer, of 1638. The King's 12 000 acres were leased out in

[57] A. Fraser, *Cromwell, Our Chief of Men* (1973), pp. 54–5; Darby, *Draining*, p. 64; J. W. Gough, *The rise of the entrepreneur* (1969), p. 263; J. Korthals-Altes, *Sir Cornelius Vermuyden* (1925), p. 98; Harris, *Vermuyden*, pp. 73–4; M. Noble, *Memoirs of the Protectoral-House of Cromwell* (1787), i, 107–8; *Fenland notes and queries*, iii, 159; Sir Philip Warwick, *Memoirs of the reign of King Charles the first* (Edinburgh, 1813), pp. 277–8; W. Dugdale, *A short view of the Late Troubles in England* (Oxford, 1681), p. 460; J.L., *A Discourse concerning the great benefit of Draining and imbanking* (1641), p. 6.
[58] P.R.O., S.P. dom. 16/367, fols 71–2; 370, f. 54; P.C. 2/48, f. 337.

sections by commissioners at Peterborough, around Lady Day 1638, to a number of local people, but complaints soon followed of the tenants' inability to profit from the leases and hence pay their rents, or to retain a hold on the lands. Some of the lessees in the fens of Yaxley and Sawtry, in Huntingdonshire, and Maxey, in Northamptonshire, encountered the problem of local commoners still regarding the lands as commonable and destroying their bridges and passage ways. But not all the blame was heaped on the commoners for the tenants' grass and hay allegedly lay under water because of the failure to carry out work promised at Peterborough.[59] Far more serious and widespread disorder followed the Huntingdon sessions of sewers in April 1638 at which Bedford's drainage of the level, according to the terms of the original contract, was declared imperfect. The commoners interpreted this judgement as an invitation to recover their fens: 'divers disordered and Mutinous persons in sundry parts of the great Level of the fens', it was observed, 'have taken Encouragement to disturb and interrupt the workmen' engaged in enclosing the Earl's lands, and his earlier enclosures were levelled and some of his works overthrown. Acting on the King's express command, two messengers were sent into the level on 16 May to arrest offenders and convey them before the board.[60]

Drainage works in Cambridgeshire were attacked at the end of May 1638 by 'divers of the meaner sort' of Wicken, Burwell, Swaffham Bulbeck and Bottisham. Immediately acting upon information received, two local justices, and a jury hastily assembled by the sheriff, held a riot enquiry on 1 June, but the jury, probably composed of local men not unsympathetic to the action taken by fellow commoners, 'for want of sufficient evidence and proof' found only against Thomas Shipp, a Burwell ringleader, who was imprisoned in Cambridge Castle for want of sufficient sureties for his appearance before the board. However, with one rioter identified, the authorities could usually extract information about others, and Shipp was accordingly examined before the deputy lieutenants and some Cambridgeshire justices at Newmarket on 11 June. He confessed his guilt and went on to reveal the identities of six fellow rioters who, with six or seven others, had levelled the Queen's recent enclosures in four places. A Burwell widow, fulfilling the auxiliary function women

[59] Ibid., E. 178/5970.
[60] Ibid., S.P. dom. 16/395, f. 77I; 390, f. 89.

commonly served on such occasions, had brought the rioters food to sustain them. Upon being reprimanded, two of the rioters were said to have replied 'that though other townsmen had given away their Right, they would cast them down again'. Yet four Wicken commoners, who had demolished embankments, acted on the understanding that 'they did it in their own Right of Commonage; and that if his Majesty's Royal assent were thereto, and that his Majesty's proclamation in Print were published that they might know his Majesty's pleasure therein that it should be taken from them, they would ditch it up again, at their Charges'.[61] This emphasis upon absolute obedience to the King's wishes concerning the fens may have been the result of false optimism engendered by the Huntingdon judgement of the previous April, which had received royal backing, disputing the effectiveness of Bedford's scheme.

The above rioters apparently enjoyed at least the sympathy, if not active support, of both the local justice and the curate of Wicken – Isaac Barrow of Burwell, esquire, and his son-in-law, Robert Grimer. Both men enjoyed considerable local influence: Barrow's standing was believed to be such that he could 'rule them all with a word of his mouth' and Grimer enjoyed similar authority in Barrow's absence. But this influence was not brought to bear, as law and convention required, in proceeding unequivocally against the rioters. A Wicken constable later testified that when several rioters had been brought before Barrow, he neither committed them nor bound them over 'but persuaded them that two of them should voluntarily go to prison, promising them that he would see that they should want nothing, and that he would endeavour to get them out of prison'.[62] Ironically, Barrow was a cousin of that staunch pro-drainer, Sir Miles Sandys, senior, who experienced at first hand Barrow's obstructive, or at best perfunctory, attitude. As his authority was restricted to the Isle of Ely, Sir Miles referred the examination of a Haddenham informant called Barker, who claimed knowledge of the Wicken riot and of treasonable sentiments uttered by one Hovell of Bottisham, to his cousin in the shire. At first Barrow did nothing, but two days later, 'having better bethought himself', he requested Barker's return with

---

[61] Ibid., P.C. 2/49, f. 249; S.P. dom. 16/392, f. 54.
[62] A. G. Matthews, *Walker revised* (Oxford, 1948), p. 80; P.R.O., S.P. dom. 16/375, f. 46 (for which *Cal. S.P. dom.* suggests 1637 as the date of this document but the correct date is 1638).

a view to examining him on oath and taking steps to secure Hovell. Minimal progress was made on Barker's second visit beyond the hearing of his sworn testimony, and the possibility of gathering more evidence against Hovell from a Bottisham man was ignored. In the event, Hovell was committed to Cambridge Castle by another justice and Sir Miles himself bound Barker over to testify against him at the next assizes.[63]

When two messengers eventually arrived in Wicken to make arrests, both the neighbouring justices (including Barrow) and the high sheriff were away in London, leaving only the constables to assist them. One of the latter warned the messengers against placing their lives in jeopardy by entering the town because the townspeople were ready to do battle and had received offers of help from Soham, Burwell and Swaffham. Grimer was also asked to accompany them 'to persuade his parishioners to peace and obedience', but he proved even more reluctant than his father-in-law to take effective action, and was castigated in the messengers' subsequent report. When called upon to assist, Grimer

> was very averse first saying it did not concern him to meddle in such a business, requiring to see our warrants, and after he had seen it, he persuaded us to desist from the execution thereof, telling us that his parishioners were desperately bent to do mischief, and when he saw that that argument would not serve, he told us it would be lost labour to go, for we should find never a man that we looked for in the town and as he was going with us, all his discourse was, against the draining and taking in of the fens. He was also often going back from us, and when we came near the Town's end he said I perceive they are up in Arms already, you are best therefore to make haste through the Town and keep your Horse backs not meddling with any of these men, but only pass through and away.[64]

The curate emerges from this report as blatantly sympathising with, and sharing, his parishioners' opposition to drainage and enclosure, and when the messengers finally confronted a crowd prepared with pitchforks, poles and stones, Grimer behaved more like the crowd's spokesman than an upholder of the law. At the crowd's request, he read out the privy council warrant but gave no help in the attempt to arrest John Moreclacke (or Mortlock), 'a principal Actor',

[63] P.R.O., S.P. dom. 16/392, f. 28.
[64] Ibid., 375, f. 46.

who had bragged that 'he would obey no Warrant from any Lords and . . . being told that it was a Warrant from a Secretary of State by his Majesty's special Command, he answered again that he would obey no Warrant at all from anyone whatsoever'. Moreclacke kept the messengers and constables at bay with a pitchfork, while Grimer's contribution was to advise the messengers to 'best make haste away' as he sought to excuse Moreclacke's behaviour on the grounds that 'he did not refuse to obey the Lords of the Council's Warrant, but the Lords Adventurers'. In such circumstances, the messengers became simply the object of ridicule (one of Barrow's servants 'did scoff at us, and make himself merry to see us thus abused') and were impotent in the face of the townspeople's resolution that 'if any one were taken away, they would all be taken'. Warned to expect the same reception in Soham, the messengers rode out of town as a large crowd of women, and several look-outs on top of the church, were preparing to shower them with stones. Although Moreclacke's wife may have had more than Barrow and Grimer in mind when she asserted that 'the Chief of their Parish had a hand in this business though they would not be seen in it', there is no record of any subsequent privy council action being taken against either of them, or indeed against any Wicken inhabitant.[65]

A meeting of deputy lieutenants and justices at Newmarket, summoned by the privy council to investigate recent riots and punish offenders, reported back on 11 June with information concerning the Burwell and Wicken riots. However, they were not able to ascertain if any disturbances had in fact occurred in Swaffham Bulbeck and Bottisham, as earlier reports suggested, and reassured the board that the whole area was now peaceful.[66] But the same could not be said for the Isle of Ely about which Sir Miles Sandys, senior, writing from Wilburton on 6 June to his son in London, added the dramatic postscript – 'Whilst I was writing this letter, word was brought by my Lord of Bedford's workmen, that the country rose up against him, both in Coveney and Littleport, by the example of Wicken men. And I fear that if present order be not taken at the beginning, it will turn to a general rebellion in all the fen towns, whereof you shall do well to acquaint the lords.'[67] Sir Miles's pessimism was not shared by the

[65] Ibid.
[66] Ibid., 392, f. 54.
[67] Ibid., f. 28.

Earl of Exeter, who had been entrusted with the task of restoring order in the level. In a letter from Huntingdon to the King on 9 June, Exeter gave the following, much more considered, judgement and sound advice, and was probably in no small measure responsible for a shift of government policy in the following months:

> In my opinion your Majesty shall not need to fear a general revolt, for though divers that look upon them do allow of their work, being glad of the reformation, knowing their intents to be no further, and in that respect will levy no arms against them, yet in my opinion they are otherwise touching their allegiance dutiful subjects and in the end if upon the suppressing of these tumults, which grow upon the rage the poor people bear to these enclosures, your Majesty show a public reformation by law, the effect will be to your Majesty's great honour to the great contentment of your people and the placing of your self and posterity in peace and security.[68]

Thus, in sharp contrast, Sir Miles Sandys, a local landowner and active participant in Bedford's undertaking, and a man totally insensitive to the commoners' case, was in favour of the privy council taking immediate suppressive action, while the Earl of Exeter exhibited some understanding of both the causes, and limited objectives of the riots, and why the local gentry were reluctant to proceed against offenders, and counselled compromise.

The riots that had so alarmed Sir Miles Sandys had begun on Monday, 4 June, in Whelpmore Fen, in the Isle of Ely, which, with the adjacent Burnt Fen, was enjoyed as common by the inhabitants of Ely, Downham and Littleport. An estimated forty or fifty men had levelled the undertakers' enclosure ditches as a foretaste of more extensive action planned for the next day. The rioters had presumably felt the need to boost or exaggerate their local support: Nicholas Sayer (or Sayre) recruited a fellow Littleport man for the riot; Thomas Cooke of Ely (also prominent in the 6 June riot) boasted that they were 100 strong on 4 June; and as many as 600 men were expected on the following day. According to the plan of action, men were to be assembled that day under the guise of playing football in Burnt Fen and were to take their lead from Edward Powell, alias Anderson, of Ely (and not Nicholas Sayer, as one Littleport man expected). Powell was to bring 100 Ely men with him and have 'the first blow at the ball', which he would provide, possibly as a signal to begin levelling.

[68] Ibid., f. 42.

But 5 June was incident-free owing partly to pre-emptive action by local justices arresting and imprisoning two of 'the chief movers', and partly to the fact that torrential rain fell on that day, and even a planned rescue of rioters in the custody of Littleport constables was abandoned. However, action had merely been postponed to 6 June when about 200 men filled in enclosure ditches in an apparently well orchestrated riot. Most rioters came from Ely and a Suffolk town about 11 miles to the east, Lakenheath, which enjoyed common rights in the Suffolk section of the Whelpmore and Burnt Fens. Two Ely men had previously visited Lakenheath and had returned with the proposal that both towns should meet in Burnt Fen 'to play at football', and the impression of 'one Town holding privy intelligence with another' was confirmed by similar reported contacts with Mildenhall, in Suffolk, and Littleport. The football itself probably served as a signal to drum up a crowd; John Bryce, blacksmith, was observed on the morning of 6 June bouncing and kicking the ball through much of his native Ely before returning with it into Whelpmore Fen. The great majority of rioters were in fact Ely men, the only outsiders mentioned being fourteen or fifteen Lakenheath men (well short of 100 originally promised) who seemingly confined themselves to giving moral support. Action was concentrated on filling in enclosure ditches, 'not hurting any man's person or goods' as the justices freely acknowledged, until the rioters agreed 'we have thrown down enough here come let us go into Sheild and make ways there'. Four supposed ringleaders were arrested and joined the others in Ely gaol, but the local resentment this produced threatened a serious breakdown of law and order in Ely. Rumours of an intended rescue necessitated a strong watch on the gaol at night, and local justices were reportedly warned that if they 'did take that course to send so many to the gaol that it would be the means to have a thousand people to rise'. The townspeople were said to have become 'desperately careless, and nourish bad spirits amongst themselves', and justices' warrants were 'resisted by some, neglected by others, and some that are charged in his Majesty's name to aid the Constables make light of it and refuse it'. But Ely constables evidently performed their duties to the best of their abilities, baulking only at the prospect of trying to arrest men brandishing pitchforks or the like, and may thereby have earned some local unpopularity which their presentment of three townsmen at an Ely sessions, for refusing to watch over the gaol holding the rioters, did little to dispel.[69]

One of the two ringleaders arrested on 5 June was Edward Powell, alias Anderson, who would have led the rioters if everything had gone according to plan. Although described as an Ely labourer at his interrogation on 7 June, Powell was evidently an educated, literate man who was reasonably articulate and had some familiarity with the law. Earlier in the year he had been brought before an Ely justice, John Goodrick, accused of giving the town crier 2d to assemble townspeople in the market-place the next morning for a journey to Newmarket (where the King was spending Lent) with a petition concerning their fens, 'for the losing of the fens would be the losing of their Livelihoods'. When charged, Powell had insolently retorted, 'If I deny it the Crier's evidence being but one man, is no evidence; and if I confess it, what harm. For, what was he (Mr Goodrick) and the rest of the Justices, they were but the Bishop's Justices and not the King's.' Goodrick tried to prevent disorder by going into the market-place around 5 a.m. the next day, where about sixty people with cudgels had already gathered. From the front of the crowd, Powell protested that there was nothing illegal about being in the King's market-place and taunted Goodrick 'I was yesterday in your hands, and heard what you would say; now you shall hear what I have to say; I will complain of you to the King, for the King my master bade me tell him of any that hinder me in my petitioning of Him, and you now hinder me and the King shall know it.' A valuable legitimising purpose was served by Powell conducting himself among the local poor 'as one having ordinary access and speech with the King', and popularising the fiction that 'the King at Newmarket leaned on his shoulder and wept' at his account of the suffering caused by fenland enclosure. But Powell did not naïvely expect Charles automatically to concede their case for, in reply to an inquiry as to whether the King would grant their anti-enclosure petition, he was said to have warned 'If He do not, it will cause a great deal of blood to be spilt.' Goodrick's own behaviour raises one or two questions, such as why he had not committed Powell to gaol, or even bound him to keep the peace, on the previous day, and Powell was probably hoping to appeal to a sense of local solidarity, and concern for the commoners'

[69] Cary, *English Atlas* (1793): Suffolk; *Fenland notes and queries*, ii, 355–9; P.R.O., S.P. dom. 16/392, fols 45, 45I; 409, f. 50; Camb. U.L., Ely diocesan records, Ely 10 assize files, 1638.

plight, when he asked (presumably with a reasonable expectation of compliance) if Goodrick could 'keep home and take no notice of what we do?'

Powell managed to evade arrest in March by going to London and entering a recognizance for his good before the chief justice of the Isle of Ely, but he could make no such evasion in June and spent twenty-one days in Ely gaol until bailed to appear at the sessions. At his examination on 5 June, he was said to have declared to the justices – 'I will not leave my Common until I see the King's own Signet: I will obey God and the King, but no man else, for we are all but Subjects. Why, may not a man be inspired? Then, why not I, to do the poor good about their Commons?' And on entering prison, he taunted 'I will come out again in spite of you all.' These and other 'foul speeches' were weighed against him at an Ely sessions on 24 July, during the course of which he scandalised the court by interjecting, as a local justice, William March, stood up to give evidence against him, 'Mr March, before you take your oath, answer me to this, were you never forsworn in all your life?' The bench took advantage of the presence in Ely on drainage business of the attorney-general and the King's solicitor to seek advice and they recommended a trial of the indictments against Powell by jury. He was accordingly found guilty and sentenced to a £200 fine and imprisonment in Ely gaol from whence local justices, 'doubting some further mischief about him, if he remained a prisoner at Ely', secured his removal to Newgate, later congratulating themselves that since his removal 'the poor people are very quiet and in good order'.[70]

From Newgate prison, Powell addressed several letters to fellow Ely commoners begging for help, and two of them, both addressed to his 'worthy and much esteemed and assured good friend' William Hitch (the Ely clergyman who was to find fame when interrupted by Cromwell in 1642 as he officiated in the cathedral), were annexed to the bishop of Ely's report to the board about Powell. In the first, probably written in early November, Powell explained that he was being kept in prison because of his refusal to name his fellow male-factors despite daily offers of inducements followed by threats. He called upon his fellows to raise £20 locally which, he was convinced, would secure his release if given 'under hand . . . to such, as are both able, and willing to procure the same'. Hitch was asked to read the

[70] P.R.O., S.P. dom. 16/409, f. 50.

letter to the inhabitants of Trinity parish and then pass it on to St Mary's for a further reading. Although drawing attention to the lamentable condition of himself and his family, which would ultimately force him to reveal names if relief were not forthcoming, the letter elicited no response and was followed up by a brief note, written in terms of the utmost urgency on 29 November, renewing the plea and giving an ultimatum that he would turn informer if he did not receive a favourable reply immediately. As both letters fell into the bishop's hands, they could have been intercepted or handed over to the authorities by Hitch, and perhaps Powell's appeal never reached the commoners, and there is also the puzzling fact that the two letters were not written in the same hand. Whether or not help eventually arrived, he was probably reluctant to trade information for his freedom and remained in custody until 8 May 1639.[71]

Order was restored in the Great Level in the crisis summer of 1638 not only by the arrest and severe punishment of ringleaders like Powell, but also by the willingness of the government to make important short-term concessions to the commoners. At a Huntingdon sessions of sewers held on 18 July, a qualification was added to a previous order made in April (prohibiting entries into fens allotted to the undertakers) to the effect that commoners could retain possession of such fens where they could prove that drainage works were deficient pending a sewers adjudication. The King superseded Bedford as undertaker at the same sessions but, as more urgent national affairs came to monopolise his attention, drainage works were allowed to fall into neglect, and commoners resumed their fens, with the result that the level remained free from disturbances until the first half of 1641.[72]

The Holland Fen, 1638; the Lindsey and Ancholme Levels, 1639

Undertakers in other schemes also faced challenges from aggrieved commoners towards the end of the 1630s. In November 1638, five of the drainers' labourers employed in the King's portion of the Holland Fen were threatened by three commoners on horseback who allegedly said 'Must we suffer the fens to be taken away in this order, we are assured the King knows not of it, and we must come and batter you

---

[71] A. G. Matthews, *Walker revised* (Oxford, 1948), p. 82; P.R.O., S.P. dom. 16/409, fols 50I–II; P.C. 2/50, f. 341.
[72] Albright, p. 57; Harris, *Vermuyden*, pp. 78–9; B.L., Additional MS. 5821, f. 101.

all out of the fen'. When a labourer replied that the three of them could not drive them out of the fen, they countered 'that if one Town could not do it, they would bring 3 or 4 towns more'. Continuing their menaces, the commoners disregarded the labourers' appeal that they were merely poor men striving to make a living and claimed that 'the great ones' who had hired the labourers 'hid themselves' and could not be seen in the fen so that the commoners would be sure to overwhelm them.[73]

Some of the commoners in the southern half of the Lindsey Level, after drainage had been judged completed on 14 March 1639, resisted agents who tried to remove their cattle prior to enclosure. The privy council was particularly anxious to suppress such riots, 'which in these times may prove of a dangerous consequence', and instructed the justices of the Kesteven and Holland divisions to assist the Earl of Lindsey's efforts to retain his enclosures. Poor offenders were to be imprisoned until they found sureties, while those of 'better condition and quality' were to be proceeded against at the sessions or assizes, or reserved for the board's attention.[74] Yet the attacks continued: on 8 June livestock were driven into a Billingborough enclosure of Sir William Killigrew's by four husbandmen; in October two commoners committed further disturbances against enclosures there; and, in the same month, Thomas Hall, gentleman, was guilty of misdemeanours in Donington Fen, 'though not altogether in so riotous a manner' as the Billingborough incident. The June offenders were indicted at a special sessions held at Folkingham on 5 July (as too were two of Killigrew's servants for assaults on commoners on 9 June). The two men involved in the October incident were committed to the Fleet, and Hall to the custody of a messenger, until they entered bonds never to disturb the undertakers again. The privy council referred all future complaints against undertakers to the determination of local commissioners of sewers, yet when Hall addressed himself to the commissioners in early 1640, proceedings were allegedly stopped by Lindsey's invention so that he was left without any means of legal redress. Hall became a leader of commoner opposition to the drainers, acting as their solicitor in the 1640s and 1650s and, although a man of modest means, was chosen knight of

---

[73] P.R.O., S.P. dom. 16/402, f. 18.
[74] Ibid., 422, f. 104; P.C. 2/50, fols 400–1.

the shire in 1654, his enemies believed, because of 'his factious humour'.[75]

First reports of trouble emanated from the Ancholme Level in May 1639 when several men 'of poor and mean condition', urged on by others, were said to be threatening Monson's enclosures by driving in cattle, surreptitiously throwing down banks and fences at night and openly promising further levelling. Apprehensive of disorder spreading in those unsettled times, the privy council instructed local justices to proceed against poorer offenders locally, and bind over the more substantial for a board appearance. The level was thus temporarily pacified until the following summer.[76]

Fenland enclosure had been achieved by a mixture of chicanery, coercion and persuasion, with royal and conciliar connivance or assistance, and the suppression of local resistance to it followed a similar pattern. Fenmen were deprived of a recourse to law to defend cherished property rights when they failed to gain a trial of title, had lawsuits stopped by conciliar intervention or were ultimately deprived of their liberty. Whatever the level of political consciousness of most commoners, wider constitutional issues were inevitably raised by fenland drainage and enclosure – the inviolability of property, the subject's freedom of access to the law and protection from arbitrary arrest and imprisonment – and local reaction to it played some part in bringing on the collapse of Charles's government as fenland enclosure came to be associated with ship money and other excesses of the personal rule.[77] By that stage, fenland commoners, sharing the general optimism that grievances would be rectified, had begun addressing appeals to Parliament, while some of the less patient recommended their attacks on works and enclosures.

[75] Ibid., K.B. 9/817/285-6, 288-9; P.C. 2/50, f. 693; ibid., 52, f. 477; S.P. dom. 16/452, fols 73, 89; ibid., 451, f. 65; ibid., 18/73, f. 91; H.L.R.O., Main Papers, 5 August 1641 petition of Nicholas Rowe and Thomas Hall; ibid., 23 May 1642 certificate of the sheriff and justices of Lincolnshire; *A Breviate of the Cause*, p. 6.
[76] P.R.O., P.C. 2/50, f. 391; S.P. dom. 16/422, f. 23.
[77] Holmes, *Lincolnshire*, pp. 134-7.

3 Lords, Commons and Commoners

As political tension mounted from the collapse of the personal rule to the final outbreak of civil war, all the drainage schemes became targets of renewed offensives, with commoners combining appeals to Parliament with direct action. While the commoners looked to the House of Commons for a sympathetic hearing and expected them to remedy their grievances, the undertakers sought the assistance of the House of Lords, which took over the role previously discharged by the privy council (and, where necessary, Star Chamber) of protecting their interests and suppressing riots and disorders on their lands. These contrary appeals to Commons and Lords eventually resulted in a constitutional clash between the two Houses which helped to heighten the political temperature. But the riots themselves were a most potent stimulant of political division in these pre-war years; fenland riots were at the forefront of a growing wave of rural protest and tumult principally directed against the enclosure of common land which, combined with increasing disorder in the capital, convinced a section of the ruling elite that their future lay with the King, as a symbol of order and orthodoxy, rather than with a Parliament, which appeared too tolerant of, or was believed to be blatantly encouraging, social and economic protest and heterodoxy.[1] As far as the vast majority of fenland commoners were concerned, their main pre-occupation throughout these months probably extended no further than the desire to rectify wrongs sustained at the hands of the under-takers by whatever means or opportunities those troubled times afforded.

The Short Parliament and its aftermath

Fenland drainage became an electoral issue in the choice of the Lincolnshire knights of the shire to serve in the Short Parliament.

[1] B. S. Manning, *The English people and the English Revolution* (1976), pp. 123–8, 135–8.

Voters were advised to 'Choose no ship sheriff, nor Court Atheist, no fen drainer, nor Church Papist'. Hence in some quarters, fenland undertakers were regarded as fit companions for ship money sheriffs, evil courtiers and crypto-catholics as betrayers of liberty and property, and the courtier dominance of some drainage schemes made them obvious and immediate targets for attack. Before Parliament met, preparations were being made in the Lindsey Level to petition against the undertaking as a county grievance, with towns reportedly combining to hire counsel against the undertakers. Powerful figures like the Earl of Lincoln, Sir Henry Fiennes, and Lady Dymock, were ranged against the undertakers ready to mount a parliamentary offensive. One Lincolnshire MP, Sir John Wray, seized the opportunity of a Commons debate upon the grievances of the kingdom, on 2 May 1640, to mention three of particular concern to his county: ship money; depriving the trained band of their arms; and the situation whereby 'we stand not ensured of our *Terra firma,* for the fen-drainers have entered our lands, and not only made waste of them, but also have disseised us of part of our soil and freehold'. Around the same time, a local informant was warning Robert Long that 'you shall hear many more complaints in Parliament than for the present you imagine, for such meetings and combinations are among the people as you can not suppose'.[2]

Some Lindsey Level commoners, probably anticipating parliamentary support, took immediate steps to regain their fens. They began by driving cattle into the undertakers' grounds on 14 April 1640 to consume their grass, and were within two weeks keeping one of their agents extremely busy trying to protect their crops, as his breathless note testifies – 'the country begins to Rise up in arms and makes nothing for 20 of them to come and cut our Land eau banks and stand by it and will not suffer our men to stop it; I am just now going to the Justices about it.' The Earl of Lindsey blamed these disturbances partly upon 'some ill affected persons' who had recruited support among 'the meaner sort of people', and partly upon the encouragement such people had received 'by occasion of this parliament, boasting that what they do will be pardoned by the general pardon usually granted at the end of the parliament'.[3]

[2] E. S. Cope and W. H. Coates (eds), 'Proceedings of the Short Parliament of 1640' in *Camden Society,* 4th series (1977), xix, 227–8; *A Breviate of the Cause,* p. 7; P.R.O., S.P. dom. 16/450, f. 90; 451, f. 65; B.L., Add. MSS. 11, 045, f. 99.
[3] P.R.O., S.P. dom. 16/450, f. 90; 451, f. 67; 452, f. 32.

Disorder spread over the level during the summer: at the beginning of May, cattle were driven into growing crops in Dunsby Fen and forcibly kept there; embankments were cut to flood crops and the grounds reclaimed as common pasture after the waters had subsided; towns were reported to have joined in a bonded association to defend one another; and there were fears that the commoners were about to pull or burn down the undertakers' houses.[4] Alarmed at both the timing and scale of these riots, the privy council adhered to the standard practice of sending for the more substantial offenders while leaving the rest to local justice. Two-thirds of the thirty-six offenders sent for by warrant came from Bourne and the rest (with one exception) from Donington. Heading the latter was Thomas Hall, a gentleman with a previous board appearance for disturbing the undertakers, and another gentleman, William Trollop of Bourne Park, was listed among the Bourne offenders. Trollop was required to enter a £500 bond to answer charges in Star Chamber but was exonerated (and the bond cancelled) when he succeeded in proving that he had gone down to London shortly before the rioting. During the Interregnum, it was claimed that Hall and the rest had been classified as rioters after the dissolution of the Short Parliament, 'it being then a dangerous time to oppose Prerogative power', whereas they had actually made peaceful entries into the enclosures.[5] Nevertheless, the undertakers were convinced at the time that they were facing a crisis, urgently requiring pursuivants to effect arrests or 'there will be no living here'. Some Bourne men were later proceeded against in Star Chamber, but this did not deter their fellow commoners from continuing to drive cattle into enclosures, regardless of possible distraint and even sale.[6]

Other parts of Lindsey Level experienced the forcible resumption of previously enclosed grounds by commoners in June and July. A Swaton man, with just one other, was probably testing the validity of recent enclosures in the fens of Swaton and Helpringham when he made entries on 9 and 10 June. Both men claimed authority for their action from the Earl of Lincoln via one of his bailiffs, John Cole of Swaton, who had assured them that the Earl had directed that

[4] Ibid., 463, f. 46; 452, f. 27.
[5] Ibid., P.C. 2/52, fols 477, 485–6; ibid., 53, f. 85; S.P. dom. 16/452, fols 73–4, 89; ibid., 453, fols 32–3; 455, f. 111; 476, f. 100; *A Breviate of the Cause*, p. 7.
[6] P.R.O., S.P. dom. 16/453, f. 116; ibid., 416, f. 6; H.L.R.O., Main Papers, 22 February 1648 petition of Sir William Killigrew.

Lindsey's enclosures should be disturbed. They were each fined £5, and imprisoned pending payment, at a Boston sessions of sewers presided over by Sir William Killigrew and a fellow undertaker on 21 August, and similar penalties were threatened against others if they failed to make amends for their offences within a fortnight. Any prospect of these entries leading to a trial of title was removed by a privy council order of 12 June forbidding vexatious suits over the undertakers' enclosures and referring grievances to a sewers' adjudication.[7] But as violations continued, the board was again forced to intervene and order the arrest of sixty-three offenders from Donington, and six other towns in the vicinity, on 28 June. A Morton gentleman, Peregrine Coney, and four neighbours were attached in August and subjected to intimidation while in custody, and two were allegedly freed after paying thirty shillings to a pursuivant and signing a disclaimer of title to the undertakers' grounds. Coney and the two others were threatened with committal to the Fleet at their board appearance, unless they entered a £1000 bond never to disturb the enclosures again.[8] Enclosures in Dunsby Fen were the scene of renewed trouble in July, resulting in two commoners being placed in the sheriff's custody until they had paid fines of £10 and £5 respectively.[9] On 24 July the privy council's attention was directed to the anti-undertaker activities of two local gentry, Robert Cawdron of Great Hale, esquire (previously named as joint leader, with Lady Dymock, of fenland petitioners to the Short Parliament), and Thomas Wilson of Kyme, gentleman (Lady Dymock's bailiff). Both men were committed to the Fleet for violating enclosures in Great Hale Fen and Kyme Fen, and inciting others to follow their example, after hopes of a parliamentary redress of grievances had been confounded by dissolution, and there they remained until bound over to appear with Lady Dymock to answer charges in the Exchequer.[10]

The Lindsey Level had been grouped with the Holland Fen and Ancholme Level, on 12 June 1640, as fens where the undertakers faced commotion as disaffected commoners drove cattle into their enclosures, cut banks, mowed and carted away hay and spoiled crops,

---

[7] P.R.O., S.P. dom. 16/463, f. 46; K.B. 29/289/138; P.C. 2/52, fols 548–9.

[8] Ibid., P.C. 2/52, fols 595, 686; H.L.R.O., Main Papers, 12 January 1641 petition of Peregrine Coney, gentleman, and others of the parish of Morton.

[9] P.R.O., S.P. dom. 16/463, f. 46; 464, f. 38; K.B. 29/289/138.

[10] Ibid., P.C. 2/52, fols 663, 676–7, 686; S.P. dom. 16/451, f. 65; 461, f. 60; 465, f. 70.

and pestered them with vexatious suits.[11] No further details were available concerning the Holland Fen disturbances, but the Ancholme disorders had apparently begun in the previous month shortly after the completion of drainage work. As the surveyor was engaged in setting out the undertakers' lands, Sir John Monson was

> by some unruly spirits, much opposed, either by vexatious suits commenced, or threatened against him or his Agents, by discharging his workmen for making of new drains, Cutting his banks, putting Cattle into his ground, mowing and leading his meadow, without giving him rent or other satisfaction, and wilfully refusing the Commissioners' warrants in aiding the surveyor to set out the grounds, according to several decrees.

As a direct result, Monson's fellow undertakers proved reluctant to meet their part of the drainage costs when its profitability had been placed in jeopardy. Following further disorders in early June, the privy council intervened to require all local officers to restore order and send in offenders' names for Star Chamber, or other appropriate proceedings. According to Monson, commoner opposition had only manifested itself once work had finished, yet this was to ignore the disturbances of May 1639 when work was still in progress.[12]

The Long Parliament
Expectations of a remedying of the fenmen's grievances, momentarily frustrated by the dissolution of the Short Parliament, were reawakened when elections were held for a new Parliament. The premier knight of the shire for Lincolnshire, Sir John Wray, an active opponent of court policies since 1627, and one of those commissioners who had been severely critical of Vermuyden's Isle of Axholme works in 1630, resumed his previous parliamentary stance and presented a county petition to the House on 9 November 1640 attacking fenland drainage and enclosure and harassment by pursuivants.[13] As the number of petitions from both commoners and drainers mounted, the House of Commons nominated a committee, under the chairmanship of William Ellis, on 3 December, to examine rival claims, hear evidence and report back to Parliament. However, the committee's

---

[11] Ibid., P.C. 2/52, fols 548–9.

[12] J. Thirsk, *English peasant farming: the agrarian history of Lincolnshire from Tudor to recent times* (1957), p. 190; Lincs. R.O., Monson 7/17/18, 21; 7/18/3.

[13] Holmes, *Lincolnshire,* pp. 139–40; W. Notestein (ed.), *The journal of Sir Simonds D'Ewes* (New Haven, 1923), p. 19; P.R.O. E. 178/5412.

slow deliberations afforded little solace to commoners impatient for reform. Commoners from the Lindsey Level, for example, submitted evidence to this committee, and waited while they listened to the other side, but the committee never apparently proceeded to a report.[14]

While the committee for the fens were examining the commoners' allegations, the Earl of Lindsey was addressing himself to the Upper House, complaining of attacks on enclosures, the molesting of tenants and agents and refusals to pay rent since the beginning of the parliamentary session. His fellow peers sprang to his assistance by ordering, on 6 April 1641, that he and his tenants were to remain in peaceful possession of the enclosures pending a parliamentary adjudication. But the order failed in its purpose and was disparaged in the fens; six days later, local commoners invaded an enclosure in Morton Fen belonging to Sir William Killigrew's youngest brother, Henry, and four Bourne men contemptuously defied the order when it was served upon them by two of the undertakers' servants. The Bourne men were sent for by the Lords on 19 April to answer for their 'high contempt', but one of them was allegedly encouraged to break free from the messenger by Posthumus Preistman, a Common Pleas attorney, who challenged the order's legality and incited disobedience to it. Preistman was also suspected of having been implicated in the disturbances themselves (having drawn 'divers poor men' into entering bonds to secure him harmless), as well as instigating and advising rioters in the East and West Fens, and was called to account at the Bar of the House. Sentence was pronounced upon two of the Bourne men on 12 May: they were committed to the Fleet and ordered to stand in the pillory for two hours in the New Palace Yard at Westminster and at Bourne on a market day, with a paper on their heads inscribed 'For disobeying and using scornful speeches against an order of the Upper House of Parliament'. Upon a plea for mercy, and with Lindsey's favourable intercession, they were spared the pillory and required instead to make a humble submission on their knees both at the Bar of the House, and publicly before a justice at Bourne; a third offender, who had been disobedient but not contemptuous, received a similar sentence.[15]

[14] *Commons' jn.*, ii, 44, 74, 110; vi, 333; *The Picklock*, p. 3; *Certain papers concerning the Earl of Lindsey his Fens* (1649), pp. 2-4, 6.

[15] *Lords' jn.*, iv, 208, 221, 247, 251, 264; T. Birch (ed.), *The court and times of Charles I* (1848), i, 461; P.R.O., K.B. 9/824/132-3; H.L.R.O., Main Papers, 14 May 1641 petition of Thomas Drinkwater and Robert Harwood; ibid., 4 June 1641 petition of Mathew Clerke of Bourne, gentleman.

East and West Fen commoners also looked to the Long Parliament to remedy their grievances. Shortly after Parliament had convened, Edward Ironside, gentleman, led the inhabitants of his manor of Thorpe near Wainfleet in petitioning against Sir Anthony Thomas's discreditable enclosure of a third of their fens. The irrepressible Robert Barkham succeeded in obtaining a full Commons's investigation of the way he had been treated and, on 3 February 1641, the House voted that the terms of imprisonment imposed upon him by the privy council were a grievance and illegal and ordered those councillors who had signed the commitment orders to contribute, alongside Sir William Killigrew and Sir Anthony Thomas, to his compensation. A week later, Barkham was declared free to proceed at common law against the undertakers and the Duchy injunction was dissolved. The equally resolute Nehemiah Rawson led local commoners in their petitioning of the Commons on 11 December 1640, urged their case before the committee for the fens and eventually (on 27 May 1642) secured an order requiring the judges of King's Bench, and the Duchy, to explain their obstruction of the commoners' proceedings at common law.[16] In vindicating Barkham and Rawson, the House of Commons was both specifically attacking the nefarious means used to sustain some of the fenland undertakings, and airing the wider issues of arbitrary imprisonment, the withholding of the subject's rights to a legal defence of his property and the role of courtiers, privy councillors and judges in the excesses of the personal rule.

Frustrated by the delay of a parliamentary hearing, the commoners resorted to direct action in late 1640 or early 1641 in the East and West Fens. They assembled 'in great Troops' to march into the patentees' grounds to level enclosures and destroy crops, and had since repeatedly given notice of their resolution to return 500 or 1000 strong to demolish houses, cart away corn and kill outright, or bury alive, any who dared oppose them. The patentees placed a strong and constant guard over their grounds and appealed for parliamentary

---

[16] H.L.R.O., Main Papers, [1640] petition of Edward Ironside, gentleman; 'The case of the lords, owners, and commoners, of 22 towns in the soke of Bolingbroke' in Thompson, *Collections*, p. 152; *Sir William Killigrew his answer*, p. 12; *The Picklock*, p. 14; *The Anti-Projector*, p. 5; Bodl., *Two Petitions . . . from Thousands of the Lords, Owners, and Commoners of Lincolnshire; against the Old Court-Levellers, or Propriety-Destroyers, the Prerogative Undertakers* (1650), p. 4; *Commons' jn.*, ii, 74, 589; P.R.O., S.P. dom. 16/473, fols 50–1.

protection, with the caveat that such riots 'may (as hitherto it often hath in like cases) prove very dangerous to this Commonwealth, and beget a Rebellion'. The Lords again responded sympathetically by ordering, on 17 April 1641, that the patentees were not to be disturbed further unless Parliament, or a law court, declared otherwise. As little respect was accorded this order as that for the Lindsey Level, and six transgressors were brought down to London at the end of May and kept in close custody for about a week. Describing themselves as 'poor husbandmen', they sought the Lords's permission to be heard through counsel, as they were 'ignorant men not well knowing how to speak before such an assembly', but the request was denied and, on 4 June, these humble fenmen were brought to the Bar of the House to apologise on their knees for their disobedience.[17] This action of the Lords in coming to the assistance of the undertakers in the Lindsey Level, and the patentees in the East and West Fens, was construed in the Lower House as a breach of privilege. The Lords's order of 6 April, quieting the undertakers' enclosures in the Lindsey Level, had been made without reference to the House of Commons, where the commoners' earlier petition was still pending, and hence led the Commons to refer the Lords's order to the committee of privileges on 15 May. The committee reported back, on 29 June, that the order had been an attempt by the Lords to appropriate sole jurisdiction over a matter which was still under consideration in the Commons, and it was voted a breach of Commons's privilege and not binding. It was also decided to inquire into the Lords's imprisonment of commoners from the East and West Fens and to confer with them over the privileges issue.[18]

The same question of Commons's privilege was raised in the House following riots in the Great Level in April 1641 and prompted a decisive intervention by Oliver Cromwell. It was Bedford and his associates, rather than the commoners, who had first turned to the Long Parliament complaining about the King's action in supplanting them. They secured a parliamentary condemnation of the King's proceedings and the introduction of a Bill on 7 May 1641, restoring Bedford as undertaker but the Earl's untimely death halted its

[17] P.R.O., S.P. dom. 16/487, f. 37IV; *Lords' jn.*, iv, 220, 248, 264; H.L.R.O., Main Papers, 4 June 1641 petition of Thomas Abbott, etc.
[18] *Commons' jn.*, ii, 147, 191-2; *A Breviate of the Cause*, p. 8.

progress.[19] Shortly before the first reading, Bedford and the Earl of Portland had been forced to seek urgent protection from the Lords for their enclosures within the Isle of Ely manor of Whittlesey. As joint manorial lords, they had reached some agreement with their tenants (confirmed by Exchequer decree) for the enclosure of about 20 000 acres of marsh and fenland in the vicinity of Whittlesey and Thorney. However, since Parliament's assembly, there had been threats or attempts to flatten fences and banks and drive in cattle. On 22 April 1641, the Lords ordered that the Earls' possession was not to be disturbed but, despite publication in local churches, the order was flagrantly disobeyed by rioting Whittlesey commoners, and the inhabitants of Ramsey in Huntingdonshire. The latter, claiming that some of the enclosed land lay within their parish, drove in cattle and brought actions of trespass and replevin against the Earls' bailiffs and servants when they impounded them. The Lords responded by calling on local officers to protect the enclosures from further disorder and ordered the staying of all lawsuits commenced by the Ramsey commoners until the following term. It is quite conceivable that the Whittlesey disorder may actually have been provoked by two of the Earls' associates, George Glapthorne and Francis Underwood, who were said to have enclosed about 1000 acres of common since 22 April, and were believed to have further enclosures in mind. On 31 July, eleven Whittlesey commoners petitioned the Lords on behalf of their fellows to call a halt to further enclosures, pending a parliamentary hearing, and grant them access to grounds enclosed since 22 April. They firmly denied having ever consented to the original enclosure decree which, as the commons were 'their chiefest means of livelihood', had 'very much impoverished' them. Although requiring Glapthorne and Underwood to reply to the charges, the Lords insisted that none of the enclosures were to be disturbed in the interim, and on 26 November the dispute was referred to the committee for petitions for deliberation.[20]

---

[19] *Commons' jn.*, ii, 137, 196; *The state of the Adventurers' Case, in Answer to a Petition exhibited against them by the Inhabitants of the Soke of Peterborough* (undated); *The Anti-Projector*, p. 4; *An Answer to a Printed Paper dispersed by Sir John Maynard entitled The humble Petition of the Owners and Commoners of the Town of Isleham* (1653), p. 7; P.R.O., S.P. dom. 16/480, f. 88.

[20] *Lords' jn.*, iv, 224–5, 269, 312, 336, 453; H.L.R.O., Main Papers, 31 July 1641 petition of some of the poor inhabitants of Whittlesey; ibid., copy of order of 31 July 1641; ibid., order of the Lords of 22 April 1641.

Somersham and its neighbourhood, in the east of Huntingdonshire close to the Cambridgeshire border, witnessed major disturbances that same April. The manor of Somersham was part of the jointure the Queen had received on her marriage to the King. Her agents had enclosed part of the commons and leased the grounds to the Earl of Manchester, who was lord of the adjacent manor of Holywell-with-Needingworth, with a view to draining them. Early in 1641 the commoners complained to the Commons that the enclosures had been made without their consent and that they, and neighbouring tenants, had been deprived of their common rights, and their petition was referred to the committee on the Queen's jointure. In the meantime, the commoners of Somersham, and the neighbouring villages of Earith, Colne and Bluntisham, had been threatening to level the enclosures and drive in cattle, thus obliging the Lords to order on 2 April that the Queen's possessions in Somersham were not to be disturbed (an order shortly afterwards extended to cover the Earl's enclosures in Holywell-with-Needingworth). Nevertheless, the commoners put their earlier threats into effect on 21 April when 'a great multitude of people', summoned by the ringing of a bell, gathered at Somersham, carrying shovels, spades and crowbars, to throw down the Queen's enclosures. A gentleman from nearby Pidley, Robert Clarke, who farmed part of the enclosures, happened to be at Somersham when the bell was rung and hurried down to the enclosures, with another farmer, ahead of the rioters where he cited the recent order in an attempt to dissuade them from levelling, only to be told 'that that order was only or but from the Upper House and that the Lower House was not acquainted therewith'. The rioters also declared that they 'would break open the fences and feed the said grounds and in case the rent must be paid they would bear a part thereof'. This willingness to pay part of the rent perhaps betokens a reluctance on their part to alienate local men of substance (although it would presumably only be paid pending the legal confirmation of their common rights), and this, and their self-assurance that the worst that could happen was that they would be required to re-erect the fences, was probably part of an attempt to minimise their transgression in their own minds. They turned a deaf ear to Clarke's entreaties and systematically threw open all, or most, of the enclosures in Somersham Fen. On the following day, the Queen's enclosures in the Little and West Fens near Earith were also levelled by another 'multitude' largely from Earith, who made passage ways into all the severals. On 27 April the Lords called upon the sheriff to restore order and resolved to send for those who could be identified as having disobeyed them. Yet violence spread the next day to the heath-land of Somersham where commoners from Colne, Somersham, and St Ives tore up hedges and resumed their commons. On this occasion, a local justice appeared on the scene and instructed one of the tenants to note rioters' names for future legal proceedings. The House of Lords ordered the arrest of eight ringleaders on 5 May, but messengers charged with this duty were assaulted and put to flight, barely escaping with their lives. Moreover, the levelling continued with those formerly sent for by the Lords going into hiding, and avoiding any further open involvement, while they sent 'their Wives and Servants in the Absence to do the like'. In such circumstances, the Lords could do no more than authorise the use of the trained bands to restore order and arrest rioters.[21]

On 22 May Denzil Holles presented a petition to the House of Commons from Lord Mandeville (the Earl of Manchester's son) and Sir Thomas Hatton (representing the Queen) complaining of the riots and requesting an order that the enclosures be maintained until the dispute had been resolved. In the ensuing debate, Cromwell played a prominent part, arguing that

> this much concerned the privilege of this House and of all the commons of England: for after the petition by the inhabitants of the said towns preferred here, and that it was in hearing before a committee of this House, the Lords made an order in the House of Peers to settle the possession, which made the people to commit this outrage, which he did not approve nor desire to justify; and that since they had made another order to settle the possession again by the sheriff and by force of arms with the trained bands.

The House was unanimous in condemning the rioting but because the Lords had breached 'the privilege of this House by sending down orders to settle possession after this House was possessed of this cause, it was thought fit for the present to forbear any order in it'. The constitutional point made by Cromwell had, therefore, carried the day and as a result the House made a stand on its privileges rather than taking action to punish the rioters and restore the Queen and the

---

[21] H.L.R.O., Main Papers, 5 May 1641 affidavit of Robert Clarke of Pidley, Huntingdonshire, gentleman; ibid., first and second affidavit of John Cranwell of Earith, yeoman; *Lords' jn.*, iv, 204, 219, 227, 236, 252.

Earl of Manchester to their lands. In the following June, Cromwell presented another petition, this time from the commoners, and asked that the committee for the Queen's jointure might be renewed to consider it. The House agreed and later referred a counter-petition from Lord Mandeville to the same committee. Cromwell was a member of this committee and its chairman, Edward Hyde, subsequently wrote a brief account of Cromwell's conduct when the commoners appeared before it. In Hyde's view, Cromwell 'appeared much concerned to countenance the Petitioners, who were numerous, together with their witnesses' and openly sided with them throughout the hearing, advising them on procedure and 'seconded, and enlarged upon what They said with great Passion'. Lord Mandeville, who was present to represent his father's interests, was allowed to sit with his hat on in deference to his social position. The commoners and their witnesses, on the other hand, were seen through Hyde's socially prejudiced eyes as 'a very rude Kind of People' whom he was compelled as chairman to rebuke sharply for repeatedly interrupting Mandeville's counsel and witnesses 'with great Clamour, when They said any Thing that did not please them'. Hyde's intervention was condemned by Cromwell who 'in great Fury reproached the Chairman for being partial, and that He discountenanced the Witnesses by threatening them'. When the rest of the committee exonerated Hyde from the charge of bias, Cromwell, 'who was already too much angry', gave vent to his notorious temper and proceeded to reply to Mandeville's defence of the enclosures 'with so much Indecency, and Rudeness, and in Language, so contrary, and offensive' that eventually 'his whole Carriage was so tempestuous, and his Behaviour so insolent, that the Chairman found himself obliged to reprehend him; and to tell him, if He proceeded in the same Manner, He would presently adjourn the Committee; and the next Morning complain to the House of him'.[22]

Through the summer months of 1641 there was much more persistent rioting in both the Lindsey Level, and the East and West Fens, with the commoners gaining the advantage over their opponents. On 2 June, the Lindsey Level undertakers secured the first Commons's reading of a Bill to settle their possession of the

[22] J. L. Sanford, *Studies and illustrations of the Great Rebellion* (1858), pp. 367–72; Manning, *The English people and the English Revolution,* op. cit., pp. 129–31; Edward Hyde, Earl of Clarendon, *The Life* (Oxford, 1759), pp. 40–1.

14 000 acres in the southern half of the level. At the same time, an urgent appeal to the Lords for the maintenance of order produced yet another directive to local officers on 4 June to suppress riots and safe-guard the undertakers' enclosures. The effectiveness of this order was quickly put to the test; on 9 June, the sheriff of Lincolnshire was obstructed and assaulted by seven locals when he tried to restore order in Hacconby Fen, and on the following day a group of Rippin-gale commoners drove livestock into one of the undertakers' enclosures.[23] Although the House of Lords renewed their call to the sheriff and undersheriff to restore order, the sheriff himself apparently entertained doubts about the lawfulness of the under-takers' enclosures which paralysed his will to act. The undertakers protested that the sheriff, when called upon to act in Pinchbeck, had stopped within a quarter of a mile of the place to consider whether the Lords's order actually authorised him to assist in driving the commoners' cattle out of their grounds and, apparently deciding that it did not, had returned home without lending any assistance. The sheriff was summoned by the Lords to reply to these charges as the continuing deterioration of order in the level was blamed on his neglect and inaction which had made their orders the object of local scorn and irreverence.[24] On 30 June livestock were herded into two enclosures in Helpringham Fen (belonging to the Earl of Lindsey and Sir William Killigrew respectively) by two men and fifteen women from Donington. Ten of the latter were wives, with husbands perhaps keeping a discreet distance, including the wife of William Fox, clerk, and two other wives whose husbands had been engaged in riots the previous summer.[25]

By July the undertakers and their tenants in the Lindsey Level seemed on the verge of being overwhelmed by the commoners. On the 8th, Lindsey again appealed to the Lords for emergency action to combat a rising tide of disorder as evidenced by the way commoners had recently 'assembled themselves together in Companies and troops consisting of many hundreds' to demolish banks and destroy crops and, with the sheriff powerless to resist, were currently threatening to pull, or burn, down houses belonging to undertakers

[23] *Commons' jn.*, ii, 164; *Lords' jn.*, iv, 264; H.L.R.O., Main Papers, 4 June 1641 copy of order for sheriff, etc. of Lincolnshire; P.R.O., K.B. 9/824/130, 136.
[24] *Lords' jn.*, iv, 282, 297; H.L.R.O., Main Papers, 2 July 1641 petition of the Earl of Lindsey.
[25] P.R.O., K.B. 9/824/204, 287; P.C. 2/52, f. 595; S.P. dom. 16/452, f. 73.

and their tenants. The Earl's fellow undertakers also petitioned the Commons on 10 July appealing for the protection of their crops from further destruction until the harvest and thereby provoked a prolonged debate revealing considerable antipathy to the undertakers among MPs. 'Many spoke against this petition', Sir Simonds D'Ewes observed, 'showing that the country first petitioned here in this House for redress, and after that, the cause depending here, the undertakers got out an order from the Lords to settle their possession.' D'Ewes contributed to the debate himself arguing that 'we were not now to enter into the body of the cause, to examine the right; for admitting, which I did conceive, that these undertakers had no colour of title, yet now we were to preserve the corn and the peace of the kingdom; which I desired might be done any ways, so as they who reaped the corn might give security to the other side to answer the value of it.' While the House could not condone riotous attacks upon property, it studiously avoided a pro-undertaker stance. The sheriff and justices of Lincolnshire were instructed 'to preserve the peace of both sides', repress riots and safeguard the current crop of corn and rape-seed. At the same time, the House referred to the committee of privileges consideration of how far the undertakers had infringed its privileges by entering upon the commoners' grounds, by virtue of the Lords's order, while the commoners had a petition pending in the Lower House. In a show of impartiality, the House added on 15 July that it did not intend to prejudice the rights of either side in the dispute and referred the complaints of all parties to the same committee.[26] The undertakers therefore turned to the Upper House where, in a more sympathetic atmosphere, Sir William Killigrew secured the introduction of a Private Bill on 2 August to prevent the riotous destruction of crops, enclosures and works in the southern half of the level. The Bill stipulated that the 14 000 acres were to remain in Lindsey's possession, pending a parliamentary adjudication, and laid down stringent penalties for future rioters. The destruction of drainage works would be made a felonious offence, and those who levelled enclosures or destroyed crops would be convicted upon the oaths of two witnesses, before a single Lincolnshire justice, and committed to gaol for three months without bail, and their

[26] H.L.R.O., Main Papers, 8 July 1641 petition of the Earl of Lindsey, his tenants and assignees; Manning, *The English people and the English Revolution*, op. cit., pp. 128–9; Sanford, *Studies and Illustrations of the Great Rebellion*, op. cit., pp. 372–3; *Commons' jn.*, ii, 205, 211–12.

eventual release would be conditional upon their finding sureties for their good behaviour. Provision was also made for dealing with uncooperative justices with suspected commoner sympathies. Any justice who, having been called upon to perform his duties under the Act, refused or neglected to do so would incur a penalty of treble damages which the injured party would be able to recover by action of debt in any Westminster law court. The Bill was committed after a second reading on 5 August but the commoners, led by Thomas Hall and Nicholas Rowe, requested a postponement of further proceedings until Michaelmas term to give them time to prepare their case against it, as they were sure that it was another attempt by the undertakers to block their recourse to law under the guise of suppressing riots. The undertakers had previously secured privy council orders to prevent the commoners from gaining a judgement upon the legality of their proceedings, and the present Bill had been introduced after a Commons's decision to postpone its consideration of the commoners' case. The timing of the Bill also presented the commoners with practical difficulties as the harvest claimed all their attention and their principal counsel was on circuit and had all their documentation with him. The Lords accordingly agreed to a postponement and the Bill in fact progressed no further.[27]

About a week after the second reading of Killigrew's Bill, the undertakers in the Lindsey Level faced the kind of upheaval they had dreaded as the inhabitants of Donington launched a major offensive and disorder rapidly spread to other parts of the level south of Kyme Eau. The Lords's order of 6 April had been read out on a busy Donington market day by one of the undertakers' servants, and in other towns bordering on the fens by the sheriff and local justices, in an attempt to forestall violence. Some awareness of the privileges issue raised by this order in the Lower House had apparently percolated through to the commoners who were said to have asserted that 'They had believed too many Orders of the higher house already' and the present order 'was not worth a Pin. But if they had an Order from the House of Commons they would obey it.' Rioting commenced on 12 August when about sixty-four Donington commoners, armed with long staves and pitchforks, invaded the undertakers' lands. In deference, perhaps, to the Commons's

---

[27] *Lords' jn.*, iv, 337, 343; H.L.R.O., Main Papers, 5 August 1641 petition of Nicholas Rowe and Thomas Hall; ibid., draft of 'An Act for the preventing of Riots, etc.'

previous order against the destruction of crops, the rioters simply carted them away after they had been harvested by the undertakers' tenants. About forty cartloads of corn, rye, hemp and flax were removed over a period of four or five days, any of the tenants' servants who stood in their way were beaten and there were reported threats to raze to the ground undertakers' houses. The rioters, with ranks occasionally swollen to almost 100, were a mixed throng of men and women whose activities had evidently been carefully planned and co-ordinated by two prominent Donington men, Henry Carre, mercer, and William Fox, clerk. Carre, described as a chief instigator and activist, had been implicated in the Donington riot of May 1640, and Fox had been among the Donington rioters sent for by council warrant on 28 June 1640, while their wives had been more recent offenders in Helpringham Fen, on 30 June 1641. Both men, it was claimed, 'do daily call the poor people together, promise them wages, and appoint them when to meet and on what ground they shall commit the riots'. Carre was the dominant figure: it was he who hired the carts for transporting away the crops and the first cartload was deposited in his barns, and it had been Carre who had earlier forbidden the undertakers' tenants to plough the grounds and had caused their cattle to be impounded. Carre and Fox were later attached by a messenger, acting on a warrant of the House of Lords, but escaped from custody. On his rearrest, Carre was reported to have said 'that the said warrant was but an order from the upper house of Parliament and that they would not be carried to London with such a thing', to which his wife added 'that her husband should not go, but if the Lords had any thing to say to him, she would answer them'. True to his calling, Fox refused to go with the messenger on the grounds that 'he would obey god rather than man'. Such behaviour emboldened their fellow prisoners to refuse to accompany the messenger or enter bonds for their appearance before the Lords.[28]

Local sentiment generally favoured the rioters in Donington where an innholder, Richard Stokes, who had been represented in the riots by his wife, spoke disdainfully of the Lords's warrant to one of the arrested men brought to his inn by the messenger, advising him that

[28] *Commons' jn.*, ii, 263; *Lords' jn.*, iv, 428; H.L.R.O., Main Papers, 25 August 1641 affidavit of John Smith; ibid., 6 September 1641 affidavit of John Smith and others; ibid., 8 September 1641 affidavit of Jasper Heily, messenger; ibid., 8 September 1642 paper endorsed 'Sir William Killigrew's business Affidavits'.

he need not obey it 'for it had no seal and that it might be made under a hedge' and 'they were all fools if they obeyed the warrant'. Furthermore, Stokes told him 'not to expend one penny in the said cause, but let them that sent the messenger pay him' and, turning to the messenger, taunted him to put his name into the order 'and he would undertake for all his Townsmen now sent for'. He also warned the messenger not to attempt to remove the prisoners or the townspeople would rise up and rescue them 'and deal worst with them [i.e. the messengers] than the inhabitants of Bicker did deal with Sir Edward Heron, a JP, whose horse they dangerously hurt with a scythe, but they intended to mow off the Justice's legs and hang the scythe about his neck'. Yet the rioters' own local justice, William Lockton, esquire, behaved in a blatantly partisan manner: He committed one of Sir William Killigrew's Dutch tenants to Lincoln gaol for eight days for an alleged assault upon a Donington woman (a former prisoner for riot) who had been involved with others on the previous day in the forcible harvesting of the Dutchman's crop of rye, and simultaneously released the arrested intruders; and, in the wake of further disturbances, he exploited various legal technicalities to block the hearing of evidence against several offenders who appeared before him. If the witnesses could not specify the offenders' forenames, or a name had been misspelt in the warrant by so much as one letter, Lockton refused to hear testimony against them and would not even 'ask their names himself, being urged to it, but did threaten to bind the evidence to their good behaviour for not knowing the delinquents' Christian names'. Meanwhile, he was allegedly meting out arbitrary justice to the undertakers' servants and tenants. One servant was bound to his good behaviour for calling one of the committed rioters a rogue as was a tenant for resisting the riotous expropriation of his corn. When binding over James Fossett, a particularly assiduous agent of the undertakers, Lockton was said to have remarked 'that by God he could make nothing of it, yet he must bind James Fossett to the good behaviour to please the Country'. The case made against him also included the accusation that he had exclaimed 'that the Undertakers did slight and affront him, but by God's blood he cared not a fart for the best Undertaker in England' and had assured some rioters in his own home of his partisanship by swearing 'By God's blood neighbours you shall not be wronged'. Lockton was sent for by the Lords and was put out of the commission of the peace on 8 September, with the proviso that his exclusion was 'for the present' and he could be restored later if the Lord Keeper was satisfied as to his fitness.[29]

Rioting soon spilled over from Donington into other parts of the level as neighbouring towns turned upon the undertakers, destroying works and bridges and carting away (or burning on the spot) their corn and fodder. By 6 September an estimated £20 000 worth of damage had been done in recent riots and the names of 300 rioters had been gathered, excluding women and boys. A few prominent offenders, and especially those who had disparaged their order, were required to enter bonds of £100 each for their appearance before the Lords. The rest were to be left to the assizes, yet one of these, Kenelm Phillips, whose committal to Lincoln Castle had been ordered pending sureties for his appearance at the assizes, and a bond against further riotous behaviour, managed to evade arrest and remain at home with apparent impunity. When Carre, Fox and five others appeared before the Lords on 8 November, they were sentenced to be committed to the Fleet; to pay compensation to Sir William Killigrew; to make a public acknowledgement of their offence in dis-obeying the Lords's order before a justice on a Donington market day; and to find sureties for their future good behaviour. A week later Carre and four fellow prisoners petitioned the House from the Fleet; they confessed their guilt, expressed contrition and begged for freedom, as they were 'men of small estates', living by husbandry, who had been impoverished by the expense of retaining counsel, attending upon the House and paying fees to its servants (which had already cost them nearly £80), and their wives and children faced ruin. In a counter-petition, Sir William Killigrew and his fellow undertakers asked the Lords to ensure that all their expenditure on witnesses and legal costs, of which they submitted a detailed account, was met by Carre and the others because they were mostly 'sufficient men , and the rest, maintained in their disorders, at the charge of the towns where they are inhabitants'. The undertakers were also anxious that the ringleaders' public submission at Donington (preferably before two justices), and the rest of their sentence, should be fully executed as their fellows had recently pulled down two of the undertakers' houses and, on the very day of their

---

[29] *Lords' jn.*, iv, 375–6, 390; *Commons' jn.*, ii, 263; H.L.R.O., Main Papers, 25 August 1641 affidavit of John Smith; ibid., 6 September 1641 affidavit of John Smith and others; 8 September 1641 affidavit of Alsop Crosse, messenger.

appearance at the Bar of the House, a third house had been demolished and even Sir William's £3000 house was under threat. The petitioners were eventually released upon their submission and payment to Sir William of £30 in compensation (which fell far short of his own estimated costs of nearly £180), and they returned to Lincolnshire to make a public submission at Donington and enter bonds of £100 for one another to keep the peace.[30]

The House of Lords were, at the same time, coming to the assistance of the undertakers in the East and West Fens in a vain attempt to protect works and enclosures. On 8 June the House ordered that the undertakers, and the late Sir Anthony Thomas's heirs, were not to be disturbed in their enclosures until a parliamentary or legal settlement had been obtained, but the commoners here shared the same slight regard for their orders as their counterparts in the Lindsey Level. When Anthony Walsh, gentlemen, and two others (acting on behalf of Lady Thomas and her children) tried to expel the commoners' cattle from Sir Anthony's enclosures on 16 June, they encountered stubborn resistance. An angry crowd met Walsh's call for obedience to the recent order with an outright refusal and chased him for 2 or 3 miles crying out for his blood for showing them the order. Three offenders expressed sentiments (later echoed in the Lindsey Level) to the effect that 'they did not care for any order that issued out of the upper house of parliament, but that the same was made under a hedge'. Others derided it in similar terms: one commoner scornfully pulled a paper from his pocket saying that it was as good an order as the one shown them; another said that the order 'was not worth a wisp of grass'; and yet another used 'many opprobrious and daring words of the same, saying who durst put his cattle off the grounds'. Fleeing over banks and through ditches, and even abandoning his horse to the commoners' wrath, Walsh eventually found refuge in a nearby house. Since that incident, more of Lady Thomas's grounds were invaded and her rents fell off as tenants were expelled. Commoners also directly reasserted common rights in both the patentees' and the undertakers' grounds by cutting turf, or digging for clay, or driving in cattle. On 3 July Lady Thomas asked

---

[30] *Lords' jn.*, iv, 390, 393, 410, 428, 439; H.L.R.O., Main Papers, 6 September 1641 affidavit of John Smith and others; 8 September 1642 paper endorsed 'Sir William Killigrew's business Affidavits'; 15 November 1641 petition of Henry Carre, etc.; ibid., petition of Sir William Killigrew, etc. and annexed account; P.R.O., P.C. 2/52, f. 595.

the Lords to dispatch further instructions to local officers for securing her grounds and named six riot instigators worthy of investigation. The latter were summoned before the Lords, along with three or four 'principal Actors', on the understanding (to be followed in similar cases) that the plaintiffs were to bear the costs if the suspects were acquitted. Three instigators and three activists were eventually brought before the House to be bound over for a future appearance.[31]

The West Fen was the scene of repeated attacks upon the patentees' lands in August. In an earlier effort to prevent violence the Lords's order of 17 April had been read out in all churches bordering on that fen, and Nehemiah Rawson had been given specific notice of it, yet on 2 August a crowd from Sibsey gathered in the patentees' grounds to fill in sections of enclosure ditch and drive in cattle, and symbolically rejected the newly introduced arable husbandry by threatening to burn any ploughs found there. This action was repeated on 7 August in other grounds by about seventy commoners who proceeded there 'with a fiddler playing before them' and, declaring that 'they had an order to cast down the Ditches', made passage ways for their cattle into the patentees' corn. Further attacks followed during the first half of August as between sixty and seventy commoners divided into groups of twenty or thirty, on three separate days, to cart away the patentees' flax, and the burning down of houses and destruction of crops was reported to be the next stage. Humphrey Walrond, and other patentees, turned in desperation to the House of Commons and, on 13 August, secured an order for the restoration of peace in the county, yet with the rider that it was not the House's intention 'to prejudice the parties interested in point of title to the land, or to hinder the commoners in the legal pursuit of their interest'. The Commons's order was first put to the test on 27 August when two justices were called upon to help save a grain crop, belonging to Robert Webster, gentleman, from a large crowd of rioters engaged in its destruction. The latter not only refused to obey the justices' commands to keep the peace, 'but utterly contemning the same' threatened their opponents with violence. Some of the rioters were arrested and promptly gaoled at Lincoln, but three days later, while most of the justices were attending the Lincoln assizes, about 200 men and women forced their way into Humphrey

31 *Lords' jn.*, iv, 269, 320, 430; H.L.R.O., Main Papers, 3 July 1641 petition of Dame Mary Thomas, etc.; ibid., 30 June 1641 affidavit of Anthony Walsh, gentleman.

Walrond's grounds. One Lincolnshire justice, Sir Thomas Bishop, who had been instructed to remain in the area during the assizes, hurried to the scene and made proclamation for the rioters to disperse, but he too was defied and could only watch on helplessly as a large quantity of Walrond's wheat was carted off. One rioter, Nicholas Gardiner of Sibsey (who had been similarly active on 2 August), had reportedly vowed that the commoners would have all the wheat 'and what we cannot carry away we will burn and the house too before we sleep'. Gardiner was also overheard saying to some of his fellows 'If we do not take away all the Corn . . . I would some of us might kill or be killed', a desperate resolution that was repeated by the forty or so 'principal Instigators and Leaders'. Rioting continued the next day as local men and women, again ignoring Bishop's orders, expropriated large quantities of grain from George Kirke's tenants, and the Commons received a grave warning on 6 September that there was good reason to fear 'further and greater mischiefs' in those parts that could lead to a general rebellion.[32]

Efforts were made in the following October to restore enclosure ditches levelled in the West Fen during the summer, but the restoration work was short-lived. Local commoners were reported to have hired two men, William Crosse and William Ebbron, to fill in the restored ditches; this they did energetically, ignoring the appeal made to the Lords's order of 17 April by a tenant, John Gaddes, gentleman. Further attempts at enclosure after the departure of Crosse and Ebbron were reversed by them within a few days and, when he ordered them to desist, Gaddes was both assaulted and later brought before the mayor of Boston by warrant for defending himself with a pistol, a Scots dagger and a pitchfork. Despite having been shown a copy of the Lords's order, the mayor bound Gaddes over to the next quarter sessions. By coming to the assistance of the undertakers and patentees, the Lords had aroused the hostility of the West Fen commoners in the same way as they had invited enmity in the Lindsey Level. Two of those involved in the 2 August riot were later overheard resolving that 'they would obey no order made by the Lords for it was of no effect for they could make as good an order under a hedge' but would willingly obey a Commons's order, an

---

[32] H.L.R.O., Main Papers, [January] 1641/42 application for further order for quieting the King's possessions in Lincolnshire; 13 November 1641 affidavit of Robert Richardson; *Commons' jn.*, ii, 254; P.R.O., S.P. dom. 16/484, f. 8.

opinion believed shared by several others. The same men also confessed to having been incited by Nehemiah Rawson 'who at several times bid them do it and he would be their warrant and that they should keep possession of the same', adding to suspicions that he had been 'the Chief Ring-Leader of all these unlawful Acts'. However, they subsequently joined Ebbron and Crosse in disavowing any riotous intent in their levelling of enclosure ditches; they claimed to have acted in a peaceful manner, not more than two at a time, 'to try their right of inheritance' while not being 'well informed' concerning the Lords's order. The patentees continued to receive the Lords's backing in their struggle against commoner encroachment. On 3 December the sheriff was instructed to reinstate both patentees and tenants in possession of their grounds and preserve the peace as they restored enclosure ditches and fences. The order was to be publicised in all market towns within a 5-mile radius of the grounds together with a warning of the Lords's intention to punish severely future offenders and their abettors. At the same time, Ebbron, Crosse and the two others who had disparaged the Lords's order of 17 April were brought down to London to be committed to the custody of the usher until 20 January 1642, when the House ordered their release on condition that they paid all fees owed, and made a pledge before the lord chief justice of King's Bench never again to commit such offences. Yet, in a remarkable show of defiance, the four fenmen steadfastly refused to acknowledge their offences before the lord chief justice and maintained this stance even when brought to the Bar of the House on 2 February. If, as they themselves later claimed, they were all 'very poor men', earning a living 'by their hand labour', such audacity must have required great courage and conviction. They certainly paid a price for their stand: they were immediately committed to the Fleet and not released until the following 26 May after pleading for clemency.[33]

In the middle of a relatively peaceful fenland winter, the commoners received some recognition of the validity of their grievances against the undertakers in the form of a condemnation of the way in which large quantities of commons and several grounds

---

[33] H.L.R.O., Main Papers, 3 December 1641 affidavit of John Gaddes, gentleman; 7 January 1642 affidavit of Henny Dandyson; 8 January 1642 affidavit of Philip Hix; [January] 1641/42 application for further order for quieting the King's possessions in Lincolnshire; 26 May 1642 petition of William Ebbron, etc.; *Lords' jn.*, iv, pp. 461–2, 524, 553–4, 559; v, 85.

had been taken away by a 'falsifying and adulterating' of the statute of improvement of 43 Elizabeth I, and by an abuse of the commission of sewers whereby the commoners' consent was not obtained as the 1531 statute required. This critical reference to fenland enclosure, which formed part of the Grand Remonstrance, was not, however, intended as a blanket condemnation of the drainage schemes of the previous two decades. A later drainage apologist interpreted it as applying only to improvements made by the King as lord of several fenland manors without due observation of the statute of improvement, 'and that this work of draining [i.e. the Great Level] was not intended in this Declaration is clear because at that time Bedford's draining was countenanced by Parliament and a Bill committed for the establishing it'.[34] While commoners who were the victims of courtier-dominated enterprises, like the Lindsey Level and the East and West Fens, could rely upon a reasonable fund of Commons's sympathy, their counterparts in the Great Level (the privileges issue apart) faced a House where majority opinion clearly favoured the late Earl of Bedford's enterprise. On 16 February 1642 the House referred the problem of completing the drainage of the Great Level to the committee for the fens and, on 31 May, a drainage Bill was introduced into the House by some of Bedford's former associates. The Bill's parliamentary progress provoked some alarm among Huntingdonshire commoners who in July urged that their objections to it be considered, but the outbreak of civil war shortly halted its further progress.[35]

The Great Level had also experienced disturbances in the summer of 1641, albeit on a far less widespread and serious a scale than in southern Lincolnshire. Sir Robert Heath's enclosures in Soham Fen were once again levelled by local commoners and, on 5 August, the protection of the Lords's order of 13 July against riots was afforded to his grounds.[36] Two or three attempts were also made to sabotage the Littleport sluice beginning with an attempt around 1 August when a boat, packed with hassocks, was set on fire under the sluice but it escaped destruction as the fire was spotted and extinguished. The

[34] *The Picklock*, p. 15; *A Breviate of the Cause*, pp. 7, 9–10; *The state of the Adventurers' Case*, op. cit.; S.R. Gardiner (ed.), *The constitutional documents of the Puritan Revolution 1625–60* (Oxford, 1906), p. 212.

[35] *Commons' jn.*, ii, 421, 434, 596, 603; B.L., Harleian MS. 7006, f. 227.

[36] *Lords' jn.*, iv, 343; H.L.R.O., Main Papers, 5 August 1641 petition of Sir Robert Heath.

prime suspect was George Sutton, a Littleport labourer, who was overheard cursing those who had quenched the fire for 'if it had been to do any good they would not have been so hasty'. He may also have been responsible for a nocturnal attempt upon it in mid-March 1642, and it was again set fire to on 9 April following which Sutton was presented at an Ely sessions, but a possibly sympathetic grand jury returned ignoramus on the Bill.[37]

Once winter was over, the commoner offensive was quickly resumed in the Lindsey Level and the East and West Fens in 1642, and local authorities soon lost control of the situation – leaving commoners free to regain all their fenland with virtual impunity. The final Lindsey Level confrontation began in the spring, and reached its peak in May, when the remaining undertakers and their tenants were ejected. In a futile effort to recover grounds lost in the previous year, Sir William Killigrew persuaded the Lords, on 7 March, to send the sheriff of Lincolnshire a copy of their general order for possessions, issued on 13 July 1641, in response to daily complaints of riotous acts against enclosures and other forms of property. The order laid down that no one who had been in possession of an enclosure or any other property prior to, or on, the first day of that Parliament was to be disturbed or dispossessed except by due course of law, and future injured parties were empowered to require two adjacent justices to restore their peaceful possession until a court order was obtained to the contrary. In pursuance of this order, on 31 March 1642 the sheriff and three justices went into the undertakers' grounds in Little Hale Fen to remove encroaching commoners and their cattle. The current sheriff, Sir Edward Heron, was himself an undertaker and, in an unabashed display of bias, he took along his eldest son (as one of the justices) to restore possession of grounds in Little Hale Fen to Thomas Heron (probably the eldest son of his half-brother, James). However, shortly after their departure, twenty-two commoners returned to expel Heron's cattle and resume possession. On the following day, Sir Edward and the justices called upon Thomas Hall of Donington, as a man who had 'much power amongst the multitude', to assist them in executing the Lords's order; however, he refused point-blank on the grounds that 'he ought not to obey your Lordships' said order because his majesty had declared, that no ordinance of Parliament was to be obeyed without his majesty's

[37] Camb. U.L., Ely diocesan records, Ely 12 assize file.

assent thereunto'. Undeterred, Sir Edward and his companions attempted to restore Sir William Killigrew's possession of grounds in the fens of Horbling, Billingborough and Quadring yet, after their departure, four commoners, with faces obscured behind Spanish hunters' caps, forced their way into the grounds during the night, assaulted Sir William's servants (throwing one into the river) and ejected them.[38]

Sir Edward Heron's help was also requested in the Deeping Level where, on 13 April, the home of George Banfield, esquire, had been pulled down, and works in Pinchbeck Fen destroyed, by over 300 rioters. Banfield preferred two indictments of riot, forcible entry, ouster and detainer at the next Spalding quarter sessions but was foiled by the alleged partiality of some of the jurors. After some of his witnesses had been heard, the foreman of the jury was reported to have

> desired that any further evidence might be spared because they were fully satisfied with what they heard to find the said Indictments for the king, Thereupon one John Colson one of the said Inquest and Jury there sworn spake and openly declared in the face of the Court and country, That let whatsoever evidence be given that could be, yet they would not find the said Indictments for the king, and the Justices demanding why he would not find them, he said for it is our own cases, and the Court being moved by the Counsel for the king that the said Colson might be fined or withdrawn from the Jury the said Colson publicly and openly replied say what you will and do what you will I will be torn in pieces before I find it, and accordingly the said Colson and some others found one of the said Indictments Ignoramus and the others [sic] altered and razed and found only a bare riot, but nothing of the forcible possession, so as the said Mr Banfield could not by the Justices be restored to his former possession.[39]

This was by no means an isolated example of jurors exhibiting a pro-commoner bias for Sir William Killigrew complained in general terms 'That when any of the Commoners were indicted for riots, proved before the Commissioners on oaths, that the Jury did still acquit them.' Yet if riotous commoners found some protection in the obvious sympathy of jurors drawn from neighbourhoods prejudiced

[38] *Lords' jn.*, iv, 312, 629; H.L.R.O., Main Papers, 23 May 1642 petition of the undertakers, etc. in Lindsey Level; ibid., annexed certificate of Sir Edward Heron, High Sheriff of Lincolnshire; A. R. Maddison, *Lincolnshire Pedigrees* (1903), ii, 487–9.
[39] H.L.R.O., Main Papers, 23 May 1642 annexed certificate of Sir Edward Heron.

by enclosure, the undertakers could rely upon the partiality of members of the bench, like Edward Heron, junior, who presided over the Spalding sessions.[40]

Law enforcement agencies in the Lindsey Level had clearly lost their grip by the end of April 1642 and the undertakers turned despondently to the Lords on 9 May to beg further aid, as the Lords's earlier order had failed to restore peace, and assemblies of 'many hundreds' of commoners had expelled them, destroying works costing nearly £60 000 and demolishing several houses. Even the sheriff and justices had been assaulted while performing their duties and, with their servants, had been proceeded against as rioters for trying to restore possession to the undertakers. Riotous commoners, 'by a general confederacy', were reported to have 'at several places and sessions indicted the said Sheriff and Justices and some of their servants Ten several times for pretended riots and force although your Lordships' said orders were read to the Juries who wholly neglected the same, neither will the said Juries find or present any the offences aforesaid against the said rioters though proved by never so clear evidence'. The day of final reckoning was rumoured to be 13 May when the remainder of the undertakers' houses would be demolished and the surviving works destroyed. The Lords authorised the raising of the power of the county to prevent or suppress riots and required local officers and clergy to read out their order in all the relevant towns, villages and churches before the 13th. Yet, like its antecedents, the order was disregarded by commoners who, assaulting and wounding any who stood in their way, marched 'many hundreds in troop after Captains' into the fens to pull down eleven houses (and burn another to the ground); to overturn works and level enclosures; and to destroy crops either by turning in cattle or setting them on fire.[41]

An abortive attempt to halt the demolition of houses – and especially Sir William Killigrew's house – in the Lindsey Level was made by William Coney, a local justice. Coney's presence in

[40] *Sir William Killigrew his answer,* pp. 11–12; H.L.R.O., Main Papers, certificate of Sir Edward Heron; ibid., 9 May 1642 petition of Sir William Killigrew, and Edward Heron, esquire.
[41] *Lords' jn.,* v, 55–6; H.L.R.O., Main Papers, 9 May 1642 petition of Sir William Killigrew, etc. . . . participants with the Earl of Lindsey; 23 May 1642 petition of the undertakers, etc. in Lindsey Level; ibid., annexed certificate of Sir Edward Heron; 3 September 1660 petition of Sir William Killigrew, etc. adventurers in Lindsey Level.

Killigrew's house along with another justice initially prevented attacks on 16 and 17 May, but on 18 May the commoners, having strengthened their forces at Spalding on a market day, took advantage of Coney's temporary absence (as he presided over a private sessions inquiring into similar riots committed a fortnight earlier) to topple three houses. Around midday on the 19th, a crowd assembled ready to assail Killigrew's house by which time Coney had returned and, with the help of servants, tried to disarm some rioters as they moved towards the main body of the crowd but the weapons were retrieved by larger numbers. Eventually about 400 rioters swarmed into the yard of an adjacent inn and began pulling it down in defiance of Coney's entreaties to observe the Lords's order and disperse. The rioters also notified Coney that 'they had a greater work to do before they went out of the fen, which was to pull down Sir William Killigrew's house' and, when he warned them that it was defended by cannon with plenty of ammunition, they professed not to care or expressed disbelief until a deterrent shot was fired without bullets. But the crowd, with ranks now swollen to 500 or 600, refused to disperse without an attempt on the house, warning that 'if any of their company were killed or hurt, they would not leave a man or woman alive that was in the house' and even if they failed 'there was a thousand more would second them'. Coney made one last attempt to save the house as the crowd drew up before it around 6 p.m.; he later claimed to have been successful in persuading most of the crowd's negotiators to defer their attack for ten days in return for a payment of £10 but, while agreement was being reached, a group of rioters broke into the house and were immediately followed by the rest. Over a four- or five-hour period, the rioters wreaked destruction on the house and its contents, and even tried to coerce Killigrew's servants into helping with its demolition. Some of the latter were ducked in the drains for refusing help, as too were a number of watermen who happened to be passing down the new drain to Boston that day (whose use of a new channel of communication was probably provocation enough for the attack). The servants fled the house leaving Killigrew's property unguarded after a vain appeal to Coney for action as his 'power was not strong enough to apprehend any of the delinquents'. There are no indications that the rioters were after Killigrew's blood (and he was not in fact resident in the level at the time) and they were most probably animated by the fact that the house had been built upon enclosed fenland, and was the most expensive house so built, and that an extensive surrounding estate had been carved out of adjoining fens. Little is known about the actual rioters themselves except that they were thought to be mainly, if not wholly, from the bottom strata of society, although 'abetted by others more rich secret and malicious', and were mostly 'strangers, and few or no interested persons'. There was also a startling allegation that they had been led by one of Lindsey's own servants, referred to as captain Hull. These were the most serious riots yet in the level, and the lord lieutenant, Lord Willoughby of Parham, was required by the Lords to restore order and discover offenders, but his task was probably rendered impossible by the descent into civil war and was shortly afterwards changed merely into an obligation to report on the general situation there.[42]

There was also a renewal of large-scale rioting in the East and West Fens in the spring of 1642. The first assaults were mounted on the undertakers' lands which were the scene of nine or ten 'most barbarous and riotous insurrections' beginning on 15 March. A total of 400 or 500 rioters organised themselves into a company and 'made one John Hull their Captain' (the same man, perhaps, as the captain Hull mentioned above). They were reported to have pulled down about fifty dwelling houses and barns built upon the undertakers' lands, spoiling or appropriating their contents in the process and dragging many of the occupants forth by their heels. Corn and other foodstuffs, cattle and timber were also carried off while enclosures were levelled and many works devastated. Witnesses who had the audacity to give evidence against these rioters at subsequent sessions or assizes were afterwards assaulted by armed commoners, as too were some of the justices' and sheriff's men. The sheriff himself was rendered powerless as many of the rioters he had managed to arrest were rescued, and the commoners turned tables on him by securing the indictment of himself and his assistants in different parts of the county for riot. The undertakers again appealed to the Lords who in

---

[42] William Killigrew, *The property of all English-Men asserted, in the history of Lindsey Level* (1705), pp. 13–15; *Sir William Killigrew his answer*, p. 11; Sir William Killigrew, *A Representation to Parliament in favour of the draining of Lindsey Level* (1655); *A Reply to Sir William Killigrew's dispersed Papers, by the Owners and Commoners in Lincolnshire; A paper beginning 'The Earl of Exeter with divers other Lords and Gentlemen are Proprietors and Owners . . . of 36 000 Acres of Fen, and Meadow ground lying between the Rivers of Glen, and Kyme Eau in the County of Lincoln* (undated); *A Breviate of the Cause*, p. 9; H.L.R.O., Main Papers, 3 September 1660 petition of Sir William Killigrew, etc.; *Lords' jn.*, v, 79, 115.

June, after referring the matter to the consideration of Lord Willoughby of Parham, prepared a draft order to empower the sheriff and justices to mobilise the power of the county or, if that failed, a force of undertakers with their friends and associates. John Hull and other ringleaders were to be arrested and imprisoned without bail, and the order was to receive the usual publicity in adjacent towns and churches. In the event, the order remained in its draft stage as fenland troubles were overshadowed by national events.[43]

The patentees' enclosures in the West Fen were subjected to extensive damage on 1 April 1642 as lands restored to the patentees by the sheriff, in pursuance of the Lords's order of 3 December 1641, were once again invaded. Sheriff Heron and three justices could only look impotently on as John Hull, Thomas Pishey and Richard Sibsey joined over 300 commoners, who acted 'by a general combination or approbation of that part of the country', in demolishing houses (some worth £400 or £500 each), filling in enclosure ditches and destroying about £1000 worth of cole- and rape-seed. Dismissing the Lords's order 'for that they were made under a hedge', the rioters declared that 'they would loose their lives before they would desist'. Heron and the justices made a formal record of the riot, as required by statute, but when they met at Boston the next day to perfect it Pishey and Sibsey, with several other rioters, 'in a braving and daring manner' came into or near their meeting place. The justices therefore directed a warrant to the sheriff and the mayor of Boston for their arrest, yet the mayor, who had already shown pro-commoner leanings, refused to execute it and the sheriff's arrest of Pishey and Sibsey brought a crowd of about 1000 people from the Boston area to the house where they were being held. Uttering threats to murder the sheriff and justices, and assaulting any of their servants who came within reach, the crowd smashed the windows calling for the prisoners' release, and threatened to use instruments employed during fires to pull the house down on top of them when they refused. During the course of an almost two-hour siege, the mayor was repeatedly sent for to restore order but he only appeared on the scene after the prisoners had escaped in the tumult and brought none of the assistance necessary to disperse the rioters. As the sheriff and justices

---

[43] H.L.R.O., Main papers, 15 June 1642 petition of Samuel Thomas, esquire, and other undertakers; ibid., draft of an order to the sheriff, etc. on the petition of Samuel Thomas; ibid., affidavit of Michael Broughton of Boston, Peter Taylor of Sibsey and Leonard Paddisson of Freiston; *Lords' jn.*, v, 79, 115, 137.

headed for home, they were followed by crowds shouting abuse, and pelting them with stones and dirt, until they reached the town's limits.[44]

Both the Great and Hatfield Levels saw fresh outbreaks of rioting as the country tottered on the brink of civil war. Enclosures in Holme, Norfolk, were levelled in the early summer of 1642 by local commoners who contemptuously dismissed the Lords's order for peaceful possession and even tore up copies of it prior to filling in division ditches and spoiling crops.[45] The southern part of the Hatfield Level experienced major disorder on 25 June when a group of Misterton men, numbering at least twenty and perhaps as many as sixty, were led into Haxey Carr by John Allen to break down fences and drive cattle into crops. Between 100 and 160 acres of corn and rape-seed were destroyed with Allen rejecting the plea of a local gentleman with the taunt that 'it would do his Cattle more good than to have it preserved for hereafter'. Ten years later, it was alleged that Haxey men subsequently joined with those of Misterton to continue the destruction for a number of days until about 4000 acres had been laid waste and several houses demolished. However, there were no indications of any such co-operation at the time and the inhabitants of Haxey may, in actual fact, have deliberately refrained from joining in as the 1636 Exchequer decree only applied to the inhabitants of Epworth manor, and hence Misterton commoners could still lay claim to common rights in the whole of Haxey Carr. A Commons's order intended to suppress the riot was lost in the preparations for civil war and a large part of the undertakers' enclosures were regained as common lands. When an undertakers' servant tried to expel some of the commoners' cattle in the following September, he was set upon and beaten by about forty men including Peter Bernard, a high constable. Bernard had previously earned the displeasure of the privy council by petitioning with other commoners, in August 1629, against Vermuyden's enclosures, and he was to remain an open opponent of the drainers throughout the 1640s and 1650s.[46]

By the time the fenland counties had been drawn into a civil war that the breakdown in law and order, and the challenges to authority,

---

[44] H.L.R.O., Main Papers, certificate of Sir Edward Heron, High Sheriff of Lincolnshire, etc.

[45] *Lords' jn.*, v. 101.

[46] *Commons' jn.*, ii, 661; P.R.O., S.P. dom. 18/37, fols 11, 11III; P.C. 2/39, fols 412, 423.

occasioned by the violent reaction to drainage schemes, had helped to make inevitable, the undertakers had either been completely vanquished or were under serious pressure. Commoners in the East and West Fens and the Lindsey Level had regained all of their former commons, having successfully driven out both the undertakers and the patentees, while other levels had experienced differing degrees of an offensive which would intensify in the war years. This reaction had been largely possible because the effective centre of authority in this pre-war period, Parliament, was divided in its attitude to fenland and other popular grievances and disorders, with the Lords placing the highest priority on the restoration of order while influential voices in the Commons, although opposed to riots and law breaking in general, shied away from condemning the fenmen outright and even made sympathetic noises in their direction.

4 Civil War Allegiance and Regained Commons

THE behaviour of fenland commoners during the Civil War lends further strength to the view that the bulk of the common people were indifferent to the great issues raised at Westminster and, if they demonstrated an ostensible allegiance, it was incidental to more immediate social and economic concerns which the conflict provided a welcome opportunity to resolve.[1] Animosities generated by fenland drainage affected party alignment in a way at once more complex, and decidedly more sophisticated, than a general equation of commoner with parliamentarian and undertaker with royalist would suggest. Support for Parliament was a qualified one, enduring only so long as it coincided with opposition to the undertakers and their enclosures, and for most fenmen the chief significance of the war years was the scope they afforded for levelling enclosures and regaining commons. But the fenland disturbances that accompanied the descent into civil war turned the spectre of anarchy into a chilling reality for the political elite in counties like Lincolnshire, confirming some in their support for the King against an indulgent Parliament and many more in their reluctance to be committed to either side.[2]

The author of *The Anti-Projector,* writing after the first Civil War, claimed that commoners in all levels had been ardent parliamentarians and most undertakers had been equally strong royalists. Fenland commoners had 'furnished the Parliament with many thousand men, horses, and vast sums of money, besides the prayers of a numerous godly precious people. And those few undertakers, upon this account only, have most of them been most malicious enemies against the Parliament; for some of them had like to have slain the Lord Fairfax in the Isle of Axholme, who was rescued by the

[1] Sharp, pp. 7-9, 220-1, 247-9, 263-4; B. S. Manning, *The English people and the English Revolution* (1976), pp. 112, 163, 192; L. Stone, *The causes of the English Revolution* (1972), pp. 54-5.
[2] Holmes, *Lincolnshire,* pp. 151-7.

anti-undertakers.'[3] Petitioning in 1650 against a revival of undertaker claims in Holland Fen, the commoners reminded Parliament of
their 'cordial affections, cheerful assistance and liberal contributions
in these late unhappy differences' in stark contrast to the behaviour of
undertakers, 'all or most of them men not only of ill affected spirits,
but in these late Wars, open and violent oppugnors of the just
privileges, undoubted immunities and common peace of this
Nation'.[4] There was certainly a large element of truth in the equation
of commoner with parliamentarian, and undertaker with royalist, but
a closer scrutiny of reactions to party division in different levels
reveals a far more complicated situation than such a simple equation
would allow.

Commoners in the Isle of Axholme would appear to have been
model parliamentarians. In his journey from Beverley to Nottingham
in 1642, the King had originally intended to pass through the Isle to
Gainsborough but was forced to alter his course by the strength of
local feeling against him. An arms consignment was collected in the
Isle for the Hull garrison but was intercepted by royalists reportedly
acting on intelligence provided by the participants. Two foot
companies were raised and maintained locally throughout the war;
and a cartload of muskets and £300 in money was donated to the
cause in May 1643 by Simon Mawe and Humphrey Popplewell (two
gentlemen who both served on the early Lincolnshire committee for
sequestration) and other Belton men.[5] Among those most active in
gathering forces together to oppose the royalists at the beginning of
the war was Daniel Noddel, who held the rank of lieutenant to
captain Robert Dyneley in Parliament's forces. Noddel (1611–72)
may originally have come from either Misterton or Beckingham, in
Nottinghamshire, where there were families of that name. He had
undoubtedly received some formal education, as his expertise as a
propagandist and his legal knowledge demonstrate, and on one
occasion he was said to have addressed a dismayed French pastor at
Santoft in Latin. Yet there is no record of his having either been at

---

[3] *The Anti-Projector*, p. 6. Cf. Spittlehouse, *The Case and Appeal*, p. 8.
[4] Bodl., *Two Petitions . . . from Thousands of the Lords, Owners, and Commoners of Lincolnshire; against the Old Court-Levellers, or Propriety-Destroyers, the Prerogative Undertakers* (1650),
pp. 9–10.
[5] A. Garner, *Colonel Edward King* (Grimsby, 1970), p. 42; *The declaration of Daniel
Noddel*, p. 266; Spittlehouse, *The Case and Appeal*, p. 8; P.R.O., S.P. dom. 18/37, f.
11III; B.L., Lansdowne 897, fols 205–6.

university or having been admitted to an inn of court. When examined in the Exchequer in July 1647, his status was given as 'gentleman' and his residence Owston, in the Isle of Axholme. After Edgehill, Noddel raised local forces to oppose Sir Ralph Hansby, and his captain testified to his staunch parliamentarianism in 1652 by affirming that he 'did always express as much affection by his actions as possibly could be to the service of the Parliament to this present time and . . . that whenever the Parliament prospered he rejoiced and leaped for joy and when the Parliament did not prosper he did much mourn'. Another local observer swore that Noddel had been 'very faithful to the Parliament all the former Wars', adding that he 'did not know any man in Lincolnshire more affected to the Parliament then he was'. When Noddel, and other parliamentarians, were forced to seek refuge in Stockwith, he mounted a guard there for Parliament and later, with Dyneley, took seventy-seven Axholme royalists prisoner. It is by no means inconceivable that Noddel could have come into contact with John Lilburne during these years when the latter was a major in colonel Edward King's regiment, and that they were renewing old acquaintances in 1650 when Lilburne agreed to throw his weight behind the Epworth cause. Noddel combined his allegiance to Parliament with a persistent championing of the cause of Epworth commoners and acted as their attorney and solicitor from about 1646 to 1662.[6]

As the King had originally sanctioned the enclosures and had consistently supported the drainers in their struggles with the commoners, the Isle's disaffection to royalism could be accounted for in these terms alone. But the commoners' parliamentarianism was probably due less to their antipathy to the King, or affection for Parliament, than their perception of the excellent opportunity it afforded them for recovering their commons by force under the guise of party loyalty. An Epworth husbandman recalled in 1646 how he had often heard his fellows confide 'That they would never have taken Arms for the Parliament, but that they intended thereby to have the power in their hand to destroy the Draining and Improvement and lay all waste again to their Common.' They were to be bitterly

---

[6] P.R.O., S.P. dom. 18/37, f. 11III.

Daniel Noddel may possibly have been one of the sons of Richard Noddel (who had married Mary Kendall in Misterton parish church on 22 November 1590). [I am grateful to the Notts. R.O. for this information.] For the Beckingham Noddels see P.R.O., E. 179/160/279, 304, 322.

disillusioned when a victorious Parliament came to look with equal favour upon fenland drainage and enclosure. Many loyal commoners must have shared the resentment voiced by one prominent Haxey townsman in 1652 that 'he had fought for the Parliament, but if they did take away their Commons, he would bring a 100 men to fight them'.[7]

A corresponding line of continuity between opposition to drainage, and parliamentarianism in the Civil War, is less clearly discernible in the Great Level. The long accepted view of East Anglia as being solidly parliamentarian from the outset has been shattered by a recent study of the Eastern Association which has shown that royalist sentiment in Cambridgeshire and the Isle of Ely, in the summer of 1642, was important enough to require the intervention of a force raised from outside the county to secure it for Parliament, and there was similar evidence of pronounced royalist sympathies in neighbouring Huntingdonshire. Speculation about Cromwell being helped in recruiting the peasantry of these two counties into his regiment by his earlier championing of the commoners' cause also ignores the fact that the famous cavalry of the Association were drawn from a wider area than the fens alone.[8]

The behaviour of Isle of Ely commoners at Sutton does lend support to the commoner–parliamentarian equation. The fens of Sutton had been enclosed without the consent of the poor of the parish who hoped for a Commons's redress in 1645, but while engaged in organising a petition, 'seven of them (being soldiers) were committed to the Gaol of Ely by Sir Miles Sandys, who by force kept them and many other [*sic*] in the gaol of Ely from going forth to assist this honourable house against the Late King in the time of extremity'. These same poor men insisted that they were the most committed parliamentarians in the parish having 'paid to every assessment to the full that have been imposed on them', while the 'rich men of the parish', who had deprived the poor of their fens, 'have not all this time of the wars and troubles of the Kingdom paid one penny of rates or taxes toward any assessment or rate'. Sutton commoners in 1649 apparently saw their own struggle against rich oppressors as part of a

[7] H.L.R.O., Main Papers, 10 February 1646 affidavit of Robert Palmer of Epworth, husbandman; P.R.O., S.P. dom. 18/37, f. 11III.
[8] C. Holmes, *The Eastern Association in the English civil war* (Cambridge, 1974), pp. 33–4, 41, 54–5, 171–2; Manning, *The English people and the English Revolution,* op. cit., p. 131.

generalised struggle between rich and poor. They had 'found by woeful experience, the proverb to be true, Wealth maketh many friends, but the poor is separate from his neighbour' and therefore looked to the House of Commons 'as being the instrument under God, to be the deliverers of the poor, out of the hand of his rich neighbour, that was stronger then he'. Moved by millenarian enthusiasm, the poor of Sutton eagerly awaited the day 'when in this nation the poor do enjoy their own'.[9] But if they had supported Parliament in the naïve expectation that it would be instrumental in bringing about this transformation, their hopes were soon dashed as that body gave its approval to the Act for draining the Great Level.

Commoners elsewhere in the level may have been discouraged from joining the parliamentarians by the presence of some prominent former undertakers in command positions in that party. Although Francis, Earl of Bedford, died before the outbreak of the war, his heir, William, was appointed general of Parliament's horse, while Sir Miles Sandys, junior, George Glapthorne and Francis Underwood were all key figures in the party's organisation in Cambridgeshire and the Isle of Ely. The author of *The Anti-Projector* came close to contradicting his own generalisation that most undertakers had been enemies of Parliament when he observed that 'some Parliament men who were the Earl's participants were very active' on a committee chaired by Pelham which was considering a drainage Bill, and that another Bill was referred to a committee chaired by Robert Scawen which 'was furnished with too many undertakers of Parliament men'. The spectacle of undertakers supporting Parliament might even have resulted in some commoners opting for the King's side, especially when it is recalled that Charles had backed the Huntingdon adjudication ousting Bedford and his associates, and had been too preoccupied with national affairs to embark on fresh works himself. Many of the twenty-three Cambridgeshire men who received financial aid at a 1663 quarter sessions for lost limbs, or serious wounds, incurred while fighting for the King, came from fenland areas of the county, including Soham and other places where there had been anti-enclosure riots before the Civil War. The curate of Wicken, Robert Grimer, who had made no secret of his pro-commoner sympathies in 1638, became a staunch royalist, was

<hr />

[9] H.L.R.O., Main Papers, [1649] petition of divers poor inhabitants of the parish of Sutton, in the Isle of Ely.

ejected from his living by the Earl of Manchester in August 1644, and in 1647 published a proclamation in the King's name. As Grimer was believed to enjoy great local influence, he could presumably have mobilised the same, and capitalised upon his earlier identification with the undertakers' opponents, to recruit fenmen for the royalists. In the midst of the first war, anti-parliamentarian, and possibly pro-royalist, sentiments were ascribed to the ringleaders of one fenland riot. When Whittlesey rioters were ordered by a local justice to disperse in May 1643, their leader, Jeffrey Boyce (or Boys), and two others held their pitchforks against him, chiding 'that he was no Justice, for he was against the King, and was all for the Parliament and that they would not obey him nor any Law'. Such a statement does not, of course, necessarily imply that the rioters' leaders were ardent royalists, and in fact they were more probably taking advantage of civil war divisions to further their own objectives. Both former royalists, and former parliamentarians, became adventurers in the Great Level under the 1649 Act. In seeking to clear the adventurers of the aspersion that they were mainly former royalists, a drainage apologist generalised about pro-drainage sentiment on Parliament's side: the allegation was 'but a scandal, though some such be engaged in it, yet they are such as have made their compositions, and is not now to be objected, but there are many more that have always been eminent for their affections to the Parliament, and all the soldiery in Lynn, Crowland, and garrisons about, are adventurers and participants in this work'.[10]

Party alignment in the Lindsey Level and the East and West Fens was evidently much more clear-cut: the Earl of Lindsey, Sir William Killigrew, Robert Long, Sir Edward Heron and most fellow under-takers were staunchly royalist while the commoners were equally ardent parliamentarians. These undertakers were, in fact, depicted as the most extreme kind of royalist, blind advocates of prerogative power and 'Parliament-destroyers' who would have undermined property rights and introduced tyrannical government. Sir William

---

[10] *An Ordinance of the Lords and Commons . . . for raising and maintaining of forces . . . under the command of Sir Thomas Fairfax* (15 February 1645), pp. 14–15; *Fenland notes and queries,* iii, 58–60, 80–1; *The Anti-Projector,* p. 4; Camb. R.O., quarter sessions minute book, 1660/61–1672, f. 47; A. G. Matthews, *Walker revised* (Oxford, 1948), p. 80; *V.C.H., Cambridgeshire,* ii, 184–5; H.L.R.O., Main Papers, 29 May 1643 affidavit of John Newton of Whittlesey, Isle of Ely; 17 June 1643 depositions taken on behalf of the Earls of Bedford and Portland; *The state of the Adventurers' Case.*

Killigrew had been one of the principal people involved in the attempt on the five members, and later commanded one of the two troops of horse that guarded the person of the King during the war. The involvement of Robert Long was political and administrative, rather than military, and he was one of the Queen's party in exile. During the Interregnum, the commoners used the undertakers' former royalism to discredit them and counter attempts at regaining their lands. Sir William, on the other hand, tried to gloss over a compromising past by claiming that 'many Participants with the Earl have not fought against Parliament' (although significantly unable to instance a fellow undertaker who actually fought for Parliament), and by suggesting that royalists who had since compounded should not have their war record quoted against them.[11] In sharp contrast, the commoners could remind Parliament how 'abundance of us', or the vast majority with the exception of only 'some few persons', had been 'active and faithful in Arms, in yours and the Nation's service'. Nehemiah Rawson became a prominent member of the Lincolnshire committee and was appointed scoutmaster-general to Lord Willoughby; in 1643 he was active sequestering royalist property which he turned to his own, as well as Parliament's, profit – compensating himself, perhaps, for the earlier financial losses sustained in opposing the undertakers. A leading rioter in Bourne Fen in 1640, Thomas Kirke, enlisted in the parliamentary army on the outbreak of hostilities and was still serving under Sir Thomas Fairfax in January 1648. Areas like Boston and its surrounding countryside, the scene of earlier anti-undertaker uprisings, provided a fertile recruiting ground for Parliament.[12] Although the commoners' espousal of parliamentarianism in these two levels cannot be explained, as in the Isle of Axholme, largely in terms of

---

[11] Manning, *The English people and the English Revolution*, op. cit., pp. 95, 231–2; Holmes, *Lincolnshire*, pp. 156, 159–60; *D.N.B.*, xii, 107–8; ibid., xi, 116–17; Edward Hyde, Earl of Clarendon, *History of the Rebellion and Civil Wars in England* (ed. W. D. Macray, Oxford, 1888), ii, 348; v, 323; Bodl., *Two Petitions*, op. cit., pp. 3, 5, 7; *Certain papers concerning the Earl of Lindsey his Fens* (1649), p. 7; *The Picklock*, pp. 3–5; *A Breviate of the Cause*, pp. 10–11; *A Reply to Sir William Killigrew's dispersed Papers, by the Owners and Commoners in Lincolnshire* (undated); *Sir William Killigrew his answer*, pp. 13–14.

[12] *A Breviate of the Cause*, p. 10; Bodl., *Two Petitions* op. cit., p. 5; Garner, *Colonel Edward King*, op. cit., pp. 14, 47; B.L., Additional MS. 5508, f. 12; H.L.R.O., Main Papers, 31 January 1648 petition of Thomas Kirke of Bourne; Manning, *The English people and the English Revolution*, op. cit., pp. 178, 244; Holmes, *Lincolnshire*, p. 158; *A Perfect Diurnall . . . 5–12 September 1642.*

expediency because the undertakers had been expelled prior to the Civil War, the prospect of enclosures being restored following a royalist victory was presumably incentive enough for commoners to work for a parliamentary triumph.

The Civil War certainly afforded aggrieved commoners an ideal opportunity to launch attacks upon recent drainage works and enclosures. Enclosures in Wildmore Fen were levelled at the beginning of the war and later drainage banks in the Deeping Level were cast down 'by the tumultuous rising of the tenants and others'. Recently finished Ancholme Level works were also abandoned to commoner depredation when Sir John Monson left to join the King in Oxford.[13] Isle of Axholme commoners conveniently combined allegiance to Parliament with opposition to the drainers during the first war. Lilburne later acknowledged that 'the Commoners being in Arms for the Parliament in 1643, did take advantage of the Time, and as they had been put out of possession by force, and could not through the Tyranny of those Times have any Legal Remedy, so by force they put Themselves into possession again of above 3,000 Acres'. At the very start of the war, two sluices, one on Bycker's Dyke and the other on Snow Sewer, were pulled up to flood a great part of the Isle of Axholme. The commoners argued that it was a necessary measure to prevent royalists from marching into the Isle (the inhabitants being 'much secured by the Water that the King's soldiers could not get to them that Way'), much to the indignation of participants and tenants who believed it was principally aimed at forcing them to abandon their lands. The sluice on Bycker's Dyke was pulled up first by a group from Epworth, including a constable, acting on the orders of a Belton man called Kingman (possibly Richard Kingman, or Kinman, gentleman) who was a captain in Sir John Meldrum's regiment. Kingman had apparently acted without authority from his superiors for Meldrum opposed the drowning of the Isle (having already assured a Dutch settler that 'the Islemen do not love thee I find for they have entreated me very much to drown this Level but I will not'), and he was supposedly furious at the action. In early December 1642, the participants managed to persuade Meldrum (the local commander-in-chief) to give them control of a sluice on Snow Sewer which several Epworth and Owston

[13] J. Thirsk, *English peasant farming: the agrarian history of Lincolnshire from Tudor to recent times* (1957), p. 190; *D.N.B.*, xiii, 642–3; P.R.O., E. 178/5433; S.P. dom. 25/78, fols 815–16; E. 134/17 Chas. II/East. 14.

men had designs on. This did not prevent it from being pulled up, allegedly at night, in the spring by men from Epworth, avowedly to protect the Isle from a rumoured royalist advance under Sir Ralph Hansby. As a swollen River Trent poured into the level, two tenants desperately tried to close the sluice but were prevented by an armed guard set there by two local leaders, Thomas Peacock and Thomas Burton. Both tenants were warned to 'stand off at their perils' as the guards were determined to carry out their instructions 'till they had drowned the said Level and had made the Tenants thereof to swim away like Ducks'. After 6000–8000 acres had been flooded, the gates were closed again so as to retain the waters. The commoners were later said to have acted with the approbation of two members of the Lincoln committee, Sir Christopher Wray and Sir Anthony Irby (the former being Sir John Wray's half-brother, and a fellow critic of the Axholme drainers in 1630, and the latter his brother-in-law) who had given additional orders for the felling of trees. But twelve armed men employed to keep the sluice closed subsequently refused to obey an order from the same committee for its re-opening to allow the waters to drain away, keeping it firmly shut for about ten weeks and threatening to shoot any participants who attempted to execute the order. Peacock and Burton (who derived their authority from Daniel Noddel) did not disguise the fact that at least part of their purpose in opening the sluice was to let water into the participants' grounds to 'keep them drowned deep enough and they will be poor enough'. No help was forthcoming from local constables, like Peter Bernard, who flatly refused to give any assistance in carrying out the committee's order. The participants acknowledged that some of the commoners' own grounds had been submerged but claimed they were only meadows, and the loss was minimal compared with the thousands of pounds worth of damage they had suffered in totally destroyed crops and half-submerged buildings. Whatever motives underlay the deliberate flooding of the Isle of Axholme, the parliamentarianism of Peacock and Burton was unequivocal; both were grouped with Noddel as 'the most forward men' in mobilising forces in the Isle to oppose Sir Ralph Hansby, and all three took refuge in parliamentary garrisons when Lincolnshire finally fell and subsequently returned with their army.[14]

[14] Lilburne, *Epworth,* p. 4; Holmes, *Lincolnshire,* p. 140; P.R.O., S.P. dom. 18/37, fols 11, 11III; E. 134/3 Jas. II/Mich. 42; E. 179/140/751; E. 134/24 Chas. I/East. 4; H.L.R.O., Main Papers, 10 February 1646 affidavit of Edward Hill of Santoft, husbandman.

At various times during the first war, sluices were opened or damaged by inhabitants of the Isle of Axholme. The Turnbrigg sluice was broken down by parliamentarian soldiers 'upon the malicious information of some not well affected' to the drainage scheme, and local commoners badly damaged sluices at Althorpe and Goole and on Bycker's Dyke.[15] Some of the soldiers at the Turnbrigg sluice may have been recruited in that vicinity, and local recruits were certainly involved in at least one of three riots in the Isle in late September, and early October, 1645. On Michaelmas day 1645 about 120 Epworth commoners threw down fences and laid waste at least 3000 acres: about 500 horses and cattle were driven into the rape-crop, and among the corn stacks, and forcibly kept there for eight or ten days until all was destroyed; the homes of some tenants were pulled down and several tenants were assaulted and wounded in the process; those who offered any resistance were threatened with death and destruction; and any ploughs found were systematically cut into pieces. A number of the offenders were soldiers serving under captain Dyneley and Daniel Noddel, including some who had confided that their sole reason for joining Parliament's army was to destroy the works and enclosures and recover their commons.[16]

There are indications that local leaders in the Isle could not always rely on the ready participation of fellow commoners in these activities. Timothy Steward of Epworth, one of the Michaelmas rioters, later claimed (admittedly after deserting to the participants) that he had been 'drawn to it' by two fellow townsmen, who had also hired several others to destroy the improvements, and that the local poor 'cry out mightily since the Improvement laid down and say they are all undone'. Some Belton men may have been pressurised into joining riots on 6 and 7 October 1645. The bell-man of Belton, William Wash, allegedly visited over twenty town households on 6 October, with an intimidating escort of twenty-four men (including two constables and a high constable's son), and warned each to join in the attack upon the participants' property or their own house would be pulled down the next day. On 6 and 7 October about sixty inhabitants, armed with muskets (issued to them, perhaps, as parliamentarian soldiers) and other weapons, levelled enclosures,

---

[15] Notts. U.L., H.C.C. 6001, fols 287, 352, 407.
[16] P.R.O., S.P. dom. 18/37, f. 11III; H.L.R.O., Main Papers, 10 February 1646 affidavit of Robert Palmer of Epworth, husbandman.

herded cattle into the rape-crop and broke into pieces all the ploughs and harrows they laid their hands on. One prominent rioter, John Bernard, was reportedly urged on by his father, Peter, the high constable of Belton, who also refused to make arrests, proclaiming that 'he would not meddle with them although he had a Warrant from a Justice of peace or Judge'. A Lords's order of 10 December, for the suppression of riots within the manor of Epworth, was contemptuously dismissed by Belton and Epworth rioters with the retort that 'they did not care a Fart for the Order which was made by the Lords in Parliament and published in the Churches, and, that notwithstanding that Order, they would pull down all the rest of the Houses in the Level that were built upon those Improvements which were drained, and destroy all the Enclosures'.[17] The presence of French and Dutch settlers at Santoft was particularly resented by local commoners who tried to force them out by assaults and attacks on their property. Their crops and farming implements were destroyed and their church badly damaged by commoners who broke up and burned all the seats, smashed windows and stripped the lead from the roof and steeple. Following the general tendency to classify all rioters as *ipso facto* persons of low social status, the settlers identified their assailants as the 'meaner' sort of inhabitant, yet the involvement of persons of sufficient substance to act as constable argues a wider social base for the rioters.[18] Towards the end of October, John Allen and fellow Misterton commoners once again entered Haxey Carr; they drove 300 cattle and horses through gaps they had made in the fences to feed on the participants' crops for about a fortnight, smashed into pieces a plough and threatened to burn or pull down the houses of resisting tenants. Compared with the Belton and Epworth riots, this was a much smaller incident, with the rioters numbering somewhere between twelve and twenty-six (and carrying agricultural implements and clubs) and the acreage of crops destroyed was considerably less,[19] yet the objectives were patently similar – the returning of former commonable fenland to its previous pastoral usage by destroying crops and farming implements and expelling tenants.

[17] P.R.O., S.P. dom. 18/37, f. 11III; H.L.R.O., Main Papers, 10 February 1646 affidavit of Edward Hill of Santoft.
[18] H.L.R.O., Main Papers, 15 November 1645 petition of Peter Berchett and annexed articles.
[19] Ibid., 10 February 1646 affidavit of Jacob Vernoy; P.R.O., S.P. dom. 18/37, f. 11III.

When called upon to restore peace in the Isle in October, the Lincoln committee did not resort to the usual riot suppression measures but attempted to produce a permanent settlement of the differences between participant and commoner. The commoners were at long last to be permitted to proceed to a legal trial of their title and, in the interim, the participants' tenants were required to enter bonds to pay next year's rents to the committee who would retain the money pending a final settlement. In return for their co-operation, the tenants were given leave to sow and reap the next season's crop on the understanding that they would yield possession to the commoners if the participants had not either secured a legal judgement, or an ordinance of Parliament, confirming their title before the following Michaelmas; and to ensure the tenants' compliance, commoners were authorised to seize the grounds of any who failed to enter bonds. The participants took great exception to this arrangement and denounced it before the Lords as a device whereby their tenants had been constrained to enter bonds, in the futile hope of preserving their crops, while the committee had 'not only by this indirect manner outed the landowners of their possession for the present, but have for as much as in them lies, settled the petitioners' inheritance purchased at a very dear rate, with the commoners, who have committed all those outrages'.[20]

Conscious of the precariousness of their position, the French and Dutch settlers also looked to the Lords to protect their property, drawing attention to the recent destruction (for which they urged compensation from the riot ringleaders) and asking for the cancellation of all the bonds extracted from them by the county committee. These appeals resulted in the Lords's order of 10 December requiring the execution of the riot statute of 13 Henry IV c.7, with the assistance, if necessary, of the trained bands or nearest parliamentarian forces, and the appointment of a deputy by the sheriff to keep the Isle under continuous surveillance. However, after two days' reflection, the sheriff decided not to obey that part of the order requiring the appointment of a local deputy on the grounds that he knew of no law giving him such authority, and the rest of the order

[20] H.L.R.O., Main Papers, 6 February 1646 petition of the inhabitants of Epworth to the House of Lords; annexed copy of an order of the committee at Lincoln, 18 October 1645; and copy of an order upon the petition of the inhabitants of the manor of Epworth, 6 February 1646; 21 March 1646 petition of the participants in the draining of the Level of Hatfield Chase.

proved largely ineffective because there was only one justice residing in the Isle and local constables, who had openly identified themselves with their fellow commoners, could scarcely be relied upon to execute warrants. Local law enforcement agencies having failed them, the Lords acceded to the participants' request for direct intervention on 21 March 1646 and six prominent offenders, three from Belton (including the bell-man) and three from Epworth, were accordingly arrested and bailed for their appearance before the House which, having heard both parties, eventually discharged them on 10 December.[21]

A closely fought legal battle was being waged, in the meantime, between the participants and the commoners of Epworth over the latter's attempts to proceed to a trial of title in pursuance of the county committee's October order. The participants tried, without success, to have the tenants' bonds called into question in the Lords, but they did have some success in their efforts to deflect attention away from the question of title and on to the suppression of riots. Nevertheless, as the Lords had not placed any legal obstacles in their way, the commoners were able to commence suit against the participants' tenants, in Hilary term 1646, to have a trial of title to the 7400 acres of former commonable fenland. The participants, desperately anxious to avoid such a trial, countered by exhibiting a Bill in the Exchequer, in Trinity term 1646, to halt the commoners' proceedings and have possession established with themselves. About 223 commoners appeared to the Bill and most of them denied having given any consent to the reference to attorney-general Banks, or having submitted to his 1636 award. Legal proceedings were deliberately stretched out for a further five years by the participants (some of whom vowed that the commoners would never have a trial) but, after repeated delays, the cause finally came to a full hearing in the Exchequer. On 10 February 1651 the court decreed that all those who had submitted to the 1636 decree were to be bound by it, but the remainder were free to proceed to a trial of title, and established possession as it had been when the participants' Bill was first exhibited, which left the commoners with about 4000 of the disputed

[21] Ibid., 15 November 1645 petition of Peter Berchett and annexed articles; 21 March 1646 petition of the participants; ibid., warrant for gentleman usher; 9 March 1646 affidavit of John Gibbon; 22 July 1646 petition of Charles Broughton and William Wash; 10 December 1646 order of the House of Lords; *Lords' jn.*, vii, 705–7; viii, 36, 224, 319, 438, 584, 586.

7400 acres. After further delaying tactics, the commoners at long last secured a trial at the Exchequer Bar in the name of Thomas Vavasour, a descendant of one of the original signatories of the Mowbray indenture, and the verdict which they had sought for over twenty years passed in their favour. But the participants refused to acknowledge defeat; they and their counsel had (according to Noddel) purposely left the court, and made no defence, when they recognised that the commoners were on the point of victory, so that they could subsequently object to the verdict as having passed by default in their absence.[22]

These legal proceedings made their slow progress against a background of periodic upheaval in the Isle of Axholme. On 13 July 1646 John Allen, with forty-two Misterton men, again returned to Haxey Carr to demolish banks and fences on the grounds of two Dutch tenants, before driving 300 cattle into 60 acres of growing corn, and later, with twenty or thirty others, he fulfilled his promise to do more damage there.[23] In 1647 the scene changed to Epworth where, on 20 May, approximately forty-three men and women laid about a group of workmen with pitchforks, clubs and stones, seriously wounding two of them, as they tried to erect fences and excavate drains. In deference to the Lords's order of 10 December 1645, the sheriff dispatched two assistants to help prevent further violence, but, on 22 May, thirteen Epworth men (including three previous rioters) filled in a recently dug drain and gave a head wound to one of the sheriff's men, with a sword, and broke two of his ribs, and put the other to flight by jabbing at his horse with pitchforks. A special Gainsborough sessions on 15 June convicted twenty-four of these rioters, fined them £20 a man for each riot and bound them over to the July Spital sessions.[24]

The situation deteriorated rapidly in June 1647 as the participants, led by John Gibbon (who had bought out Vermuyden's interest),

---

[22] H.L.R.O., Main Papers, 15 November 1645 articles annexed to the petition of Peter Berchett; 6 February 1646 petition of the inhabitants of Epworth and annexed copy of an order upon the petition; 21 March 1646 petition of the participants; ibid., petition of the inhabitants of Epworth; Lilburne, *Epworth*, p. 4; *The declaration of Daniel Noddel,* pp. 262, 270; *The great complaint,* pp. 274–5; Notts. U.L., H.C.C. 8939, p. 4.
[23] P.R.O., S.P. dom. 18/37, f. 11III; H.L.R.O., Main Papers, 11 August 1646 petition of the participants in Hatfield Chase; 30 July 1646 affidavit of Edward Hill of Santoft.
[24] P.R.O., K.B. 9/838/528; H.L.R.O., Main Papers, 6 July 1647 affidavit of Edmond Awkeland; 8 September 1647 petition of the Hatfield participants.

made a vigorous attempt to recover their Epworth enclosures, thereby inviting retaliatory action from local commoners who were, in turn, directed and advised by Daniel Noddel. Noddel was by now acting as full-time negotiator and solicitor for the commoners, and had only recently returned from attending on their legal affairs in London when he was informed of Gibbon's aggressiveness, including his burning the commoners' recently cut turf, distraining and selling their cattle and assaulting and imprisoning any who resisted.[25] On 18 June the activities of about eighty workmen in repairing enclosures near the town of Epworth, under the protective eye of the sheriff's deputy, brought a menacing crowd on to the streets. The deputy hurried to Epworth with two workmen to read the Lords's order establishing possession with the participants and to command their dispersal, but an assembly of around seventy-three townsmen (including five recently fined May rioters) replied with murderous threats, narrowly missed the deputy, but hit his horse with a staff, and forced one of the workmen to abandon his horse. Over sixty men pursued the deputy into the fens where they came up against the sheriff himself who had been sent for to preserve the peace. The sheriff's proclamation to disperse was also ignored as the rioters demolished enclosures until a superior number of workmen, whose working implements were probably equal to the rioters' pitchforks, clubs and staves, repelled them. Two rioters, who had also been involved in the May disturbances, were subsequently caught and imprisoned for two days until local justices ordered their freedom. At some stage that day, Gibbon, with another participant and three tenants, forced their way into a close belonging to one of the above two rioters, who was assaulted and wounded in the process, and distrained livestock belonging to another former rioter. Noddel preferred an indictment for riotous entry and assault for this action against Gibbon and his fellows on 15 July at the Spital sessions, where the indictment was allegedly found upon evidence supplied by convicted June rioters after the justices had ordered the deputy sheriff to be quiet and mind his own business when he tried to intervene. Warrants were accordingly issued for their arrest and imprisonment, and a tenant was later gaoled for a month, until allowed bail, while

---

[25] Stonehouse, pp. 90–6; G. H. Overend, 'The first thirty years of the foreign settlement in Axholme, 1626–56' in *Proceedings of the Huguenot Society of London*, ii, 314–15; P.R.O., S.P. dom. 18/37, f. 11I.

Gibbon and another tenant were fined under protestation.[26]

A set battle between Noddel, at the head of a force of commoners, and Gibbon and his men, was only narrowly averted on 25 June 1647. Divergent accounts of that day were given by Noddel and the participants' witnesses, with the latter's being perhaps somewhat closer to the truth once the inevitable exaggeration has been discounted. Noddel blamed Gibbon and his men for setting events in motion by assaulting an Owston commoner and seizing his horse as he journeyed along the highway, leading the commoner to seek a warrant for Gibbon's arrest which Noddel, attending to his client's interests, sought to execute on 25 June. Accompanied by about 200 men drawn from Haxey, Epworth and Owston for assistance and self-defence, he entered grounds in Haxey called Langham Hill to help the constables of Owston and Haxey execute the warrant. Strenuously denying any unlawful intent, Noddel had made it clear to the commoners 'that what he might by Law do for them he would faithfully perform his duty therein but would not do any thing for them but what by Law he might safely do', and had urged them to abstain from violence unless Gibbon proved obstreperous and they were forced to defend themselves. After conferring together at Haxey, Noddel and his men decided to request a meeting with Gibbon in Haxey Carr to discuss his recent abuses. However, Noddel acknowledged that he had worn a sword at the time (as his status as a parliamentarian officer entitled him) and that some of his companions carried guns, forks, long staves and clubs. It is difficult to believe that such a numerous, and well-armed, company could have had purely peaceful intentions and it may well have been that Noddel, on his return from London, was experiencing some difficulty in controlling the rising passions of commoners, subjected to renewed pressures by the participants, while still frustrated in their efforts to secure a trial of title. The participants' own witnesses certainly had no doubts as to the commoners' violent intentions. One testified to having seen Noddel enter Haxey Carr at the head of over fifty commoners mounted on horseback, with a further 500 following on foot, and that one of the horsemen carried guns while others had clubs, forks and long staves. A meeting at Langham Hill had been

[26] P.R.O., K.B. 9/839/199–200; K.B. 29/297/27; H.L.R.O., Main Papers, 8 September 1647 petition of the Hatfield participants; 6 July 1647 affidavit of Edmond Awkeland.

arranged for 8 a.m. but, after waiting there until 10 a.m. while Gibbon prudently kept away, Noddel and most of his men returned home, leaving behind a group of about thirteen commoners who were still inquiring after Gibbon 'in an insolent manner' at 3 o'clock in the afternoon. The purpose of this meeting was supposedly to extract from Gibbon an assurance that previously levelled enclosures would not be restored, and there were rumours of a plan to murder him and two other men (employed as guards on enclosures) if he proved unco-operative, for the commoners had decided 'that if we cannot get our Common by law we will get it by Club law'. There were also reports that the commoners had resolved to pull down all houses built in the level by the participants and their tenants if agreement were not forthcoming. An ambush had, in effect, been carefully prepared that day; men lined the banks waiting to surprise Gibbon and his company, and a cartload of muskets had been brought into Haxey Carr and hidden in sacks according to one report.[27]

That a confrontation was narrowly averted on 25 June was largely due to the peace-keeping intervention of the steward of Epworth manor, William Geery, esquire. Geery had had previous discussions with some inhabitants about the commons of Epworth in which he had tried to dissuade them from violence, and had reached an arrangement whereby the commoners would give him prior notice of any action they contemplated. This pledge was honoured on the morning of the 25th, giving him time to head off a clash by speeding to Santoft to exhort Gibbon's men to stay out of Haxey Carr, as the commoners were bent upon using force and the very mention of Gibbon's name provoked murderous thoughts. He succeeded in persuading the men (who were awaiting the arrival of Gibbon with the sheriff) to remain where they were and thereby defused what could easily have been one of the bloodiest encounters so far. Yet the explosive potential remained as the events of the next few days demonstrated. On 26 June two Epworth men (former May rioters) dragged a servant off his horse, and beat him about the head, before sending him home with the message that if his master (an enclosure guard) had been there, he would have been killed. The same day a crowd from Epworth drove cattle into enclosures, through gaps made by three rioters in the participants' fences, and announced that they

---

[27] P.R.O., S.P. dom. 18/37, fols 11, 11I, 11III; H.L.R.O., Main Papers, 6 July 1647 affidavit of David Zeland of Haxey; ibid., affidavit of Edward Hill of Santoft.

would return the day after next to cart away freshly mowed grass 'and
see who durst oppose them'. A passage way was constructed by
dumping straw into sections of ditch and then covering it with sods of
earth, thereby enabling an orderly procession of about forty carts,
with two commoners in each, to transport the grass away on 28 June,
while one of the participants' men stood by helpless and afraid to
venture close enough to identify offenders. The Lords came to the
participants' aid; they ordered the arrest of all traceable offenders,
who were to answer before them for their contempt of the House's
orders, and also summoned two supposedly pro-commoner justices.
Noddel and two others were taken in custody to London, but were
released from restraint on 25 October following the intercession of Sir
Thomas Fairfax, whose help had been sought by Noddel in the
previous June (possibly with a view to expediting an Exchequer
verdict on the question of title).[28]

The year 1648 was a relatively incident-free one in the calendar of
commoner and participant struggles in the level as it became engulfed
by the second Civil War. The parliamentary commander, Edward
Rossiter, failed to drum up the kind of local support that had been so
evident in the first war as the commoners were doubtless disappointed
at the way Parliament had failed them in the matter of their
commons. Hence Rossiter's efforts to raise a company of foot to help
secure the Isle of Axholme against the royalists foundered as 'the
Islanders are backward, being many of them grown ill-affected', so
that the enemy was able to sweep into, and plunder, the Isle, and
support for Parliament elsewhere in Lincolnshire was at best luke-
warm.[29] When Epworth commoners recommenced their anti-
participant offensive in the following year, it was on a very much
smaller scale than previously. On 6 April seven Epworth men
assaulted a tenant and demolished his home, and six of these men
went on to expel one of Gibbon's tenants that same day, and another
later in the year.[30] The continuity of personnel and minimum
numbers involved in these incidents raises the possibility that a small

[28] P.R.O., S.P. dom. 18/37, f. 11III; H.L.R.O., Main Papers, 6 July 1647 affidavits
of Edmond Awkeland, David Zeland and Edward Hill; 27 September 1647 order of the
House of Lords for hearing complaints of participants, etc.; 9 November 1647 letter of
Sir Thomas Fairfax to the Earl of Manchester; *Lords' jn.*, ix, 427–9, 451, 494.

[29] Holmes, *Lincolnshire*, pp. 201–3; H.M.C. 13th report, Portland MSS., i, 467:
*Packets of Letters from Scotland, Newcastle, Lincoln and Lancashire to Members of the House of
Commons . . . 26 June 1646*, p. 5.

[30] P.R.O., K.B. 9/849/259, 261, 263.

group had been delegated to act on behalf of their fellow commoners. In September, the sluice at Idle Stop was opened by four commoners, putting the level at risk, and another five commoners seriously weakened the banks of a drain by removing wooden supports, while men employed on drainage works had to endure threats and interruptions.[31] But it was not until 1650 that local commoners braced themselves for a final onslaught upon the participants and their tenants.

Unlike their counterparts in the Isle of Axholme, commoners within the Great Level did not grasp the opportunity afforded by the slide into civil war to engage in the large-scale destruction of works and enclosures which had, after all, been largely neglected since the 1638 Huntingdon adjudication. During the course of the first war, rioting was confined to the Whittlesey enclosures of the Earls of Bedford and Portland in the Isle of Ely, where there was a major disturbance in May 1643, a lesser incident in the summer of 1644 and a minor one in the spring of 1646. The most serious rioting began on 15 May 1643 when between seventy and 100 inhabitants of Whittlesey and places nearby, including 'divers loose and disorderly persons' recruited in Ramsey, gathered in the northern part of the Whittlesey fens carrying agricultural implements and staves. The nearest justice who appeared on the scene was George Glapthorne, a leading drainage advocate whose enclosing activities in July 1641 had caused great local resentment.[32] In the circumstances, it was hardly surprising that the rioters defied his call to disperse and obey the Lords's orders and proceeded to cut up, and bury in the enclosure ditches, flowering cole and rape. Three men threatened him with their pitchforks, jeering that they would not recognise him as a justice because of his strong parliamentarianism 'and that they would not obey him nor any Law, and many of the Company . . . cried out and said that shortly he would be served as Felton served Buckingham'. One rioter apparently stood out from the rest as 'the principal actor and Ringleader', Jeffrey Boyce (or Boys) of Whittlesey, who described himself as a poor labouring man, and the rioters generally appear to have come from lower ranks of peasant society.

Rioting continued the next day as 150 or 160 Whittlesey and Ramsey commoners converged on other fenland enclosures which

---

[31] Notts, U.L., H.C.C. 6001, fols 443, 445.
[32] H.L.R.O., Main Papers, 31 July 1641 petition of some of the poor inhabitants of the town of Whittlesey.

they levelled in two companies and destroyed the rape- and cole-crop. The rioters had become even more audacious and were threatening to fill in all enclosure ditches, and to pull up the great sluice and demolish the dam to submerge the crops 'before they went home or else they would loose their lives'. Although they did not carry out this threat, they did turn large numbers of cattle into the rape- and cole-crop and tried to put an end to their cultivation by intimidating the tenants and their servants. One of the latter was warned never to plough in those fens again or they would cut the legs off both himself and his horse, for 'it was Commons heretofore and they would have it so still or else they would loose their lives', and a French tenant was told that 'he should be sure not to have his crop again' if he continued ploughing there. The special local animosity which George Glapthorne and Francis Underwood had earned as enclosing gentry prompted the rioters to pull down two of their houses built in the fens. A Whittlesey rioter was observed placing a shovelful of burning embers by the side of a rick of wood and hassocks, close to the dwelling house of Sir Peter Brettagne, which shortly afterwards ignited, but the vigilance of one of Sir Peter's servants saved the house and its contents.

Jeffrey Boyce, and all but two of the named rioters, were involved in both days' violence during which the Earls and their tenants sustained damages estimated at £1000, excluding the prevention of tillage for the following year which would have added a further £4000. But serious though the destruction had been, if £4000 was the correct value of the total crop, there was still three-quarters of it left untouched and this probably explains the rioters' resolution on 16 May to continue their violence with double their numbers the next day. It had, after all, become crystal clear on the 16th that local law enforcement agencies were impotent, leaving the rioters 'not suppressible by the ordinary Course of Justice', and the movement to destroy all the enclosures was gathering impetus. George Glapthorne was therefore compelled to travel to Wisbech to request assistance from Sir John Palgrave, the local parliamentarian army commander, and military aid was certainly needed on 17 May when between 400 and 500 rioters were summoned into the fens by the ringing of a bell to recommence their levelling.[33] Before the arrival of a contingent of

[33] Bells were sometimes rung in fenland regions in times of serious flooding as a signal for people to line their banks and struggle to preserve them. This was, for example, a common practice on the northern side of Wisbech. (Camb. R.O., R. 59/31/9/3, f. 6.)

soldiers (variously estimated at eighty, or 100 or 200) from Wisbech, Glapthorne's associate, Underwood, tried to persuade the crowd to disperse but his efforts came to nought as the rioters had designs upon the enclosures of two other men who, like Underwood, had earned special hostility. The soldiers' arrival did put a stop to further violence and the crowd drifted away muttering threats about returning after the soldiers had left to cut down the rape and cole. Given the situation, the soldiers could not return to Wisbech (which was about 14 miles away) and had to be billeted in the town of Whittlesey for about a month at considerable cost to the townspeople.

Thirteen Whittlesey ringleaders and instigators, including Boyce, were later arrested and brought to the Bar of the Upper House on 10 June where they pleaded not guilty and asked to be assigned counsel. A week later, after hearing witnesses, the Lords found Boyce and his associates guilty of riotous disobedience of their orders and committed them to the Fleet, while confirming the Earls and their tenants in possession of their enclosures and granting them leave to seek damages from the rioters. Copies of the Lords's judgement and their order confirming possession were sent into the locality to be read out by the clergy, and the sheriff or his deputy, not only in Whittlesey and Wisbech but also in Ramsey and Peterborough. As 'poor labouring men and without any other means of living', imprisonment hit the rioters and their families particularly hard, forcing them to make a desperate plea to the Lords on 31 July in which they claimed that, despite their submission and offer of bail, their release was being held up by their inability to meet the demand of £265 for the messengers' fees, on top of the fees required by the warden of the Fleet and the cost of maintaining themselves in custody, 'which said fees in value far surmount all the petitioners' estates'. The prisoners were eventually released shortly after entering recognizances on 6 September 1643 not to engage in, or foment, unlawful assemblies or disturbances in Whittlesey.[34]

The fens around Whittlesey were the scene of further upheaval in

---

[34] H.L.R.O., Main Papers, 29 May 1643 petition of Earls of Bedford and Portland; ibid., order of the House of Lords; ibid., affidavit of John Newton of Whittlesey, gentleman; 10 June 1643 order of the House of Lords; 17 June 1643 depositions taken on the behalf of the Earls of Bedford and Portland; 26 June 1643 draft order and judgement in the case of the Earls of Bedford and Portland; 31 July 1643 petition of Jeffrey Boyce, etc. prisoners in the Fleet and annexed recognizances; *Lords' jn.*, vi, 83, 86, 88, 107. (The list of rioters given in *Lords' jn.*, vi, 107 is in error being in actual fact a list of the July 1641 Whittlesey petitioners against the enclosure of their fens.)

early summer 1644 when rioters from the town disturbed enclosures
settled on Nicholas Weston by his father, the Earl of Portland. The
Lords reaffirmed their earlier orders for these fens when Weston
appealed to them on 10 July, and ordered the deputy lieutenants and
justices to ensure that they were observed.[35] The same grounds were
disturbed in a comparatively minor incident in early April 1646 when
four commoners drove over twenty horses and cattle into Weston's
enclosures. The rioters were probably hoping to set in motion a trial
of title but, having acted in violation of the Lords's order of 10 July
1644 confirming the Earls' enclosures, they were accordingly
summoned to answer for their contempt, while the governor of the
Isle of Ely was instructed to restore Weston's peaceful possession.[36]
For the remainder of the decade, there were apparently no further
violent encounters in the Great Level directly connected with the
drainage and enclosure of fenland and tumult only returned in the
wake of the 1649 Act and the enclosures it sanctioned.

Experience of the drainage schemes did not politicise the great
mass of commoners in the fens, any more than their forest counterparts, and turn them into unswerving parliamentarians in the Civil
War. The possibility that the clock might be turned back, in fens that
had previously attracted great courtier interest, may have persuaded
some fenmen to rally to Parliament in the first war against un-
compromising defenders of royal power, and Isle of Axholme
commoners may initially have seen support for Parliament as the best
means of facilitating the recovery of their fens, but any ostensible
parliamentarian enthusiasm had largely been dissipated by the time
of the second war. The struggle to regain former commons, and resist
undertaker pretensions, continued into the Civil War from the 1630s,
mirroring the situation in many forests,[37] and indeed for most fenmen
their war was with enclosure, loss of common rights and enforced
change, rather than with King or Parliament.

[35] H.L.R.O., Main Papers, 10 July 1644 petition of Nicholas Weston to the House of
Lords; *Lords' jn.*, vi, 625.
[36] H.L.R.O., Main Papers, 17 April 1646 affidavit of Robert Turbutt, gentleman;
Lords' jn., viii, 275–6.
[37] Sharp, pp. 220–5, 241–6, 249–50.

5 Commoners, Adventurers and Soldiers

ALL the fenland schemes initiated during Charles I's reign had been thrown into varying states of disarray by the time of his trial and execution. The return of peace, though, brought a major revival of interest in the fens, as former undertakers renewed pressure for the recognition and protection of their interests, and commoners either struggled to recover the remainder of their commons or rose in revolt against a new series of enclosures. While the drainage lobby was generally able to rely upon the support and influence of powerful Interregnum personages, including Cromwell himself, their commoner opponents successfully enlisted as champions of their cause a prominent figure in the presbyterian party, Sir John Maynard, and two Leveller leaders, John Lilburne and John Wildman, whose fenland involvement is examined in Chapter 6. Contingents of the same military force that maintained national order were employed in the fens to preserve peace and protect the interests of drainers once again enjoying official favour, and the combined weight of military and government support in the 1650s ensured that undertakers in the Great Level, after an initial trial of strength, gained the upper hand.

Although the East, West and Wildmore Fens were virtually abandoned and reverted to their former condition, an attempt was made by some undertakers, led by Sir William Killigrew, to retrieve their losses in the Lindsey Level and the Holland Fen. The Rump had initially declined to read a petition from Lindsey Level undertakers, somewhat disadvantaged as former courtiers and royalists, but on 21 May 1649 petitions from both undertakers and commoners were read and referred to the committee for the fens chaired by John Goodwin. The committee urged both parties to attempt some form of amicable agreement with a view to securing parliamentary approval for the Lindsey Level scheme, and on 27 August a number of commoners accordingly met together at Donington to draw up a document for presentation to the undertakers. Among those in attendance were six of the local gentry, including Thomas Hall, Robert Cawdron and William Trollop, all pre-war opponents of the undertakers, and at least two of the lower ranks present had a similar background. Although not departing from their previous denunciation of the undertakers' proceedings as illegal (a case reportedly proved before the fens committee under its first chairman), those present offered to negotiate terms with the undertakers provided that they could share in the enterprise. But this proposal did not have unanimous approval for some of the relevant towns were not represented at the meeting 'and divers Owners there present' signified their dissent from the document. Sir William Killigrew's reaction was astonishment at their impudence in refusing to reach an accord 'unless themselves may become (after works done at our charge) joint undertakers with us', meaning in effect that former destroyers of drainage works would become participants, and thus 'They have torn our coats from our backs and would now have a large share of our coats to help us mend what they have torn.' His counter-proposal was to offer them the option of becoming joint-undertakers in the unfinished, northern section of the level, or of taking over there completely (with a suitable reimbursement of the undertakers for money already spent), but he was adamant that 'it were madness to speak of admitting any of them Undertakers with us in our first Level which we have drained and sold'.[1]

In the absence of a compromise agreement, the committee for the fens was forced to listen point by point to the accusations and counter-accusations of both sides in the Lindsey Level, which occasionally became intemperate, as on 15 May 1650 when an exchange between Carew Raleigh, MP, and William Howett, a commoner, resulted in the former being committed to the Tower for a few days, and the latter's behaviour being investigated by a parliamentary committee. Sir William Killigrew sought to play upon the fears of MPs, and other men of property, by warning 'that if multitudes of men shall be suffered to pull down houses at their wills, which were erected by the authority of a Decree of Sewers, they may do as much against a Decree of Chancery, and then where is our property so much talked of'.[2] But the commoners had by this stage enlisted as their spokesman

---

[1] *Commons' jn.*, vi, 204, 212–13; *Certain papers concerning the Earl of Lindsey his Fens* (1649), pp. 2–8.
[2] *Sir William Killigrew his answer, passim*; *D.N.B.*, xvi, 648; *Commons' jn.*, vi, 413.

Sir John Maynard who adroitly managed their case before the committee for the fens. He denounced Sir William and his associates, 'the Old Court-Levellers, or Propriety-Destroyers, the Prerogative Undertakers', as the real enemies of property in *The Picklock of the Old Fen Project*, and developed a similar line of argument in two parliamentary petitions of 1650, almost certainly written by him, from the commoners of the southern half of the Lindsey Level and the Holland Fen.[3] At the same time Sir John was committed to the commoners' cause in the Great Level (where he had an estate at Isleham, in Cambridgeshire) which led Sir William Killigrew to the conclusion that his intervention in the affairs of the Lindsey Level, where he 'hath no interest in those fens now in question', was tactical 'in hope after our overthrow, if this design take effect, to repeal Bedford Act'.[4]

Sir William and his associates had also been busy trying to recover property in the Holland Fen and, by 1651, had prepared a Bill that they hoped to steer through Parliament. To counteract the undertakers' growing influence, the commoners organised an intensive lobbying of Parliament and allegedly incited their fellows at Boston 'to come up in great numbers to make new clamours, by telling them that they have a good cause, and but few friends in Parliament' and that if their views were not heeded they should 'bring up their wives and children to the Parliament door, and there leave them'.[5] The Lindsey Level report, prepared by Goodwin's committee, was finally communicated to Parliament on 26 March 1652 and, after further consideration, two proposals were put to the House on 9 April: a proposal (which was rejected) to empower commissioners to view the whole level and ascertain both how much of the northern section had already been drained, and how it might be completed for the commoners' benefit; and a proposal (approved by Parliament) to settle the southern section of the level. A Bill to that effect was accordingly drafted but neither it, nor the Holland Fen Bill, made

---

[3] *The Picklock, passim*; Bodl., *Two Petitions . . . from Thousands of the Lords, Owners, and Commoners of Lincolnshire; against the Old Court-Levellers, or Propriety-Destroyers, the Prerogative Undertakers* (1650). The authorship of the latter is ascribed to John Lilburne in a contemporary hand on the title page, yet the line of argument closely resembles that of *The Picklock* and there is no other evidence connecting Lilburne with the fens of south Lincolnshire.

[4] *Sir William Killigrew his answer*, p. 16.

[5] *A Paper delivered and dispersed by Sir William Killigrew* (1651).

any parliamentary progress and attempts to revive interest in the former in 1654–5 foundered.[6]

One final offer of compromise was made by Killigrew and his fellows on 25 August 1654; the inhabitants of all towns bordering on the Lindsey Level were exhorted to reject the leadership of men who opposed the undertakers for their own selfish ends and were offered three main concessions in return – the purchase or lease of grounds at favourable rates, a chance to participate in the drainage of the northern section of the level, and the freedom to graze their livestock on the undertakers' 14 000 acres from Michaelmas to Lady Day 'at such easy rates as shall make appear our real affection to you'.[7] Such terms were hardly magnanimous as the commoners were already in possession of virtually all of the undertakers' grounds, and had been so since May 1642, and there could scarcely have been much appeal in the prospect of paying, no matter how favourable the rates, for the use of lands over which they had previously enjoyed free common rights. As compromise proved impossible, the undertakers concentrated upon securing an Act of Parliament as their only means of recovery, and both sides were again drawn into the parliamentary arena. In elections to the first Protectorate Parliament, the commoners managed to secure the return of Thomas Hall, a veteran champion of their cause, and some of them turned up at the doors of Parliament to hand out tracts to members which argued against Sir William Killigrew's attempt to resurrect the Bill sanctioned by the Rump and extract compensation for the repair of drainage works.[8] Sir John Monson also made a petitioned parliamentary defence of his Ancholme Level undertakership, but he too met with no success during the Interregnum in his efforts to regain lands lost to the commoners.[9] With commoners enjoying an undisturbed possession throughout the 1650s, a general peace settled over all these fens which was disturbed only twice: in July 1653, when the great sluice at Boston was badly damaged by persons unknown (threatening the Holland Fen with inundation), and in April 1656, when efforts to con-

---

[6] *Commons' jn.*, vii, 111, 118; Sir William Killigrew, *A Representation to Parliament in favour of the draining of Lindsey Level* (1655).

[7] B.L., Additional MSS 21427, f. 207.

[8] Sir William Killigrew, *A Representation to Parliament*, op. cit.; P.R.O., S.P. dom. 18/73, f. 91.

[9] *Commons' jn.*, vii, 402; H.L.R.O., Main Papers, 15 December 1654 petition of Sir John Monson to the House of Commons.

struct works sanctioned by a court of sewers in Little Hale Fen (within the Lindsey Level but unrelated to the earlier undertaking) provoked local trouble.[10]

The drainers achieved their greatest success in enlisting parliamentary support in the Great Level where years of persistent lobbying, by Bedford and his fellow undertakers, were eventually rewarded by the Act of 29 May 1649. The drainage lobby had made their first parliamentary moves towards the end of 1643 when, with Bedford recently back in Parliament's camp after his brief defection to the royalists, a short drainage ordinance was committed. Spokesmen from the six relevant counties ensured that there was 'an extraordinary appearance against the undertakers' but the manoeuvres of the latter's friends on the committee deprived them of a reasonable chance to present their case. They quite justifiably took exception to the committee's first chairman, Robert Scawen, formerly solicitor to Bedford's father, the fourth Earl (a service recognised by the grant of a £40 annuity), and most of Scawen's dozen or so successors in the chair were believed to have had an undertaker bias, as indeed had the committee as a whole. The following tactics had allegedly been employed to deprive the undertakers' opponents of a fair hearing:

no witnesses were fairly examined for the six Counties, but leading Interrogatories obtruded upon them: not one Town of ten were examined at all, when the six Counties attended there were commonly two or three undertakers, who adjourned the Committee in Westminster Hall on purpose to vex and tire the people; when the people had spent their money and were gone out of town, then the Committee sat in one corner or another, so that their solicitors were fain to watch them. The Committee-men were often feasted by the undertakers, and our lands were offered to be sold at two years value to Parliament men, which was often complained of to the Parliament by some worthy Patriots. This great (not good bargain) increased very much their faction.

Yet despite all these manoeuvres, Parliament did not give its approval to the ordinance and it 'withered away to nothing'.[11]

Success only came to the drainers in the form of the 1649 Act after almost four years of intense activity, beginning with a first reading in

[10] P. Thompson, *The History and Antiquities of Boston* (1856), p. 633; P.R.O., K.B. 9/871/265-7; 878/162-3. Little Hale Fen was to be the scene of further disturbances in June 1673 (K.B. 9/926/347-9).
[11] *The Anti-Projector*, p. 4; M. F. Keeler, *The Long Parliament 1640-41* (Philadelphia, 1954), p. 335; P.R.O., PROB. 11/332/41 will of Robert Scawen.

the Commons, on 15 August 1645, of a drainage ordinance for the Great Level. This measure had been prompted by a pro-drainage petition, purportedly emanating from the commoners themselves, but the latter condemned it as a contrived device seeking to convey the impression that 'it proceeded from the major part of the owners, and commoners, but it was a mere imposture of the undertakers' faction, and not one of a hundred [consented to it]'. After a second reading on 28 April 1646, the ordinance was referred to an investigatory committee of which no undertaker was to be a member. But this did not exclude the undertakers' friends, supporters or future associates from membership, including Cromwell, who was now unequivocally in favour of drainage, Robert Scawen, Henry Darley, the later co-author of a patently one-sided report into the riots in the Hatfield Level, and Sir Edward Partridge (or Partherich), a direct beneficiary of renewed drainage and enclosure. Partridge was of Kentish origins and was perhaps unconnected with the fens until his appointment to the committee but later submitted rival proposals for drainage to Vermuyden's, built up an estate in the level and took up residence at Ely where he died a man of considerable substance.[12]

The opposing side also had at least one friend on the committee in the person of the eloquent Sir John Maynard (a member from 7 May 1647) who had earlier appeared before it, in June 1646, to urge the case against the proposed drainage and for the next seven years remained one of the undertakers' principal opponents. The reasons for Sir John's stand are somewhat obscure, unless one accepts at face value his public posture as a defender of property rights against arbitrary intrusions. His earlier courtly career certainly made him appear an unlikely candidate for the role of champion of oppressed commoners, and it was later claimed that when Charles I supplanted Bedford as undertaker in 1638 'Sir John Maynard an old Courtier, was not a little active and busy to advance the late King's interest'. On the outbreak of war, Sir John opted for the Parliament's side and helped raise troops in Surrey, but he was very much on the right of that party, subsequently becoming a leading presbyterian and favourer of a treaty with the King. He was one of the eleven MPs charged with disaffection by Fairfax on 16 June 1647 and in the

---

[12] *Commons' jn.*, iv, 229, 243, 525; *The Anti-Projector*, p. 4; Keeler, *The Long Parliament 1640–41*, op. cit., pp. 298–9; W. M. Palmer, *The Fen Office Documents* (1939), p. 154; Harris, *Vermuyden*, p. 98.

following February he was impeached of high treason. Refusing to recognise that the House of Lords had any jurisdiction over him, he demanded a jury trial citing Magna Carta and the petition of right (documents that he drew on frequently in his defence of the fenland commoners), was fined £500 and remanded to the Tower, and then resumed his Commons's seat upon his release on 3 June 1648. During the early days of the Rump (for which he had little affection), Sir John was said to have espoused the fenmen's cause 'not so much to oppose the Draining, as to make use of it against the Parliament, for in the King's time he was the greatest promoter thereof that could be for the King'. But although the fens provided some useful ammunition with which to discredit the new regime, his opposition to drainage, discernible as early as June 1646, probably cannot be dismissed as political expediency, despite the interesting parallels that might then be suggested between his career and that of Cromwell, with expediency pushing them in diametrically opposed directions. One of the reasons advanced for Cromwell's animosity towards Sir John in 1648 was that he had opposed him 'in the project of Draining the Fens when Cromwell appeared against 50 000 of his countrymen whom formerly he had stood for', and there was some scurrilous speculation that Cromwell coveted Sir John's Isleham estate which he would forfeit as a convicted traitor. Sir John would presumably have found common cause with his fellow landowners and commoners in opposing schemes for the Great Level which adversely affected them, yet his opposition to drainage also extended to the Lindsey Level and Holland Fen where he had no lands (although Sir William Killigrew discounted it as a tactical opposition with the Great Level his real concern). Whatever his motives, Sir John Maynard was a formidable opponent with substantial political experience, and an expertise as a political pamphleteer that the first Duke of Buckingham appears to have first recognised and drawn upon in his service. Sir John's preeminence as spokesman and propagandist for the commoners was somewhat analogous to Lilburne's position in the manor of Epworth and, although politically opposed, the two men were old Tower prison acquaintances; it was Sir John who, in August 1648, procured Lilburne's release after a masterful pleading of his cause while Lilburne suggested that Wildman devote a pamphlet to Sir John's case as a means of discrediting the army leadership. But their political differences remained, and Sir John could not resist an oblique attack on the Levellers when denouncing pro-drainage petitions, purportedly proceeding from the country, which really came from 'only a few of the Undertakers' faction, like to the Agreement of the People'.[13]

The committee for the Great Level began its work on 16 May 1646 when it invited the six relevant counties to respond to the ordinance and was subsequently bombarded with forty-nine petitions against it from most parts of the level. Among those who appeared to argue against the ordinance were Sir John Maynard; George Quarles of Ufford, Northamptonshire, esquire, on behalf of the inhabitants of the soke of Peterborough; a Mr Barnard, on behalf of nineteen towns in Huntingdonshire; a Mr Cony, on behalf of thirteen towns (and 1100 petitioners) in the Isle of Ely; and a Mr Peck, representing towns in Norfolk. On the other side were George Glapthorne and Francis Underwood, seasoned campaigners for drainage and enclosure: the former, under cross-examination by counsel for the commoners, categorically denied being 'any adventurer or sharer' in the proposed undertaking which, although perhaps technically correct at the time, masked his real intention to become actively involved after the passage of the 1649 Act; and Underwood and two other drainage advocates before the committee had previously served as officers in Parliament's army. Lieutenant-colonel William Dodson, a native of the Isle of Ely, who had been employed on the original 1630s undertaking and was to resume his interest in the level after 1649, had served with Cromwell from the beginning of the war until his presbyterianism ruptured their relations, while Underwood himself had achieved the rank of major and the other former officer, captain Roger Pratt, had lands around Downham, in Norfolk. The committee was besieged by the commoners' spokesmen clamouring to be heard; one spokesman begged the committee on 11 November 1647 to appoint separate days for each county to produce its witnesses as he had earlier failed to obtain a hearing because all the counties had appeared at once. Nevertheless, eleven days later, as the

---

[13] *Commons' jn.*, v, 166; *An Answer to a Printed Paper dispersed by Sir John Maynard entitled The humble Petition of the Owners and Commoners of the Town of Isleham* (1653), p. 7; *D.N.B.*, xiii, 155–7; *The state of the Adventurers' Case, in Answer to a Petition exhibited against them by the Inhabitants of the Soke of Peterborough* (undated); *Sir William Killigrew his answer*, p. 16; John Harris, *The royal Quarrel, or England's Laws and Liberties vindicated, and maintained, against the tyrannical usurpations of the Lords by that faithful Patriot of his Country Sir John Maynard* (1648), p. 6; *The Picklock*, p. 7; M. Ashley, *John Wildman* (1947), pp. 56–7; Camb. R.O., R. 59/31/9/3, f. 5.

counties' spokesmen stayed away presumably to avoid lending credibility to its spurious impartiality, the committee felt it had heard enough evidence to recommend drainage as both feasible and profitable to the commonwealth. The committee was also to give a favourable hearing to objections raised by the participants' counsel to indemnity clauses urged by counsel for the country; the participants objected in particular to provision being made for trial of the effectiveness of the proposed works by jury and succeeded in having exclusive powers of adjudication vested in commissioners. After the committee had reported back on 6 March 1648, the Great Level ordinance received a second reading and was referred to a grand committee of the whole House. Three or four days of debate followed in March and April, but more pressing national problems relegated it to the background until 8 May 1649 when amendments were read and it was recommitted – while Lindsey Level undertakers failed in their efforts to gain a parliamentary hearing on that very same day. The ordinance finally completed its parliamentary progress on 29 May and was ordered to be printed; the demand for copies was so great that the House was obliged to sanction the printing of an additional 500 on 23 October.[14]

The circumstances in which parliamentary approval was obtained caused acrimonious exchanges between the Act's opponents and supporters. According to the former, the House had been 'very thin' at its passage with only about forty-three members present 'and some of them were parties interested, and the undertakers of all the Levels, like birds of a feather flocked together and watched their opportunity when many of the uninterested Parliament men were absent'.[15] The other side replied that only four Members of that Parliament had a direct vested interest in the Act's passage, as adventurers under it for a total of 3050 acres, and they had been 'excluded by Order of Parliament, to have any Vote at the debate of the business', and only one of them had sat in the House during the debate and passage of the Act. Whatever the precise circumstances surrounding the passage of the 1649 Act, drainage apologists were able to answer their opponents' criticisms from a position of strength once having

14 Camb. R.O., R. 59/31/9/1, fols I–VI, X; R. 59/31/9/3, fols 3–6, 9–10, 23–4; Harris, *Vermuyden*, pp. 96, 98; C. Holmes, *The Eastern Association in the English Civil War* (1974), pp. 199–202; *Commons' jn.*, v, 471, 474, 481–2, 492, 509, 526; vi, 201, 204, 210, 212–13, 219, 300, 311; *The state of the Adventurers' Case*, op cit.
15 *The Anti-Projector*, p. 4.

received Parliament's blessing. Replying to objections that the consent of the majority of commoners had not been obtained as 43 Elizabeth I c.11 required, the Act's supporters argued that, given the scale of the enterprise, it was not really feasible and that was why an Act of Parliament, which embodied 'the consent of the whole Nation', had originally been thought necessary. Furthermore, as Parliament in Elizabeth's 43rd year had laid down one set of regulations, so successive Parliaments might see it as being in the public interest to make others, and such legislation would become impossible if the consent of private individuals was mandatory for people were 'for the most part covetous, and self-seekers; minding their own private before the public concernments'. Those who, like Sir John Maynard, argued that the Act constituted an attack upon property rights laid themselves open to the charge that

> men who broach such principles as that Acts of Parliament (wherein all men's consents are included) destroy propriety would be carefully heeded in time lest the consequence . . . interrupt the great affairs of this Commonwealth, if such an unsound, destructive principle (That a Commoners' right cannot be bound by an Act of Parliament) should be taken up by tumultuous giddy people.

From a practical point of view, an Act of Parliament was absolutely essential if the enterprise was to attract sufficient investment for undertakers, wary of possible interruptions to the enterprise's progress, were said to have resolved 'not to engage their Estates further in it, but by Authority and countenance of Parliament'.[16]

The 1649 Act in effect gave statutory recognition to William, Earl of Bedford, as the lawful successor to the undertaking of his father, Francis, and declared the 1638 Huntingdon decree null and void. The recompense of 95 000 acres was restored to the Earl and his participants, termed 'adventurers', who were given 10 October 1656 as the completion date for drainage, and on 25 January 1650 Vermuyden was appointed director of works.[17] Adjudication commissioners, appointed under the Act in the hope of mollifying aggrieved commoners, held their first meeting on 10 July 1650 and in the following year visited the northern part of the level before adjourning to their permanent meeting place in the Middle Temple. Although they received over 200 petitions, the commissioners were

---

[16] *An Answer to a Printed Paper dispersed by Sir John Maynard*, op. cit., pp. 1–3, 6, 7–8, 12.
[17] Harris, *Vermuyden*, p. 90; Darby, *Draining*, pp. 67–8, 70.

inevitably viewed by the commoners with a mixture of scepticism and distrust or, at best, regarded as poor substitutes for regularly constituted sewers commissioners and juries. Some of them were denounced as interested parties, being either undertakers themselves or 'sharers, or creditors directly or colaterally', but the Act's defenders refuted this aspersion on the commissioners' impartiality. Nevertheless, the institution of adjudication commissioners continued to be regarded as 'a most intolerable grievance', requiring commoners to 'dance attendance a 100 miles from their homes every 7th day after the Term, to attend them for 4 or 5 hours, to spend their monies, and have no aggrievance redressed, sometimes no Committee appearing', and a return to traditional procedures was urged whereby the Great Level 'was 7 levels, and each Level had their several Commissioners and Jurors, and acted only in their proper Counties'.[18]

The northern part of the Great Level was the first to receive the drainers' attention, provoking organised resistance in the soke of Peterborough in the spring of 1650. Ultimate responsibility was ascribed to Sir John Maynard who organised, and most probably composed, a local petition to Parliament before work began opposing the whole undertaking, but the pressure of business prevented the MPs entrusted with it from presenting it to the House before workmen had been dispatched into the Peterborough fens. Four prominent Northamptonshire gentry co-ordinated local resistance; two brothers, Francis and George Quarles of Ufford, esquires, were first recruited by Sir John and they in turn enlisted two other esquires, John Cleypole of Northborough and William Leafield of Longthorpe. These four gentry were accused of using their position as justices to foment local opposition to drainage at both quarter sessions, and at a hundred court presided over by George Quarles as steward. The Earl of Exeter was also approached but he refused his backing (which did not, it was reported, prevent them from claiming it) and warned the justices that 'their undertaking would come to none effect'. Three of the latter subscribed notes sent to each town within the soke calling for voluntary contributions, 'indifferently computed', to a defence fund, and nominating a few townsmen to

[18] S. Wells, *The History of the Drainage of the Great Level of the Fens called Bedford Level* (1830), i, 212–13, 279–80; Camb. R.O., R. 59/31/9/9I, II; *The Humble Petition of the Inhabitants of the Soke of Peterborough . . . against the Undertakers there* (1650), pp. 2, 4; *An Answer to a Printed Paper dispersed by Sir John Maynard*, op. cit., p. 1; *The Anti-Projector*, p. 5.

further the business and liaise with others during the next quarter sessions. The adventurers described these notes as 'warrants', citing them as confirmatory evidence of abused authority, but the justices repudiated the description, for there was no word of command in them or any penalty stipulated for non-compliance. They also denied any intention of making the meeting of town nominees part of quarter sessions business, explaining the timing as simply a question of convenience at a time of general confluence in the county. However, this attempt to concert opposition may have fallen flat for, if the adventurers' observations were correct (and it certainly suited them to minimise local opposition), the principal town of Peterborough failed to contribute its mere £11 to the fund and the response generally fell short of expectations.[19]

The soke came closest to violence on 17 April 1650 when Francis Quarles and John Cleypole, at the head of 100 commoners, ordered about a thousand of Bedford's workmen (in the name of the Earl of Exeter, according to one account) to abandon their work in Borough Fen, which many of them apparently did. A Crowland gentleman present, Richard Kendall, believed that the commoners would have fallen upon the workmen had they not been so numerous with military backing on hand at Crowland, for they 'gave out in a jeering way before they came, that they would come that day to pay the workmen their wages, meaning...to beat them'. But Kendall's evidence is suspect as he later confessed to having made a false allegation against William Leafield concerning the day's events and 'would have expressed the same in his Affidavit, but that some that stood by him, gave him a twitch, and wished him to forbear to express the same'. Moreover, Francis Quarles denied that he and his fellows had had anything else in mind when they discharged the workmen, other than to register peacefully their clear disapproval of the works pending a parliamentary decision on the matter.[20]

There are indications that the leaders of resistance in the soke may not have enjoyed the kind of mass following they boasted. The adven-

[19] *The Humble Petition of the Inhabitants of the Soke of Peterborough*, op. cit., pp. 1–7, 12–13; *The state of the Adventurers' Case*, op. cit.; W. C. Metcalfe (ed.), *The Visitations of Northamptonshire made in 1564 and 1618–19* (1887), pp. 82, 107, 192; *Harleian Society*, lxxxvii, 1935, 118–19; Camb. R.O., R. 59/31/9/4, f. 25; *Fenland notes and queries*, ii, 403–4.

[20] *Fenland notes and queries*, ii, 402–4; *The Humble Petition of the Inhabitants of the Soke of Peterborough*, op. cit., pp. 8–12.

turers were of course only too anxious to denigrate the organisers of
the anti-drainage petition as lacking any representative authority
because they had supposedly failed to gain signatures from the townspeople of Peterborough (by far the most populous town in the soke,
and with the greatest interest in Borough Fen), and had encountered
outright refusals, or a general reluctance, to sign elsewhere. Yet, in
view of the lead given by four local gentry, the 100 commoners in
Borough Fen on 17 April was not an impressive turn-out if a gesture
of community solidarity against the works was intended. This denial
of a popular following was repeated when one of the Quarles,
speaking on behalf of the soke on 21 November 1651, asked that
progress might be made on an earlier referral to two referees of a dispute concerning the setting out of the adventurers' lands, to which
the adventurers replied that when the reference had been ordered

> it was pretended that the Complaint was made by the whole soke,
> or at least the greater part of the soke, and was conceived that the
> whole soke should have been bound to what should then have been
> done by the said referees. But the Company have since understood
> that there were not about 10 persons of the soke which were parties
> to the Complaint and that the far greater part of the soke desire that
> the lands may lie as they are already set out, so as the Company
> conceive the proceeding in the said Reference will be altogether
> fruitless.

Whatever the precise extent of local support for the Quarles
brothers and their associates, the animosity of such socially significant
individuals was a serious handicap for the adventurers and the need
to have allies on the local bench perhaps explains their anxiety to have
colonel Francis Underwood put into the Northamptonshire
commission of the peace in May 1651.[21]

The passing of the 1649 Act did not immediately lead to widespread rioting as the adventurers' opponents, like those in the soke of
Peterborough, strove to remain on the right side of the law. But peace
was shattered abruptly in the spring of 1651 when commoners
mounted resistance to extensive enclosures sanctioned by a verdict of
Peterborough commissioners, on 25 March, that about 170 000 acres
to the north-west of the Bedford River had been drained according to
the terms of the Act. A group of women rioted in an unspecified part
of the level on 14 April in opposition to the adventurers' proceedings,

---

[21] *The state of the Adventurers' Case*, op. cit.; Camb. R.O., R. 59/31/9/5, fols 47, 143.

and there was widespread riotous resistance to enclosure in northern Huntingdonshire in the same month involving the inhabitants of Yaxley, Farcet, Stilton, Holme and other towns. The adventurers' activities had also caused great resentment in the Deeping Level where inhabitants in the Market Deeping area saw their trade and commerce seriously damaged when their navigation from Crowland deteriorated as a result of the works.[22] In the same season the dowager Countess of Exeter and fellow undertakers sought help from Spalding commissioners of sewers when commoners from Spalding, Market Deeping and neighbouring towns turned cattle into their 3500 acres. Although a decree of 28 March, establishing the undertakers in peaceful possession and forbidding any further disturbances, was read out on market days in Spalding and Market Deeping and the cattle were rounded up, Cowbit and Crowland commoners subsequently followed suit and kept their cattle there by force.[23] As resistance spread through the northern part of the level, the adventurers were forced to give urgent consideration to measures for the restoration of order, including the appointment of a solicitor to attend to the prosecution of past and future offenders on the adventurers' behalf. During a temporary lull in riotous activity, reports reached the adventurers on 5 May of a fresh attempt to organise a fighting fund in the soke of Peterborough, and a few days later they were forced to employ guards on their works to prevent drainage materials from being carried off by the locals. Drains and enclosure ditches were surreptitiously blocked and the adventurers' agents assaulted as they made drifts, while the inhabitants continued to assert their common rights by persistently driving cattle into the adventurers' lands, or by cutting turf there. But one of the greatest problems facing the adventurers was the obvious impracticality of protecting the many miles of drainage works from malicious damage, such as the cutting of vital banks to overturn a season's work in a matter of hours, which prompted an attempt to secure an Act of Parliament in the summer of 1651 making it a felony to cut the banks of the Great Level.[24]

Towards the end of a summer relatively free from serious disturbances, there was renewed disorder at Haddenham, in the Isle of

[22] Wells, *Bedford Level*, op. cit., i, 213, 216–17, 219; Camb. R.O., R. 59/31/9/5, fols 26–7, 32–4, 41; R. 59/31/9/9I, f. 9.

[23] Lincs. R.O., Spalding sewers 463/2/6, 47.

[24] Camb. R.O., R. 59/31/9/5, fols 41–2, 46, 74, 80, 104, 135.

Ely, in which one of the local gentry, Thomas Castle, who had been suspected of obstructing sewers proceedings in 1619, once again attracted attention for allegedly filling in enclosure ditches, helped by his son and three labourers, on 20 August and assaulting a tenant; soldiers were later quartered in, or near, Haddenham to preserve order. The adventurers received information about another incident in the following November, the location or precise form of which is not revealed, which led to a man called Newell being summoned to London to be made an example of.[25] By the winter the adventurers were finding it increasingly difficult to recruit sufficient local labour – as a result no doubt of a combination of earlier unsatisfied wages and a growing local antipathy to the works themselves. One solution to this shortage, which the adventurers enthusiastically embraced that winter, was to employ Scottish prisoners captured at Dunbar as conscript labour. Their employment on the works was planned down to the last detail, including a scheme to clothe them in distinctive smocks in order to distinguish them from English workmen and make escape more difficult. However, the Scots, not taking kindly to the role of slave-labour, proved a most recalcitrant work-force and at the first opportunity took to their heels and headed homeward; despite a parliamentary order of 19 November prescribing death without mercy for all Scots who ran away from the works, desertions continued with the open encouragement of surrounding commoners.[26]

During the winter of 1651–2, the commoners of Ramsey and other towns in the northern part of the Great Level continued to exercise their traditional right of turbary in grounds allotted to the adventurers at Peterborough, thereby both directly challenging the latter's title and reducing the value of those grounds by leaving them scarred with turf pits. The adventurers countered by ordering the seizure and sale of all turf cut on their lands, commenced legal proceedings against those cutting turf and sought a military guard to prevent future violations. Some Ramsey commoners, unnerved by the prospect of legal proceedings, capitulated to the adventurers, offering them half of the turf as compensation for their loss; but the adventurers refused to accept anything less than the whole of the turf or its

[25] P.R.O., K.B. 9/852/293; Camb. R.O., R. 59/31/9/5, fols 140, 173.
[26] N. Walker and T. Craddock, *The history of Wisbech and the Fens* (Wisbech, 1849), pp. 147–8, 151; P.R.O., S.P. dom. 25/23, fols 25, 27–8, 31; Camb. R.O., R. 59/31/9/5, fols 111, 114–18, 128, 140, 166, 173.

value in kind and on 16 February instructed them that if they wanted the threat of legal action lifted, they should request the lord of the manor, or their neighbours, to petition the adjudication commissioners for an additional assignment of land to the adventurers as compensation for the turf pits.[27] A potentially much more serious threat to the adventurers that winter was the action taken by a commoner, later identified as Johnson, in cutting a breach in one of the banks in Carr Dyke which could have had catastrophic consequences, and it was decided to make an example of him. He was taken into custody pending trial at the next assizes and the adventurers even considered asking the General to have him tried at a court of war for his life, but decided against it as he was already being proceeded against at common law.[28]

Upheaval returned to the fens of Swaffham and Bottisham in the summer of 1652, and the ensuing winter, as the adventurers' workmen were assaulted and their works came under attack. The first riot, in May, was initially thought to have been committed by women, but it was later discovered that the rioters had in fact been men dressed in women's clothes in order to avoid detection. In the following September rioters filled in an important drain in Swaffham Fen and, by January 1653, the adventurers had come to the conclusion that military assistance was necessary if the works were to be preserved. A squadron of horse was requested from the commanding officer at Ely to be quartered in the vicinity of Swaffham, the adventurers 'conceiving this to be a principal means to suppress riots for the future'.[29] In the event, military assistance was frequently needed in 1653, a year of widespread disorder in the level, following the adjudication commissioners' declaration at Ely in March 1653 that the Great Level had been drained according to the terms of the 1649 Act (whereas the commoners attributed its favourable condition to exceptionally dry weather[30]), and the decision to employ Dutch prisoners, captured during Blake's engagement with Van Tromp, in the fens. Although 500 prisoners were employed on drainage works until peace was restored with the Dutch in 1654 (and they presumably had some familiarity with this kind of work, as Dutchmen, if they had previously

[27] Camb. R.O., R. 59/31/9/5, fols 148–9, 155, 166, 170–1, 173, 178.
[28] Ibid., fols 157, 166, 168.
[29] Camb. R.O., R. 59/31/9/5, fols 225, 239; R. 59/31/9/6, fols 10, 20–1, 37, 40, 42; P.R.O., S.P. dom. 18/39, f. 92.
[30] Badeslade, p. 54; *The Anti-Projector*, p. 5.

worked on the land), the employment of this conscript labour force probably created more problems than the Scots. On 18 July 1653 the adventurers complained to John Thurloe (one of their high-placed friends with a vested interest in the level) that the Dutch prisoners 'not only refuse to work but are encouraged by the Country people of Swaffham, Waterbeach, Cottenham and other places who are opposite to this work of draining to run away hiding them in the Corn'.[31]

The most serious rioting that year broke out in the southern part of the level, in the fens of Swaffham Prior, Swaffham Bulbeck, Bottisham and the surrounding area, which had been, and was to remain, the scene of regular disorder until the middle of the decade. On 7 February a substantial section of the Twelve Foot Drain running through Swaffham Prior and Swaffham Bulbeck was filled in, presumably by local inhabitants, during the night 'when they supposed their deeds should not be known'.[32] Workmen were expelled from the fens on 20 April by about 150 Swaffham and Bottisham men and warned not to return, and dykes and enclosure ditches were filled in. A few days later the adventurers secured a warrant from Cromwell requiring Major Packer to send a captain and a troop of horse into the area, and the troop was quartered upon local inhabitants until they had repaired the damaged works at their own expense. This means of restoring order in the southern level was also recommended for the northern part, where it was felt the people of Chatteris and elsewhere needed a timely reminder of the forces the adventurers had at their disposal by parading a contingent of soldiers before them.[33] But peace was lamentably short-lived for in early June commoners from the Swaffham and Soham area combined to level enclosures, and for much of the month there were repeated nocturnal attacks on a drain running through the parishes of Swaffham and Bottisham. A troop of horse was again required to restore order, but on this occasion the situation was considered serious enough to warrant the assignment of two further troops as a stand-by. Three of the rioters were indicted at Cambridge quarter sessions on 21 July and were later fined £20 each and imprisoned, but the deterrent effect

---

[31] J. Korthals-Altes, *Sir Cornelius Vermuyden* (1925), pp. 99–100; Wells, *Bedford Level*, op. cit., i, 250; P.R.O., S.P. dom. 25/133, f. 16; Camb. R.O., R. 59/31/9/6, fols 60–1, 68, 97, 107; ibid., records of Bedford Level, accounts 1653–4.

[32] P.R.O., K.B. 29/303/49.

[33] Ibid., K.B. 9/860/125–6; Camb. R.O., R. 59/31/9/6, fols 76–8.

of these sentences was soon nullified when the justices afterwards reduced the fines to an inconsiderable sum (allegedly paid in any case by the towns) and released them from custody. There was another nocturnal attack upon a drainage bank near Swaffham on 24 June, and a declaration of Cromwell and the council of state on 29 June, condemning the riotous disturbance of the adventurers and ordering punitive action against future offenders, was said to have been 'much slighted by the Constables and others at the said publication' in that area.[34]

The attacks continued unabated in July despite the recent declaration: a section of drain was filled in, and four iron locks broken, near Swaffham Prior on the 3rd, again during the night; newly constructed works in a fen near Waterbeach, which had been opposed earlier that summer, were demolished by the townsmen (among whom John Knight, a local gentleman, was singled out for special mention); and a Cambridge petty sessions was necessary on the 9th to indict Swaffham and Wicken rioters. The adventurers' total damages, in the form of demolished works and loss of potential profits from seized grounds in the southern level, were estimated at £8850 by this stage, and their troubles were far from over.[35] In late July, or early August, following the release of Swaffham rioters from their imprisonment in Cambridge, works in their home area were yet again attacked after dark 'by great numbers of people', and the inhabitants of Burwell, Reach, Swaffham Prior, Swaffham Bulbeck and Bottisham were rumoured to be about to follow their example. An investigatory delegation of adventurers sent to Swaffham found the local justice, Roger Rant, 'very cold and dilatory and not willing at all to take notice of my Lord General and the Council of State their late Declaration bearing date 29th of June last . . . saying (when we offered it to him) that he had seen it, but he was to proceed upon the known Laws'.

As the Swaffham magistracy was thought unreliable, an approach was made to the commander of the local regiment for a military guard and three or four soldiers were assigned to keep a nightly watch over

---

[34] P.R.O., K.B. 29/303/49 dorso; S.P. dom. 18/39, f. 92; Camb. R.O., records of Bedford Level: accounts; R. 59/31/9/6, fols 93–4; *By the Lord General and the Council of State. A declaration respecting those who do assemble together in a riotous manner, and by violence dispossess the Adventurers for draining the great Level of the Fens* (1653).
[35] P.R.O., K.B. 29/303/49; Camb. R.O., records of Bedford level: accounts; R. 59/31/9/6, f. 120; R. 59/31/9/9I, f. 47.

the Swaffham works. As events were to demonstrate, this guard, which commenced duty on 17 August, was hopelessly inadequate given the commoners' determination and the soldiers' unfamiliarity with the local terrain. When a soldier and a few workmen began erecting a shelter for the guard near works in Swaffham High Fen on 25 August, they were approached by Edmund Drury, a local gentleman, who forecast that it would be toppled in a matter of days and that all the earth would be thrown back into the drain they were guarding. Answering the taunt that the drainers had learned a 'new trick' of spreading excavated earth over the surrounding fen (rather than leaving it heaped near works only too convenient for rioters), Drury coolly replied that a couple of spadefuls of earth flung in from each side was all that was needed to block the drain. Furthermore, the presence of an armed guard would not deter levelling commoners who would come, armed with fowling pieces, sixty or eighty strong, 'and what could 3 or 4 soldiers do against such a number', and if the commoners were able to match the soldiers in arms 'they would not care for 2 or 3 thousand of them'. Two days later about eighty commoners, carrying muskets, short pikes and swords, entered the fen around midnight; the cover of darkness both helped conceal their identities and enabled them to capitalise on their own familiarity with the fen's contours, in contrast to the soldiers' ignorance, which had earlier obliged them to alert assistance by firing into the air 'having lost themselves in the night' in the fen. The rioters shot at and wounded two of the guards (one of whom sustained a dangerous head wound) and pursued and caught the others who were forced to help throw earth into the drains as the rioters uttered 'very high and insolent speeches'. Later efforts to discover the offenders' identities proved fruitless, and all that Major Robert Swallow could report to Commissary-General Whalley after his investigations was that 'the business is so much in the dark, and so subtly and Cunningly carried on by the country that no Considerable discovery is as yet made neither is there much probability of it for the future'. The adventurers also failed to produce offenders' names but were convinced that further investigations would reveal that they were 'the meaner sort of people' of Burwell, Swaffham, Reach and Bottisham who had been 'set on and abetted by the better sort of the said towns' of whom Edmund Drury was their prime example.[36]

[36] P.R.O., S.P. dom. 18/39, f. 92, 96; 40, fols 19, 191–II, 58; Camb. R.O., records of Bedford Level: accounts.

News of the Swaffham riot reached a delegation of ten adventurers at Ely at about the same time as a reported attempt to break down the doors of the double sasse at Salter's Lode (which, had it succeeded, would have jeopardised the entire southern level). The delegation advised their fellows in London on 30 August to seek help from higher authority, as 'all other means here used having hitherto proved fruitless and ineffectual by reason of the contrary interest and disaffection of the Civil Magistrates in these parts'. They also warned that the commoners generally in the southern level were beginning 'to be very high and riotous and no doubt are fomented by some of your Enemies above, and do all talk of Sir John Maynard's petition being received and that the whole matter is to be re-examined and they hope revoked and made null'. The petition referred to was the Isleham petition addressed to the Nominated Assembly which the adventurers saw as a deliberate ploy to encourage opposition to them in the level. The delay in bringing the petition to a hearing was likewise seen as 'but an artifice of the said Sir John's to gain time, and in the interim to take advantage of any trouble or disturbance in the State as they did in Yorkshire and Lincolnshire [i.e. in the Hatfield Level]'. The adventurers were confident that once this petition had been discountenanced by the Assembly 'there would be no colour left for opposition and this side would by degrees grow calm and settled as the North side is'.[37] Sir John Maynard's central role in promoting opposition was also recognised by Anthony Hammond, esquire, 'conservator' of the southern level, who reported how local people 'growing troublesome, and by influence from Sir John, do combine against us, do raise money to bear the charge, and are framing very large and clamorous petitions against us, so that when he comes to make good his petition, instead of reason, he will produce a multitude of other complaints'. An analogy was similarly drawn with fairly recent events in the Hatfield Level for Hammond believed that, as long as Sir John's petition remained unheard, 'his party here will take the advantage of any trouble or misfortune that may happen to the State to rise and destroy our works as they did in Lincolnshire, for I conceive we are in the same danger of him that the State is of Lilburne the only likely man to make a Change'. Hammond therefore begged John Thurloe, as a friend, to exercise his influence as

[37] *An Answer to a Printed Paper dispersed by Sir John Maynard entitled The humble Petition of the Owners and Commoners of the Town of Isleham* (1653), p. 9; P.R.O., S.P. dom. 18/39, f. 92.

secretary to the council of state on the adventurers' behalf, and suggested how local disaffection might be dealt with. He pointed out how the assistance of civil and military authorities had failed to restore order in the past, 'the first wanting will and affection to do us any good, and the other power and Orders from their Superiors', and there was always the accompanying problem of where to quarter the soldiers 'unless they might lie in private houses, which they did a while, but they [i.e. the commoners] got them removed, that they might the better play their pranks'. Even proceeding against rioters by a special commission of oyer and terminer was inadvisable because there was always the possibility that 'the Jury will serve us, as they did in the case of John Lilburne, and there we are worse then we were before'. Hammond's solution to the problem was both simple and contemptuous; 100 known rioters and malcontents should be pressed for service in the Navy 'they being all water men and having little to do at home, do make these night excursions and shew their valour against my Lord General's men, which were much better employed against the Dutch'.[38]

The task of proceeding against Swaffham rioters was given to Commissary-General Whalley who delegated the responsibility to a group of army officers at the beginning of September. The latter were largely unsuccessful in tracking down the guilty parties; Edmund Drury was the only person they found any real evidence against, and that was insufficient to warrant either his detention in prison or his being sent up to London, although he was bound over in a £1000 surety to appear before the council of state if required. Some other suspects were taken into custody to await further evidence from the guards when they returned from testifying before the adventurers in London. Yet in the very course of these investigations, there was a further attack upon works in the same neighbourhood: part of the Twelve Foot Drain near Swaffham Prior was filled in after dark on 1 September.[39]

The adventurers also encountered hostility in other parts of the Great Level in the summer of 1653. A large flock of sheep belonging to Sir Edward Partridge were impounded in May by a dozen commoners from Ely, Littleport and Chittisham (most probably acting on the advice of Thomas Aungier of Ely, gentleman), as a

[38] P.R.O., S.P. dom. 18/39, f. 96.
[39] Ibid., 40, f. 19; K.B. 29/303/49.

reassertion of their title to Burnt Fen, and on 30 August Commissary-General Whalley was ordered to dispatch two troops of horse into the Isle of Ely to disperse rioters who were attacking works, but there was nothing resembling the scale or frequency of the Swaffham riots in the Isle.[40] In Huntingdonshire, enclosures in Warboys Fen, temporarily saved from attack in the spring of 1653, were eventually levelled by local commoners in January 1654 on the grounds that they exceeded the adventurers' entitlement in the fen.[41] The adventurers' Norfolk lands came under attack in April 1653; works in Methwold Fen were thrown in around the same time as, a few miles to the north, the commoners of Stoke Ferry, Dereham and Wretton were engaged in a similar offensive, and detachments of soldiers were needed to restore order.[42] Commoner opposition in early May to an attempt to make a drift of Peterborough Little Fen, as a preliminary to enclosure, was allegedly 'countenanced' by Humfrey Orme, esquire, and four gentlemen (William Hack, Robert Powell, Thomas Dickison and Richard Alfield) who were also present when rails set upon banks and forelands to mark out the adventurers' lands were pulled down.[43] On 10 September the council of state was asked to empower commanding officers in the Great Level to investigate all disturbances committed within the previous two years aimed at overthrowing works and send the guilty parties in custody to London.[44] An uneasy peace descended over the level in the winter quarter of 1653 punctuated by occasional reports from local agents of fresh outrages being planned. Works in Soham Fen were believed to be under threat in October but, with the authorities forewarned, the commoners apparently bided their time, and on 14 December a foot company were set to guard the sluices and works at Salter's Lode following a warning that some commoners were threatening to destroy those vital works 'now upon this change of government [i.e. the end of the Nominated Assembly]'.[45]

During the course of 1653 the adventurers met mounting resistance with an unfaltering determination to punish rioters and restore order

[40] Camb. U.L., Ely diocesan records, Ely 14 assize files 1653; P.R.O., S.P. dom. 25/70, f. 302.
[41] B.L. Additional MS. 37482, f. 6; Camb. R.O., R. 59/31/9/6, f. 127.
[42] P.R.O., S.P. dom. 25/69, f. 10; Camb. R.O. R. 59/31/9/6, f. 80; ibid., records of Bedford Level: accounts; R. 59/31/19/A, fols 10–11.
[43] Camb. R.O., R. 59/31/9/6, f. 83.
[44] P.R.O., S.P. dom. 18/40, f. 58.
[45] Camb. R.O., R. 59/31/9/6, fols 110, 122.

in the Great Level, and relentlessly pursued these ends with little scruple as to means. The employment of soldiers to suppress riots, and guard both works and enclosures, was adopted as a regular procedure at the beginning of the year and a great deal of effort and money was invested in pursuing rioters through the law courts and gaining favourable verdicts. Quartering men in an area served the dual purpose of deterring offenders and punishing recalcitrant towns by subjecting them to a hated imposition. Thus Hammond was advised on 22 June to quarter 440 Dutch prisoners *en route* for Ely, at Swaffham, Waterbeach 'and other parts most averse to the Company' as a punitive measure. But quartering was such a sensitive issue that the local commander-in-chief was ordered by his superiors in July not to quarter men outside of the Isle of Ely or place them other than in inns and alehouses. Yet these restrictions caused considerable consternation for the most troublesome area lay outside of the Isle in places where there were no inns, and few alehouses, with the result that the adventurers were 'so far from expecting any assistance to suppress disorders in those places where they are, that it begins to be taken notice of already by the Country and they receive encouragement to proceed in their riotous proceedings'.[46] As military help was paid for and rewarded out of company funds, the adventurers' accounts bear witness to both the regularity of that assistance, and the variety of ways in which it was deployed. The sum of £5 was, for example, paid to six soldiers 'carried from London to drive the fens at 13s 4d per week'; ensign Bootie received a 'gratuity' of £8 10s 'for the foot guard that defended the great Dam and Sasse over Ouse'; soldiers guarding Methwold Fen were paid £13 6s 8d to suppress riots and carry offenders before one of the local justices; and works in the notoriously disturbed fens of Swaffham were guarded for eleven nights in August by corporal Rudgeley at the rate of 10s a night. These accounts also shed some light upon the adventurers' activities in prosecuting or defending suits arising from riots, like the expenses incurred proceeding against Swaffham rioters at petty, and later quarter, sessions or the costs of proceeding against the town of Swaffham upon the statute of Northampton. Ironically, these same records contain evidence of an officially condoned use of bribery to secure favourable legal verdicts, of which the best example is the sum of £100 paid out to the Huntingdon jury in Hilary term 1653. This

---

[46] Ibid., fols 42, 98, 107.

amount was vastly in excess of other jury payments which varied from £4 12s to a Cambridge jury on the statute of Northampton, to 15s for a petty sessions jury, and 6s for a quarter sessions jury empanelled for the trial of Swaffham rioters. The sheriff of Cambridgeshire was rewarded on 5 July with a £5 'gratuity' for his care in giving the adventurers possession of their allotted land near Waterbeach, and rewards given to soldiers, in addition to their pay, were not unusual. Colonel Humphreys and his troop received £45, and Major Tyson and his company £20, as 'gratuities' in 1654, and in one account, covering the period 31 May 1653 to 20 November 1656, 'Gratuities to soldiers' is the largest item, totalling £78 15s.[47] By these means, the adventurers were at least able to get on top of the situation by the end of 1653 and, although there was intermittent rioting in 1654 and in subsequent years, it was never again on the same scale or as widespread.

The fens of Soham were the first part of the Great Level to experience disorder in 1654 when an enclosure ditch recently dug for Sir Robert Heath's son and heir, Edward, was filled in during the night of 31 January. In the absence of identifiable offenders, the sheriff was ordered to levy distresses upon the villages nearest to the enclosure to pay for its restoration and meet Edward Heath's damages.[48] In the following March and April violence returned to the fens of Swaffham where, on 13 March, a bridge was burnt down and a small part of the drain below filled in, and other sections of drain were cast in on 1 and 2 April. The levying of distresses on adjoining villages was again authorised when the undersheriff's efforts at Cambridge on 8 April to discover the identities of the guilty parties came to nought.[49] Works near Willingham were thrown in at the beginning of May necessitating the quartering of a guard of horse to preserve order and further distraints to pay for the damage.[50] The Protector and his council brought their full weight to bear in defence of the adventurers in the ordinance of 26 May that laid down that, in the event of any further attacks, the adventurers were to be awarded double damages, recoverable by the distraint and sale of offenders' goods or, in the absence of sufficient property, their commitment to a house of

---

[47] Ibid., R. 59/31/19/A, *passim* but see especially fols 2–6, 9, 11; R. 59/31/21/1(j); ibid., records of Bedford Level: accounts; R. 59/31/9/6, f. 104.
[48] P.R.O., K.B. 29/303/48.
[49] P.R.O., K.B. 29/303/49, 49 dorso; Camb. R.O., R. 59/31/19/A, f. 5.
[50] Camb. R.O., R. 59/31/9/6, f. 156.

correction until satisfaction had been received. Moreover, if the destruction of works was judged 'perverse and malicious', those offenders were to be proceeded against as felons (as the adventurers had urged on Parliament in the summer of 1651) provided that they were prosecuted within four months of the offence. The adjudication commissioners, established under the 1649 Act, were also given extended powers to pass judgement on all matters connected with disturbances to any adventurer's possession and imprison recalcitrants until they conformed.[51] A dozen printed copies of this ordinance were dispatched to Major Alexander Blake on 7 June after he had reported the recent destruction of a bridge over Bevill's Leam, between Whittlesey and Ramsey, while around the same time the quelling of a fenland disturbance at Brandon, in Suffolk, and nearby Hockwold cum Wilton, in Norfolk, again required military assistance.[52]

There were no other reported incidents in the Great Level until the beginning of 1655 when three Mildenhall (Suffolk) commoners were said to have cut a 12-foot-wide ditch in Mildenhall Fen which caused £500 worth of flood damage to hundreds of acres of cole-seed and grain. In the spring, another three commoners were accused of opening the doors of a sasse at Crowland during a period of flooding, thus placing an extensive part of the northern level at hazard, and having done about £200 worth of damage to the Peakirk bank. Both sets of offenders were subsequently summoned before the adjudication commissioners, acting under the new powers given them in the 1654 ordinance.[53] Twenty bullocks were riotously rescued on 2 July by five Soham men as they were on their way to the pound after being found grazing on enclosed fenland.[54] Extensive flooding occurred in the south level around harvest time after the doors of two sluices (one at Bottisham and the other at Swaffham) had been broken off by persons unknown, who risked the penalties of felony under the 1654 ordinance, but the offer of a substantial reward apparently produced no results. On 16 November the inhabitants of March, in the Isle of Ely, prevented a workman from enclosing approximately 21 acres of fenland recently awarded as recompense for the damage done by the

[51] C. H. Firth and R. S. Rait (eds), *Acts and Ordinances of the Interregnum 1642–60* (1911), ii, 899–902.
[52] Camb. R.O., R. 59/31/9/6, fols 159–60.
[53] Ibid., R. 59/31/9/9II.
[54] *Statutes of the Realm*, v, 510; P.R.O., K.B. 9/866/54.

same inhabitants in digging turf pits.[55]

Activity directed against the adventurers in 1656 took the form of interfering with or damaging crucial sluices in the vicinity of Salter's Lode. In February a sluice door was thrown off its hinges, the doors of another sluice were maliciously shut and four locks set upon gates leading to a major drain were broken, actions that subsequently resulted in the imprisonment of one offender and levying of damages on three others.[56] In the same year, there was a major reorganisation of the government of the Great Level when a well-attended meeting of adventurers at Ely on 29 September decided to restructure it according to the laws and customs of Romney Marsh. The Earl of Bedford was chosen as governor of the company and John Thurloe, deputy governor, presiding over twenty-three 'lords of lands', one bailiff, twenty-four jurats, an expenditor, clerk and serjeants. Beneficiaries of this reorganisation included Major-General Whalley and Major-General Goffe, who were granted lordships of 500 acres each in the south and north levels respectively, Oliver Cromwell, with a lordship of 200 acres, and John Thurloe, with a similar grant.[57]

For the remainder of the decade there were only a few fairly minor incidents in the level. A Sutton man was accused of throwing part of an enclosure bank into a drain on 17 September 1657 and, in the following December, the tunnel under the River Glen again became a bone of contention when fourteen Bourne commoners forcibly re-opened it to let water pass through into the Deeping Level, in defiance of a decree of sewers.[58] Oak planks were removed from a sluice near Tydd St Giles in the winter of 1659–60 and in the following spring and early summer, but the fact that one offender sold the planks in Wisbech perhaps indicates motives of gain rather than hostility to the works as such.[59] Norfolk fens at Methwold were the location of riotous attempts upon drains shortly before 2 May 1660, which led local justices and a jury to conduct an inquiry with a troop of horse in attendance.[60] After the crisis year of 1653, therefore, there were few really serious outbreaks of disorder in the Great Level, and the

---

[55] Camb. R.O., records of Bedford Level, accounts 1656.
[56] Ibid., R. 59/31/9/7, fols 4, 6; ibid., records of Bedford Level, accounts 1656.
[57] J. Thurloe, *A Collection of State Papers* (ed. T. Birch, 1742), v, 475.
[58] Camb. U.L., Ely diocesan records, Ely 19 assize files, April 1658; Lincs. R.O., Spalding sewers 500/303; ibid., 477/13.
[59] Camb. U.L., Ely diocesan records, Ely 20 assize files, October 1660.
[60] Camb. R.O., R. 59/31/19/2, f. 27.

occasional surreptitious attack upon drainage works generally replaced the earlier open confrontations. The adventurers gradually reasserted their control over the level by enlisting military support when required, and going to great lengths to ensure that as far as possible either individual offenders or local communities which nurtured them paid the price of their violent actions.

Although Charles I's former courtiers and allies of the royalist cause failed in their attempts to recover fenland that had been regained as commons, a few influential civil and military supporters of a victorious Parliament advocated, and drew personal profit from, the revival of the Great Level scheme in a way that was only marginally less blatant than their pre-war equivalents. Commoners within the Great Level may have felt a similar sense of injustice to that experienced earlier in other levels when they too faced largely one-sided committees, and were deprived of the right to a jury decision on the effectiveness of new works. But when angry resentment led to violent resistance, the adventurers were able to call upon military might to restore order and protect their property.

6   Levellers and Fenmen

THE authorities were markedly less successful in bridling opposition in the Hatfield Level than they were in the Great Level, after Isle of Axholme commoners decided to resume their offensive against the participants in 1650. Until that year Epworth commoners not only seemed satisfied with 4000 of the participants' 7400 acres, but may even have offered their old opponents peace terms (which were declined) involving a grant of 4000 acres in exchange for their undertaking to maintain local drainage works.[1] However, all this changed during the second half of 1650 as successive commoner incursions were made into the participants' remaining lands, reaching their peak in 1651 when the latter, and many of their tenants, were finally driven out of the Isle. It was in this period of heightened activity that two Leveller leaders, Lilburne and Wildman, emerged as the fenmen's protagonists and designers of their strategy.

The first signs of a concerted drive against the participants were discernible in May 1650, when William Scott and between sixty and eighty-five Belton commoners systematically threw down their fences, turned cattle into crops and demolished some of their houses. A commoner was said to have exclaimed from their midst 'it was a shame the Parliament should give away their Commons, they were a Parliament of Clouts'. During October the disorder became more widespread and rioting ''twas as ordinarily done as for men to go to their labour and some of those men were daily in it'. On the 8th, Thomas Bernard and William Robinson of Belton rode into an enclosure, accompanied by twelve others on foot, and impounded cattle for which the tenants (who never dared take pasture there again) were forced to pay ten shillings each to recover. The next day there were a number of attacks launched, mainly by Belton men, upon enclosures and tenants or their servants were driven away with a beating. Bernard and Robinson joined Daniel Noddel, the constable of Belton

---

[1] G. H. Overend, 'The first thirty years of the foreign settlement in Axholme, 1626–56' in *Proceedings of the Huguenot Society of London*, ii, pp. 316–17; Hughes, pp. 23–4; Lilburne, *Epworth*, p. 5.

(Richard Mawe), and numerous others in an extensive levelling of enclosures belonging to seven tenants (three of whom were foreign settlers) and assaults upon bridges and sluices. Cattle were again impounded by rioters who had allegedly decided not to obey replevins, Exchequer orders or even 'any Order made by the Parliament for they could make as good a Parliament themselves'. Rioting continued on the 10th, when Bernard and other Belton men levelled the enclosures of at least four more tenants, violently assaulting them in the process (striking men down dead, according to one probably hyperbolic account), and killed all of one tenant's hens and removed iron from his waggons. Belton rioters resumed their work of destruction on 12 and 13 October, encouraging the men of Epworth to follow their example, and disturbances occurred on a regular basis for the rest of the year and beyond with Belton men again to the fore in riots on 17, 21 and 22 October and 28 November. During the latter, a tenant's house was partly damaged by rioters and thus began what shortly became a concerted campaign to force many tenants out of the Isle by demolishing their homes. Thomas Bernard and Richard Mawe took a prominent part in these riots, alongside other previously active Belton men, and although Noddel did not himself play a direct role, he was said to have given the rioters encouragement so that 'they reported commonly that Mr Noddel did bear them out in this business and if they would provide monies he will bear them up'.[2]

In what was to prove a futile attempt to cling on to their remaining acres, the participants secured an Exchequer injunction with a writ of assistance to the sheriff to quiet their possession pending a hearing; however, the sheriff was simply defied when he tried to act. Their tenants had no more success when they sought help on several occasions from a local justice, Michael Monckton, who allegedly not only refused to grant warrants for arrests, or to take legal steps to preserve the tenants' property, but actively encouraged rioters. Monckton's reply to a tenant's complaint about the destruction of his corn was said to have been, 'I pity your case I wish that all the spoil were John Gibbon's', and when refusing aid to two Dutchmen he proclaimed that the tenants had 'had their Commons too long'. He was also said to have used his position and influence on the bench at a Spital quarter sessions to moderate the fines set upon fourteen rioters,

[2] P.R.O., S.P. dom. 18/37, f. 11III; K.B. 9/849/25-31.

previously convicted at a Caistor sessions (to avoid a jury of Axholme men); a fellow justice, Alexander Emerson, was reported to have urged a fine of four or five marks but Monckton pressed for a 6d fine as being sufficient, and they were eventually fined 12d each. There may not always have been substance to these charges as the poverty of the offenders had been taken into account when determining the level of the fines, and Emerson himself testified that no one had pressed for a bigger fine at the time, and Monckton was not wholly negligent in the exercise of his office for he apparently bound over some suspects to their good behaviour and granted at least one warrant for the apprehension of others. Furthermore he was reported to have several times forbidden his tenants and other commoners from becoming involved in the riots, believing that 'he should see some of the Inhabitants hanged for their riotings and seemed to be very angry with them'. There is no doubt, however, that Monckton clearly sympathised with the commoners' cause; he was subsequently identified along with Lilburne, Wildman and Noddel as one of their leaders, actually penned the Epworth proposals which were submitted to the two Levellers and was one of the moving spirits behind the later agreement. His acquaintance with Noddel, and perhaps with Lilburne too, could possibly have dated from the time when he was employed as a parliamentary agent for sequestrations in Lincolnshire.[3] Monckton's stance was probably similar to that soon adopted by Lilburne of publicly condemning the riots, while privately agreeing with the rioters' objectives.

In addition to attacking the participants' enclosures, Axholme inhabitants in the autumn of 1650 resisted any attempt by collectors of sewers' taxes to levy distresses within the manors of Crowle and Epworth. In Crowle between forty and fifty commoners were reported to have armed themselves with swords, guns and headpieces in readiness to resist the collector, and in Epworth about a hundred commoners rescued distrained corn. These and similar displays of force so terrified the collector and his assistants that none of the latter dared venture into the Isle 'for fear of having their legs or arms broken if they should meet them alone'.[4]

Any account of the involvement of Lilburne and Wildman in events within the Isle of Axholme in 1650–1 is, of necessity, heavily

[3] Ibid., S.P. dom. 18/37, fols 11, 11III; Ibid., 28/211.
[4] Notts. U.L., H.C.C. 6001, fols 586–7.

reliant upon one particular source – the depositions of witnesses before a parliamentary committee (on a reference of 16 January 1652 following the reading of the participants' petition relating to recent riots) and the committee's report drawn up by William Say and Henry Darley, two of its members, purportedly deriving from those depositions.[5] Fortunately this source is to some extent counter-balanced by three tracts addressed to Parliament by Noddel, and another addressed to the council of state by the assistant solicitor for the Isle, John Spittlehouse, in which the report, its authors, and the way in which evidence was taken, were subjected to rigorous criticism.[6] The report was denigrated in no uncertain terms by Noddel as 'a most partial, wicked, and erroneous report of Master Say and Master Henry Darley... Master Gibbon's great coached and feasted friends'.[7] There was certainly good reason to doubt the impartiality of William Say, the committee's chairman, who had an estate of 800 acres in Peterborough and Crowland Great Fen and had purchased fenland in the Hatfield Level from Gibbon in December 1637 (which he sold again in March 1650). Say had acquired earlier experience in compiling evidence against the Leveller leadership in 1649 as one of the counsel for the commonwealth at Lilburne's trial.[8] His colleague, Henry Darley, allegedly tried to intimidate Noddel into betraying the commoners' trust by warning that if the committee's report 'were given in to the Parliament, he our solicitor would be ruined, as also all of us'. Noddel was offered the alternative of persuading his fellow commoners to reach agreement with Gibbon in return for a bribe of 'two hundred acres of the said lands now in question, and monies besides, as the said Darley gave out to others that told our solicitor: which if our solicitor would, that then the

---

[5] P.R.O., S.P. dom. 18/37, f. 11 the report of Say and Darley; ibid., f. 11III the depositions of witnesses.

[6] *The declaration of Daniel Noddel*; *The great complaint*; *A brief Remembrance When the Report concerning the pretended Riot in the Isle of Axholme shall be read. Humbly tendered to every individual member of Parliament, By the Freeholders and Commoners within the Manor of Epworth in the said Isle, in number near 1200 besides new-erected Cottages* (1653) [the authorship is not indicated but it was most probably written by Noddel]; Spittlehouse, *The Case and Appeal*.

[7] *The declaration of Daniel Noddel*, p. 258.

[8] *D.N.B.*, xvii, 878; G. Yule, *The Independents in the English Civil War* (Cambridge, 1958), p.117; *Cal. S.P. dom.*, 1649–50, pp. 121, 314; ibid., 1660–1; p. 428; P.R.O., S.P. dom. 19/99, f. 59; *The declaration of Daniel Noddel*, p. 269; *The great complaint*, p. 273; Hughes, p. 24; Spittlehouse, *The Case and Appeal*, p. 5. Noble records that Say may have 'dealt much in fen lands' (*Lives of the English Regicides*, 1798, ii, 164).

report should not be drawn up; and that he the said Darley would come into the country himself to agree it'.[9]

Both Noddel and Spittlehouse were convinced that Say had blatantly used his influence in the participants' favour in both the taking of depositions, and the composition of the final report. Say took upon himself the clerk's task of keeping a written record of the depositions, 'such was his zeal to promote the Participants' complaints', and Noddel was denied the opportunity to check his suspicions about Say's transcript, having never received a copy, while Gibbon, in contrast, had been lent the original. Favouritism was also shown in the order in which witnesses were heard, with the participants' witnesses being examined within a month, while those appearing for the commoners were kept waiting for nearly six months, causing them extra expense and inconvenience (and leaving them the longer exposed to bribery and other pressures to alter their testimony). The final report indisputably favoured the participants by giving greater credence to their witnesses and failing to take adequate account of those produced by the commoners, and accusations of bias and distortion are largely confirmed by a comparison of the report with the accompanying depositions. Fully subscribing to the participants' version of events, the report traced the origins of the disturbances from 1642, when the commoners first entered upon 4000 of the participants' acres, to 1650-1, and their entry upon the remaining 3400 acres, and misrepresented the Exchequer decree of February 1651 as establishing possession of the whole 7400 acres with the participants (when, in fact, it left the commoners in possession of the 4000 acres and only established the participants in the remainder pending a trial of title). Only a tiny proportion of the report was given over to the presentation of the commoners' case, and Noddel was demonstrably correct when he accused Say and Darley of having 'in ten lines locked up and imprisoned the truth of above twenty witnesses' for the commoners, while they had 'stretched out near two hundred lines, in the report out of their depositions for the Participants' advantage'.[10]

---

[9] Spittlehouse, *The Case and Appeal*, p. 6.

[10] Hughes, p. 27; *The declaration of Daniel Noddel*, pp. 262-6, 269; *The great complaint*, pp. 273-5; *A brief Remembrance*, op. cit.; Spittlehouse, *The Case and Appeal*, pp. 5-6. One of the deponents, Richard Glewe, was alleged to have proposed that if the commoners paid him well 'he can take off 5 of the witnesses of Mr Gibbon' and to have demanded £200 from the Belton men or 'he would go to Mr Gibbon's side'. (P.R.O., S.P. dom. 18/37, f. 11III.)

The story of the involvement of Lilburne and Wildman in the Isle of Axholme has been rendered somewhat obscure and confused by the polemical nature of much of the surviving evidence. It clearly suited the participants to stress the extent of Leveller complicity in the events of 1650-1 and to elevate a series of regional riots into preliminaries for a national insurrection and violent change of government. To counter these charges of sedition, the commoners recalled the former royalism of many of the participants and their tenants and accused Gibbon and his associates of being currently in league with the 'King of Scots', while they themselves could parade an impeccable record of parliamentarian loyalty. Lilburne's Lincolnshire connections date back to October 1643, when he was commissioned major of foot in Colonel King's regiment, and he possibly first became acquainted with the fenmen's cause during his service there – perhaps through contact with Noddel or other parliamentarians recruited in the Isle.[11] Noddel's later trips to London on the commoners' legal business would have afforded him the opportunity to canvass support among Levellers in the city, who certainly regarded the subject of recent fenland enclosure as important enough to merit inclusion in their petition of 11 September 1648.[12] It was Noddel who apparently took the initiative on one of these trips and enlisted the support of Lilburne and Wildman, firstly as legal advisers while the case was being heard in the Exchequer, and afterwards as direct activists in the Isle where their presence was first noted in autumn 1650.[13] The reason one leading commoner gave for Noddel's recruitment of Lilburne was 'because Lilburne was a powerful man and he having friends would give a sooner end to the business which would take off the Clamour of the Inhabitants'.[14] Yet Lilburne's power and influence was decidedly on the wane by 1650 and, ironically, he may not have been willing to devote so much time and energy to the commoners' cause had he been in any way able to influence central politics. What the commoners did gain was the unquestionable legal and political expertise of Lilburne and Wildman,

---

[11] P. Gregg, *Free-born John: a biography of John Lilburne* (1961), pp. 108, 116–17, 123; C. Holmes, 'Colonel King and Lincolnshire politics, 1642–46' in *The Historical Journal*, xvi, no. 3, pp. 462–7.

[12] J. Rushworth, *Historical Collections* (1721), vii, 1257; Gregg, *Free-born John*, op. cit., p. 249; *The humble Petition of divers well affected Persons inhabiting the City of London, etc... 11 September 1648*, p. 5.

[13] M. Ashley, *John Wildman* (1947), p. 72; Gregg, *Free-born John*, op. cit., p. 309.

[14] P.R.O., S.P. dom. 18/37, f. 11III.

and the former's propagandist skills which he used to such effect in *The case of the tenants of the manor of Epworth*, but they already had, in the person of Daniel Noddel, a man of considerable talent both as a legal adviser and a public defender of their cause.

The fenland intervention of Lilburne and Wildman raises three important questions: why were these two leading figures prepared to immerse themselves in this one particular cause at this point in time; what relationship did the cause bear to the Levellers' general programme and philosophy; and was their intervention, as their enemies insisted, part of a wider strategy? By 1650 Lilburne had temporarily retired from the centre of the political arena, and his private affairs were going badly, while the fenmen's cause, with the added attraction of 1000 Epworth acres for his services, was one of a number of enterprises currently engaging his attention. Wildman had apparently severed his links with the Leveller movement by early 1649 to build up a career, and a substantial fortune, as a solicitor specialising in property transactions and a speculator in confiscated lands, and his Epworth involvement was probably one of the least successful of his ventures.[15] Yet a specific study of their intervention has suggested that it might be vested with greater significance as providing forward leadership for a peasant movement in a region whose social structure, and radical religious and political allegiances, gave it revolutionary potential.[16] In other words, it might be argued that in 1650 two Leveller politicians decided to broaden their appeal, and move from their more familiar urban environment into rural politics, in the hope of harnessing a radical peasant movement to their wider cause. This was certainly how the Levellers' enemies in London saw it[17] and the participants lost no opportunity to highlight, or invent, seditious overtones in everything the two men did in the Isle.

Its social structure made the manor of Epworth promising territory for Leveller ideas; it was relatively egalitarian, like most of the Lincolnshire fens, and possessed a large body of freeholders whose ranks Lilburne and Wildman were to join. The fenmen's case harmonised perfectly with Leveller notions of property rights in that

[15] Gregg, *Free-born John*, op cit., pp. 303–11; Ashley, *John Wildman*, op cit., pp. 14, 17, 72–82, 156; G. E. Aylmer (ed.), *The Levellers in the English Revolution* (1975), pp. 42–3.
[16] Hughes, pp. 14, 25–7, 32–4; Holmes, *Lincolnshire*, p. 26 for a less extravagant statement of this view.
[17] See for example J. Canne, *Lieut. Colonel John Lilb. Tried and Cast: or, His Case and Craft discovered* (1653), pp. 81–93.

they were defending the property they possessed in their common rights, based upon solid legal foundations, against unlawful expropriation by wealthy allies of the late King. The Levellers had earlier condemned the enclosure of common lands, and advocated the restoration of their original communal function, as part of their indictment of men of wealth and power who exploited the poor, and recent fenland enclosures had received specific mention in this context in the London petition of 11 September 1648. A former Leveller turned moderate radical, Lieutenant-Colonel John Jubbes, had envisaged a different future for fens and other common lands in the same year; he had proposed their wholesale enclosure and division, with one-quarter going to the relevant manorial tenants, another quarter to the landless poor and the remaining half to the soldiers of the New Model Army. Any idea that the Levellers were issuing a clarion call for community of property was completely refuted by the leadership, who had imposed a ban on levelling and communism in their second *Agreement* even before the Diggers went to work on St George's Hill, but the smear was damaging enough to help retard the development of the kind of social and economic programme which some of their more radical rural supporters would have favoured.[18]

The Isle of Axholme also provided the Levellers with a receptive religious milieu as a stronghold of nonconformity, a characteristic again shared with other Lincolnshire fens and marshes. The Isle was attracting the attention of the ecclesiastical authorities as an area infested by Anabaptism in 1634 (at least one congregation was in active existence there in 1626) and Epworth, Crowle and Butterwick were all possible centres of the sect that was so influential in the development of Leveller thought. In the immediate aftermath of the first Civil War, sectarianism appears to have been on the increase in Lincolnshire, with preachers like Samuel Oates and Lawrence Clarkson combining religious with political radicalism as propagandists for the Levellers in the county. The Isle of Axholme subsequently became a fertile area for Quakerism which by the Restoration, it has been

---

[18] Holmes, *Lincolnshire*, p. 26; B. S. Manning, *The English people and the English Revolution* (1976), pp. 279, 282–3, 292–8; Aylmer (ed.), *The Levellers*, op. cit., pp. 47–8, 50, 82; R. Overton, 'An Appeale' in D. M. Wolfe (ed.), *Leveller Manifestoes of the Puritan Revolution* (New York, 1944), p. 194; 'The Case of the Army Truly stated' (1647) in W. Haller and G. Davies (eds), *The Leveller tracts 1647–53* (New York, 1944), p. 82; 'A Manifestation' (1649) in Haller and Davies, op. cit., pp. 278–9; 'An Agreement of the Free People of England' (1649) in Haller and Davies, op. cit., p. 327.

estimated, had made approximately six times as much progress there than over the county as a whole. George Fox's disciple, Richard Farnworth, met with considerable success as a proselytizer at Haxey and elsewhere in the Isle in 1652 and 1653, when he led meetings and engaged in dialogue with local Anabaptists. But of more immediate relevance to developments in the fens in the 1650s was the fact that Michael Monckton of Beltoft, esquire, the justice accused of showing favour to rioters in 1650, and a prominent trustee at the negotiations leading to a formal agreement with Lilburne and Wildman, was hounded by the authorities after the Restoration as a Quaker and was imprisoned in Lincoln Castle in 1663 and 1665 for holding meetings in his home and frequenting conventicles. Fifth Monarchist meetings were also reported in the Isle in 1663, and this radical religious tradition persisted into the eighteenth century.[19]

The fenmen's Civil War allegiance apparently added the final component to this picture of an Isle of Axholme ready to be ignited by Leveller thought and action. Noddel's radical political contacts, and the continuity of involvement of himself and a few other militant parliamentarians in the Epworth dispute, fits neatly into this picture, but it would be a mistake to read too much into a political allegiance which, for many fenmen, was probably a temporary expedient serving more immediate concerns than the future structure of the constitution and political system. It is probably equally wrong to assume that Lilburne and Wildman came into the Isle intent upon politicising its inhabitants and enlisting them in a movement that was, after all, a spent force, with scarcely any surviving organisation, rather than simply intervening to help settle a longstanding dispute to their mutual advantage.

[19] Holmes, *Lincolnshire*, pp. 43–6, 198–9, 205–6; W. T. Whitley, *A History of British Baptists* (1923), p. 48; W. C. Braithwaite, *The beginnings of Quakerism* (1912), p. 127; H. W. Brace (ed.), 'The first minute book of the Gainsborough monthly meeting of the Society of Friends' in *The Lincoln Record Society*, 1948, xi, xiv; ibid., 1951, pp. viii, 138, 143–5, 149, 151; Friends House Library, Swarthmore MSS. iii, 52–3, 58; P.R.O., K.B. 9/860/165; ibid., C. 231/6, f. 298; B.L., Additional MS. 39, 865, fols 4, 13, 15; P. G. Rogers, *The Fifth Monarchy Men* (Oxford, 1966), p. 127; W. O. B. Allen and E. McClure, *Two Hundred Years: the history of the Society for Promotion of Christian Knowledge, 1698–1898* (1898), p. 88.

Hughes claims that Monckton, the justice, and Monckton, the trustee and later Quaker, were in fact two different persons (Hughes, p. 27 and note 1) but my reading of the evidence points to their being one and the same person. Brace is rather vague on the subject of the Monckton family and Quakerism and a search among his papers has not located the Monckton genealogy referred to in his card index in the Lincolnshire record office.

The eventful year of 1651 began with yet another attempt by the participants to recover recently invaded lands. When in January the sheriff began executing an Exchequer order requiring the removal of the commoners' cattle from their property, he was persuaded by three angry commoners on horseback to halt his proceedings until he had consulted their solicitor, Noddel. Having spent the night in Belton, the sheriff was visited the next morning by Noddel whom he informed of his intentions to deliver possession to the participants and asked to restrain the townspeople from opposition. Allegedly feigning co-operation, Noddel accompanied the sheriff when he returned to the participants' lands to be greeted by the spectacle of about a dozen commoners, carefully divided into pairs, levelling enclosures. Noddel was able to turn to the sheriff and remark 'look you here is no force, and then asked the parties' names who were there and . . . asked them what will you oppose the Sheriff they answered no, will you commit any riots? no and at that present threw down the fences Mr Noddel jeering'. The advice that 'they might go by two and two' (thereby technically avoiding a riot charge) had apparently been given by Noddel who had also recommended to Upton commoners intent on levelling enclosures, 'do as we do in the Isle of Axholme fling them all down by two and two in a Company and then dispute the business afterwards'. The sheriff was perhaps only too relieved to retreat from the scene, after he had rejected pleas to seize offenders on the grounds that he was only empowered to take action against those who had been parties to the 1636 Exchequer decree. It was about this time that an Epworth man reportedly launched a verbal attack upon the central government, warning that 'if we loose our Commons whilst this Government is, the Government may alter and then we shall have it again'. February was apparently incident-free as the court of Exchequer finally issued its decree on the 10th, after a full hearing upon the participants' Bill, which (despite the participants' conflicting interpretation) was generally favourable to the commoners in allowing them to retain possession of the 4000 acres and to proceed to a trial of title. But March brought a return of attacks upon tenants' property: on the 14th a group of seasoned activists, Thomas Bernard, Richard Mawe and William Wash, with about eleven fellow townsmen, began removing pales and other timber from the home of a Dutch tenant, dismissing his warning that soldiers would restore order with the boast that they could assemble 5000 men at a moment's notice; the next day, they returned to carry away more timber (amounting to between thirty-one and thirty-four waggon-loads over the two days), turned cattle into his rye, and threatened his family; and similar actions were repeated against other tenants on three consecutive days from the 15th, 'as if it were at days work', because the timber 'was upon their Common therefore they took it'.[20]

After a lull in April, there were further violent incursions from about mid-May when eighty or ninety Belton and Epworth men destroyed a participant's crop of rye, pulled up the pales of his house and took away some livestock which they would not allow to be replevied but demanded money for their release. A servant was also dragged off to Lincoln to appear before Justice Monckton after the rioters had refused to allow him to appear before justices who were closer at hand. Following the arrival of the Exchequer decree in the Isle in May, the sheriff required Edmund Griffith, gentleman, to help restore the participants to some of their lands but ten or eleven Epworth men, despite being apprised of the decree, prevented him from driving cattle out of one enclosure. When Griffith and his men returned the next day they found even more cattle grazing there and thirty or forty commoners impeded a further attempt to drive them forth, dismissing the decree as 'an Old Order one of Gibbon's Orders not worth 2d'. The commoners had apparently agreed among themselves to defy the decree prior to its arrival, promising 'a bloody day' if soldiers were used to enforce it, and when it was subsequently read to a group of thirty or so Belton men, the reaction was predictably hostile. Thomas Bernard interjected half way through the reading that 'they had heard so much that they would hear no more neither would they obey it'; another Belton man exclaimed that 'they would neither obey the Barons nor Parliament that it was a traiterous Order'; and William Wash added that 'they could make as good a Parliament themselves'. As Griffith and his men looked impotently on, the Belton men proceeded to turn eighty cattle into the participants' corn. When, about three weeks later, one of the Belton rioters boasted of their audacity to two or three Epworth men, the latter asserted that they too 'dare do anything' which earned the rejoinder, 'If I were as you I would have 2 or 300 of you go to the Parliament and tell them so yourselves.' Not to be outdone, the Epworth men answered, 'they were better go 14 or 1500 and pull out

20 P.R.O., S.P. dom. 18/37, f. 11III; *The declaration of Daniel Noddel*, p. 265.

the Parliament out by the ears and sit as a Parliament themselves in the Isle of Axholme'.[21]

The above events and statements were immediate reactions to a decree whose meaning was not readily apparent and the commoners, quite understandably judging by past experience, assumed that it was unfavourable to them. Although the Say and Darley report implied that Noddel, Lilburne and Wildman had in some inexplicable way encouraged this hostile reception, it is significantly silent about their own reaction to the decree for Noddel at least, as the commoners' solicitor, was presumably acquainted with its contents and yet apparently failed to reassure the commoners that it was far from prejudicial to their interests.[22] Moreover, the commoners' violence hardly facilitated Noddel's pursuit of a legal solution at this delicate stage but, on the contrary, gave the other side a tactical advantage (as Noddel clearly appreciated) by focusing attention on riots and sedition and away from the question of title. The events of May and June 1651 in fact raise serious doubts about Noddel's ability to control, or effectively direct, commoner action in the Isle and serve as a caveat against the temptation to view rioters through the eyes of the authorities who almost invariably regarded them as manipulated from above, rather than reacting spontaneously to a particular set of circumstances.

The month of June saw a major escalation of anti-participant and anti-settler violence: a windmill and over eighty houses and outbuildings (mainly belonging to foreign settlers) were systematically demolished, and surrounding crops destroyed; and the town of Santoft, where foreign settlers were concentrated, was almost completely devastated, although the settlers' church was for the moment only slightly damaged. Practically all the rioters, who worked in groups ranging from twenty to 100 or more, came from Belton and Epworth, yet in one incident a Crowle man joined with Belton rioters and even took the initiative in chopping down a house, exclaiming as he did so 'down with the house and if it had been done 7 years since it had been better for us all'. The familiar faces of Thomas Bernard and Richard Mawe were recognised in the midst of one group of rioters, the latter 'being a Constable the last year and they finding him to be a very forward man was made a Constable the next year'. Determined that

---

[21] P.R.O., S.P. dom. 18/37, f. 11III.
[22] *The declaration of Daniel Noddel*, p. 262.

'if we cannot get our Commons by no other Law, we will get it by Club law', the rioters proceeded with their offensive fully confident that 'we do good work we do God's work'. Not content with forcing one family to find shelter in a dry dyke bottom for most of the summer, Richard Mawe and other rioters tried to expel them from the Isle altogether by throwing fire in among them and threatening that 'we will root you out, you shall stay no longer there'. In order to prevent rebuilding, building materials were chopped up and carted away, although some tenants were later allowed to re-erect their homes on the understanding that they took out leases from Noddel. The damage inflicted upon the church at Santoft was probably superficial as the townspeople successfully resisted demands for its demolition, but the minister's house was substantially damaged following a warning to his wife to ensure that the house was pulled down within six or eight days or they would do it for her. Attention was finally directed to a nearby windmill owned by John Amory, a French settler, which was initially visited by about forty-five rioters (including Richard Mawe) who turned the sails out of the wind but, apparently heeding Amory's plea of poverty, did no further damage once he had given them forty shillings. However, on a second visit, Robert Ryther, esquire, led between 120 and 160 fellow Belton men to the mill and, upon being refused entry, chopped through the posts of the mill and, having forced their way in, expelled its occupants and commenced demolition.[23] But this was by no means the whole story for, according to Noddel, the windmill had been taken in execution at the suit of Thomas Vavasour for costs and damages awarded him by a jury, and the later trial of title in the Exchequer was in the name of Thomas Vavasour, plaintiff, against John Amory, defendant. Immediately after the windmill's destruction Amory had rashly brought an action of trespass against one offender much to the consternation of the participants who (again according to Noddel) had intervened at once to halt the action, and had even paid the defendant's costs in case he should seek a trial, doubtless because the question of title would inevitably be raised.[24]

---

[23] P.R.O., S.P. dom. 18/37, f. 11III; 129, fols 144I-III.
[24] *The declaration of Daniel Noddel*, p. 263; P.R.O., E. 134/2 Jas. II/East. 31. Thomas Vavasour was the eldest son of Henry Vavasour of Belwood in the parish of Belton, gentleman, and succeeded to the family property at Belwood upon the death of his grandfather, Thomas Vavasour, senior (his father having died before the grandfather) in about 1635. (P.R.O., E. 134/1 and 2 Jas. II/Hil. 25; ibid., 2 Jas. II/East. 31.)

Although both the participants in their petitions, and Say and Darley in their report, implied that Noddel, Lilburne and Wildman were responsible for, or had in some way directed, this wave of rioting, no evidence was adduced to support the charge so far as the two Levellers were concerned, and both are in fact on record dissociating themselves from, and expressing clear disapproval of, the commoners' actions. Lilburne acknowledged that some, 'especially of the poorer sort', impatient of the delays and costs of the legal proceedings, had 'foolishly' pulled down many modest dwellings erected by the participants but, he emphasised, such lawless behaviour did not find favour among the more substantial inhabitants for 'that folly of the multitude none of the most discreet Commoners and tenants of the Isle do justify'. On the other hand, he recognised that the latter, in entering upon abandoned lands, were directly benefiting from the riots and ventured an explanation, if not justification, of the violence in terms of frustration engendered by lengthy legal proceedings, and of recovering by force what had originally been forcibly wrested from them. The violence could only have been an embarrassment to Lilburne who was currently preparing the ground in London for a favourable reception of the Epworth case. When negotiating an agreement with the commoners in the following October, both Lilburne and Wildman made plain their unwillingness to become involved in any defence or justification of previous violence, stressing that 'they conceived great riots were committed and that they would not intermeddle with former Riots', and Wildman 'was so far from animating the Riots that he told them they would undo themselves'.[25]

There was a certain ambivalence in Noddel's attitude to the recent events which arouses suspicions that he at least had compromised himself. The parish clerk of Belton claimed to have seen two of Noddel's letters, one of which instructed the commoners 'not to be riotous for he hopes that they should right ere long', and another which warned them against rioting 'for if they did they would give Mr Gibbon and the Participants more cause of Complaints'. With the trial of title finally approaching a hearing, Noddel would naturally have preferred the commoners to exercise restraint for tactical reasons (rather than outrightly condemning rioting as such) as he was acutely aware of the advantage the participants derived from such

[25] Hughes, p. 28; Lilburne, *Epworth*, p. 4; P.R.O., S.P. dom. 18/37, f. 11III.

violence, having 'got into a By-way (a Riot, the only fig-leaf to cover their nakedness) to gain possession in those grounds which they never yet legally had'. Even though the contents of both letters were made public in Belton, rioting still occurred thereby confirming the existence of definite limits to Noddel's ability to control local events, and a greater readiness for the commoners to act on their own initiative than the participants believed possible. Three of the participants' witnesses did in fact claim to have heard some Belton rioters say they were acting on Noddel's instructions 'to do nothing whilst he was in the Country but that they might pull down all the houses when he was gone' without fear of the consequences.[26] However, the report that Noddel advised commoners to refrain from violence is more consistent with his later published stance, with its awareness of the tactical advantages that rioting gave the participants. Part of Noddel's explanation of the commoners' actions was expressed, like Lilburne's, in terms of the exasperation felt by some at the inordinate length of the legal proceedings, Noddel having 'found this by experience, that a multitude shall never be righted so long as their remedy lies by suits of this length and continuance (if pretence of riot by a few shall take away the possession of all), for 'tis not possible but some of the ruder sort will grow disorderly, and endanger both themselves and those that deal for them'. But he was prepared to go much further than Lilburne in the direction of absolving the commoners by consistently denying that their actions had in fact been riotous and invariably referring to them as 'a pretended great Riot' or 'a late pretended Riot'.[27] The question of title provided the bedrock of this, as in the final analysis it did of Noddel's entire case against the participants: the lands where the incidents had occurred quite simply belonged to the commoners, and it was the participants who had unlawfully entered upon them and constructed houses with the commoners' own building materials. From this position Noddel could ask 'And was not the windmill, and all the houses worthy to be removed (though not in that manner) when there was neither law nor equity they should stand? Alas poor commoners! the fault (if any) was in this, that (after twenty years

---

[26] P.R.O., S.P. dom. 18/37, f. 11III; *The declaration of Daniel Noddel*, p. 259. Cf. *The great complaint*, pp. 271–3.
[27] *The declaration of Daniel Noddel*, pp. 258, 263, 270; *The great complaint*, pp. 271, 273, 275; *A brief Remembrance*, op cit.

Time you could have no trial, and Master Gibbon saying you should never have any so long as you were quick) I say the fault of a few of you was in this, that you did it by force, for which I hope there is mercy to be had.'[28] Ultimately Noddel had to acknowledge that the resort to violence, albeit understandable or even excusable, was unlawful for, no matter how good the commoners' title, their entry with force in groups of three or more constituted, in contemporary law, a riot.[29] Hence he sought refuge from this unpleasant fact in the argument that the hundred or so charged with riot constituted only a small minority of the commoners (10 per cent at the most) and, along with Lilburne, stressed that they came from the lower strata of peasant society. The first point was probably substantially correct; with the sole exception of the windmill affair, eighty or a hundred was regarded as the maximum number involved in any one incident (with a distinct impression of a high continuity of personnel from one incident to the next) and a total of ninety-eight were listed in the Say and Darley report. But the second point was most questionable; seventeen of those identified as rioters were of sufficient substance to appear on subsidy rolls and three of the Belton offenders had already served, or were later to serve, as parish constables.[30] It was manifestly in Lilburne's and Noddel's interests, as propagandists, to minimise the extent and gravity of commoner involvement in recent riots, as a counterweight to the participants' bias in the contrary direction and, bowing to expediency, they probably distorted the facts to fit the argument in at least this one instance.

The council of state quickly learned of the gravity of the Axholme situation, and on 12 July instructed the sheriff of Lincolnshire to exercise particular vigilance to 'prevent such meetings of the multitude that may make use of other pretences to begin insurrections, and carry on designs to the interruption of the public peace, and danger of the commonwealth'. Neighbouring armed forces were made available to help restore order and the commoners

---

[28] *The declaration of Daniel Noddel*, pp. 259, 265 note e. Manuscript notes [post-Restoration?] on the case of the inhabitants of Epworth include the following observation by Noddel 'That the foundation failing the superstructure ought to do so, and pleads Sir J. de Mowbray's Title.' (Lincs. R.O., Monson 7/17/52.)

[29] F. Pulton, *De Pace et Regni* (ed. P. R. Glazebrook, 1973), p. 25; M. Dalton, *The Country Justice* (1635), p. 222.

[30] P.R.O., S.P. dom. 18/37, f. 11; E. 179/139/724; ibid., 140/750-1; Lincs. R.O., town book of Belton in Axholme.

were warned against setting themselves up as 'judges in their own cases' by resorting to violence rather than the law.[31] But within a matter of weeks the commonwealth faced a much more real threat when Prince Charles invaded England at the head of a Scottish force. News of Parliament's victory at Worcester was said to have been greeted ecstatically by Noddel, no one speaking with 'more Joy and affection to that Victory then he did, and did delight to hear that Story told and that he did express as much disaffection to the Scots as possibly could be'. Local considerations were present in the elation that victory produced in the Isle, for the participants and their tenants were rumoured to have been mobilising support for the prince and threatening vengeance upon the commoners after a royalist victory. Three of Gibbon's tenants had allegedly joined a troop of royalist horse recruited in the Isle prior to Worcester, and Gibbon himself was said to have admonished one Epworth commoner with the words, 'thou art a Parliament rogue, there be many Parliament rogues in the Isle and . . . Prince Charles will come and then all in the Isle shall be put to fire and sword and that if Prince Charles came he should want 3 or 400 men he meaning Mr Gibbon would help them with horse arms and ammunition'. Two other tenants castigated the parliamentarians as 'traitors and deserved their throats were cut . . . what are they there is not a man of quality amongst them but such as have been soldiers and before these times have been tinkers and saddle-makers'. Yet the Say and Darley report maintained a discreet silence on these matters, faithfully recording the fenmen's forcible resumption of former commons while consigning to oblivion evidence that the participants were planning to reverse the situation after a royalist triumph at Worcester.[32]

Three months of relative calm gave way in October to a month of frenzied activity in the Isle, with the commoners finally gaining a favourable Exchequer verdict on their title; a special agreement being reached between the commoners and Noddel, Lilburne and Wildman for their continued assistance in return for a grant of 2200 acres of former commons; and a fresh offensive which encouraged adjoining areas to follow suit. The Exchequer verdict, obtained in the name of Thomas Vavasour, failed to afford the commoners the long-awaited

[31] P.R.O., S.P. dom. 25/96, f. 287.
[32] Ibid., 18/37, fols 11, 11III; *The declaration of Daniel Noddel*, p. 267; *The great complaint*, p. 273.

solution as the participants tried to undermine it from the outset, as having passed by default, then relied upon the partiality of one of the Exchequer barons, and finally sought to suppress all knowledge of it. Following the Vavasour verdict, Gibbon sought an Exchequer order to re-enforce the decree of February 1651, which he interpreted as establishing possession with the participants, and an order was accordingly drafted in Baron Thorpe's chamber in Serjeants' Inn which, according to Noddel, Thorpe personally amended by inserting an exception as to Vavasour in view of the recent verdict, but shortly afterwards had second thoughts and deleted the exception. When Noddel swore an affidavit to this effect in the Exchequer, Baron Thorpe, whose stepdaughter happened to have a direct interest in the disputed lands as the widow of Abraham Vernatti (a former participant and royalist captain), denied having made any such insertion and thus enabled Gibbon to denounce Noddel as a perjurer. The latter also protested that he had sent copies of the February decree and the Vavasour verdict to Say who had neither transmitted them to the council of state as important evidence bearing on the case, nor taken due cognisance of them in writing the report, but had simply let them lie in the clerk's hands.[33]

A certain amount of confusion surrounds the nature of the agreement entered into by Lilburne, Wildman and Noddel with representatives, or 'trustees', of the commoners in October 1651. The Say and Darley report endorsed the participants' view that the trustees granted 2000 acres of former commons to Lilburne and Wildman and 200 acres to Noddel, in return for a written understanding that they would defend the commoners against all suits and fines resulting from recent riots, secure their possession of the remaining 5200 acres and maintain the drainage works, and that such a surreptitiously obtained agreement constituted in effect an unlawful contract of maintenance and champerty. A particularly damaging charge was laid against Wildman (which subsequently contributed to his 1654 election as MP for Scarborough being disallowed) that he had vehemently denied to the committee ever 'having been a beneficiary of, or in any way involved in, that agreement 'till at length by a strange Providence the very Articles and whole Contract (fairly engrossed in parchment) in all particulars making good the said charge was by one of their own party produced signed with their

---

[33] *The declaration of Daniel Noddel*, p. 267; *The great complaint*, pp. 274–5.

own hands and seals, which then the said Wildman could not deny'.[34] Noddel also denied in 1653 that any such agreement had been entered into and issued the confident challenge,

> I refer this to the contradiction of the Participants' own witness in the depositions, and upon a fair examination shall produce many witnesses, that there was no such agreement made; and God will one day reveal it, whether any such agreement was made, and how the witnesses were in that point wrested. Neither is there the least proof that the 200 acres were given to me upon any such score, if the depositions were truly taken.

Viewed in context, however, Noddel was not denying the existence of an agreement as such, but was rebutting the participants' account of *the terms* of that agreement.[35]

The participants' witness alluded to by Noddel was John Thorpe, a former Epworth trustee present at the agreement's negotiation, who gave a detailed description of the proceedings and the reactions of Lilburne and Wildman to the various proposals.[36] According to his account, a key role was played by Michael Monckton who, as a fellow trustee, drew up a list of proposals for Noddel to present to Lilburne and Wildman which incorporated six main demands: first, that the two men would obtain a commission for dividing the commons up among the four parishes concerned; secondly, that they would meet the costs of a suit to make a division between Misterton and Haxey; thirdly, that they would reach an agreement with the lord of the manor for his right of the soil; fourthly, that they would 'clear them of all troubles past and to come'; fifthly, that the commoners should be guaranteed free access to the drains for their cattle in periods of drought; and lastly, that the drainage works should be maintained. At the discussions in Belton parish church both Lilburne and Wildman expressed disapproval of the terms, 'conceiving they were too high for them to engage unto', and especially the fourth proposal because they did not wish to be involved in any way in proceedings resulting from recent riots. Wildman denounced the riots as counter-productive and initially declined to be a party to the agreement until the trustees pleaded 'that if he left them they should be outbalanced by Gibbon'.

---

[34] P.R.O., S.P. dom. 18/37, f. 11; ibid., 74, fols 78–9; ibid., 25/70, fols 297–8; Ashley, *John Wildman*, op. cit., pp. 84–5.
[35] *The declaration of Daniel Noddel*, p. 265 and notes i and j.
[36] P.R.O., S.P. dom. 18/37, f. 11III.

After Wildman had amended the proposals in some undisclosed way (presumably involving at least the deletion of the fourth proposal), both men undertook to seek an Act of Parliament recognising the commoners' title, once a recovery at law had been obtained, and to meet all the costs involved in securing their 2000 acres. They were evidently most anxious to ensure that nothing irregular or illegal crept into their understanding with the commoners, Wildman in particular insisting that he was not to receive any land, or bear any of the costs, until the question of title had been resolved in a trial financed by Noddel. With the terms settled, the trustees divided into the respective parishes of Belton, Epworth, Haxey and Owston Ferry to finalise the matter and seal leases for about 1000 years to Lilburne and Wildman, and the latter was reported to have subsequently offered leases to the officers of Overton's regiment on the same terms. The final agreement is only described in broad terms; Lilburne and Wildman were granted 2000 acres 'for a settling of a peace and to protect them from suits in regard of a great Charge that they had heretofore', and Noddel received 200 acres 'for the service he had done and to carry on the work to be done' as the commoners' solicitor. There is also an enigmatic reference to Noddel having written to the trustees inquiring if they were willing to give £200, or grant 500 acres, to 'some powerful man' without actually naming anyone, or specifying what reciprocal favours were to be expected. The terms of the October agreement were in fact deliberately distorted by the participants and their friends in order to project the riots of 1650–1 as having been Leveller inspired; in the complete absence of evidence directly linking them with the violence prior to October 1651, it was construed as having been in essence a retrospective condonation of the previous riots by the two Leveller leaders and an encouragement of future outrages. In urging this, the Say and Darley report completely ignored contrary evidence that Lilburne and Wildman had throughout insisted upon legality and had totally dissociated themselves from the riots and whatever proceedings arose from them. Even Wildman's seemingly sinister later denial of involvement might conceivably have concerned (like Noddel's denial) merely the terms, rather than actual existence, of an agreement. He was certainly less enthusiastic about committing himself than Lilburne, and subsequently confined his Epworth associations to giving legal advice and acting for the commoners in London, while leaving Lilburne to attend to the surveying of the 2000 acres and negotiation of leases.

When it came to negotiating leases, former tenants of the participants were by no means excluded from leasing lands off Lilburne and Noddel. Lilburne, in fact, seemed solicitous that they should; he offered one tenant his former grounds which Noddel had already leased to another (who was to receive an equivalent acreage from Lilburne) and positively encouraged him to stay by promising that his house, demolished in the June riots, would be rebuilt. Noddel was less generous in his dealings with former tenants, allowing those who sought permission to rebuild their homes, but in one case allotting the tenant only half her previous acreage and, in another, proving implacable when faced with a request from a commoner who had failed to maintain solidarity with his fellows. William Wrootes, an Epworth yeoman, had previously been 'so threatened by those of Epworth for hiring any land of the Participants although out of that manor that he dared not for fear of his life go to Epworth', yet he had the temerity to approach Noddel for a lease of part of his 200 acres on behalf of a friend (also a former tenant) and allegedly received the curt reply that 'no one that had hired any of the Participants' lands should have any of the land in lease'. However, Noddel did in fact lease land to former tenants, while no doubt turning a deaf ear to the request of men like Wrootes who had earned a .special local animosity, and was even prepared to extend that option to foreign settlers, like one of Gibbon's Haxey Carr tenants who was offered Noddel's pledge to 'secure her against all men' if she agreed to pay her rent to him.[37] The evidence suggests, therefore, that Lilburne and Noddel were quite prepared to allow the 'participants' tenants to remain within the Isle, provided that they became their tenants, and contradicts the participants' assertion that a mass expulsion was being attempted, at least so far as these two leading figures were concerned – although the rest of the commoners may very well have had other ideas.

Lilburne took up local residence in the riot-damaged home of the minister of Santoft church as a newly established freeholder, from whence he acted as negotiator, legal adviser and propagandist for his fellow freeholders. He and Noddel were at the forefront of an incident on Sunday, 19 October, when the French minister and his congregation were prevented from entering Santoft church for their usual service. Both men were reported to have led a number of

[37] Ibid.

commoners, including Jasper Margrave and George Stovin from the adjacent manor of Crowle, to confront the minister and some of his congregation in the churchyard. According to one account, Lilburne announced to the settlers 'this is our Common, you shall come here no more unless you be stronger than we', and in another, he declared that 'he was a freeholder in that Isle as well as the rest and that they came to take possession of the Church and that the Minister should not preach there nor the people hear except they were stronger than they'. Nevertheless, Lilburne apparently tried to keep matters under control and prevent any intemperate behaviour which might rebound to their opponents' advantage. When Edmund Griffith arrived to condemn their proceedings as contrary to the February Exchequer decree, Noddel 'was passionate on the behalf of the Rioters and argued against the Decree', until Lilburne judiciously advised him 'he should not be passionate for they would have the more advantage against us'. Two men wearing swords were positioned at the church door, not to deny entry, but 'to look upon those that went in' so as 'to awe' (or intimidate) them, and eventually Lilburne conducted prayers and preached in place of the minister. Yet this incident was later inexplicably referred to in Major-General Whalley's report to the council of state as a 'very great riot', despite the fact that it was a relatively modest affair by Axholme standards, and involved no physical assaults on unpopular foreign settlers, indicating that Lilburne's call for restraint had been heeded. Furthermore, there were doubts raised in the depositions as to whether or not Lilburne and his company had been armed. The church was desecrated but not demolished; the pulpit was chopped down, the windows removed and the building allegedly converted into a cowhouse by Lilburne who was also said to have joined with Noddel in ordering that an ox be killed and hung up there in a final act of desecration.[38]

Around this time the success achieved by the commoners of Epworth manor, and the presence of Lilburne in their midst, prompted leading Crowle commoners to seek neighbourly advice as to how they might best recover their enclosed commons. A few Crowle men had already been involved in Epworth disturbances earlier that year: Thomas Wykes, yeoman (who had lived close to the Crowle/Epworth boundary) had joined with Belton rioters in June and struck the first blow in the demolition of a house; and Jasper

---

[38] Ibid.; ibid., 129, f. 144III.

Margrave and George Stovin had been implicated in the recent Santoft church incident. Both Wykes and Stovin had also been active in Crowle in 1632; the former had helped impede the enclosure of Nuttlewood (or Nethall) and Stovin had assisted in driving sheep off part of the commons, and, towards the end of the Civil War, the latter had organised a group of clubmen in the Isle of Axholme in opposition to both armies.[39] Despite the charge that Lilburne was following some preconceived design for extending the anti-participant offensive throughout the level, the initiative apparently came from Crowle, after Margrave had first approached Lilburne and Noddel at Santoft to ask their opinion of a decree concerning Hatfield Chase which they pronounced inapplicable to the manor of Crowle. Shortly afterwards, Lilburne and Noddel visited the town of Crowle at the invitation of Margrave and others, who had convened a meeting of sixteen to twenty commoners, eager for guidance, in a private room. Before their arrival a suggestion 'that if Lilburne would help them at Crowle as he had done at Epworth he should have quantity for quantity for their Land' had evidently met with unanimous approval, but no formal agreement, along the lines of the Epworth agreement, appears to have been made. Lilburne's alleged advice to those present was that they should impound cattle belonging to the participants' tenants (and, if they were replevied, impound them again) and turn their own cattle into the tenants' crops so as to pressurise them into becoming tenants to Jasper Margrave and George Stovin. The pinder of Crowle subsequently gave each tenant formal notification of the commoners' intentions and some cattle were duly impounded, and eight or nine tenants were forced to take leases from Margrave and Stovin. But the only reference made to cattle being driven into crops was one reported threat to do so, and no matter how hard the participants strove to portray it as an invitation to riot, the course of action suggested by Lilburne at Crowle was almost certainly aimed at securing a trial of title at common law by means of replevins. The actual impounding process itself was carried out with a view to remaining on the right side of the law; no more than two men, with only the staves needed to drive the cattle, were involved at any one time, and they urged the tenants, as they set about their task, to bring replevins and seek the assistance of their landlords.[40]

[39] J. Tomlinson, *The Level of Hatfield Chase and parts adjacent* (Doncaster, 1882), p. 7. Stovin was indicted under the Conventicle Act after the Restoration.
[40] P.R.O., S.P. dom. 18/37, f. 11III.

Such circumspection may not have attended Noddel's verbal utterances at Crowle for he was said to have announced to a gathering of twenty men that 'when Lilburne came to London he would lay 20s that there would be a new Parliament would call the old ones to account and that he would be one himself'. He also assured them that he 'would have Colonel Lilburne to go into Yorkshire Hatfield and Thorne and to do there as they had done in Lincolnshire and then they should give the Attorney General work enough', and when it was pointed out that those parts did not have as strong a case, 'he answered no matter for that, we will make something of it'. Noddel is not on record repudiating such damning testimony, and he may have been optimistic at the time about the possibility of fresh elections, perhaps based upon a reformed franchise, in which Lilburne would be returned as an MP and would hopefully be able to secure parliamentary recognition of the commoners' title. In fact he may have been pinning all his hopes upon a new Parliament, having allegedly confided that 'there would be a new Representative or else he had no hopes to do what he did'.[41] It is equally possible that Noddel, carried away by the euphoria of their success in Crowle, may have contemplated extending the offensive to the whole of the Hatfield Level, regardless of the absence of the solid foundation of title enjoyed by the manor of Epworth. Yet no such general offensive took place which, had it done so, would have been, in effect, an open invitation not only to commoners in other fenland areas, but to every commoner, up and down the country, who had suffered at the hands of enclosing landlords, to follow suit and forcibly recover their former commons. And it was just this image of Lilburne and his associates openly encouraging peasant insurrection that both the participants and his enemies sought to project in order to discredit the fenmen and the Levellers once and for all. In his character assassination of Lilburne, John Canne seized upon his exploits in the Isle of Axholme with alacrity and, quoting liberally from the Say and Darley report, and elaborating on certain points by frequent marginal references to Digger works, deliberately identified Lilburne with the Diggers and argued that his activities were treasonable.[42] The whole fenland episode provided, in fact, a propaganda gift to the Levellers' enemies in their denigration of the movement as communistic and subversive.

---

[41] Ibid.
[42] J. Canne, *Lieut. Colonel John Lilb. Tried and Cast*, op. cit., *passim*.

The last occasion on which Noddel, Lilburne and Wildman acted in concert was at the end of 1651 when they made an unsuccessful attempt to gain a favourable hearing of the commoners' case in Parliament. Noddel returned alone to the Isle where, on 12 January 1652, he spoke to three commoners in his house at Owston about future plans which one of the commoners, Richard Glewe, later revealed. Noddel was reported to have said

> there is none I hope in the house but friends John Lilburne Wildman and myself made our Case known to the Parliament and they look but lightly of us but we will have it printed and nail it up up on the Parliament doors and make an outcry and if they will not hear us we will pull them out by the ears, I will have Vavasour down into the Country and we will hire a mason to go with him with a pickaxe and will pull down the Church at Santoft we will lead it away and I will have a house built of it, they shall go two and two and fling down all for they had the possession and they would keep it and they would obey no Order that should come but try it at Law and they would try it as oft as they would and saith their Case would be a leading Case for all the fens in England.

Although accepted without reservation by Say and Darley, Glewe's testimony is decidedly suspect for the other two commoners present denied having heard Noddel utter any such words against Parliament, and Glewe himself stood accused of having solicited bribes from, or having tried to blackmail, his fellow commoners. Lilburne did not return with Noddel, having become preoccupied with his celebrated dispute with Sir Arthur Haselrig which eventually led to his being heavily fined and banished by Parliament, but he did maintain written contact with the fenmen. Noddel was said to have reacted to news of the banishment with the words, 'if Lilburne be banished he will not go off without a hubbub', and local rumour had it that Lilburne had written to him boasting of his ability to raise 30000 men against Parliament. If there had been any genuine expectations of an uprising, they were rapidly quashed as Lilburne peacefully left the kingdom to commence his brief exile, thus severing his links with the commoners of Epworth.[43]

Wildman continued to act in London as a legal adviser to the Epworth commoners, and appeared as their counsel before the committee for advance of money in the summer of 1652 over the

---

[43] P.R.O., S.P. dom. 18/37, f. 11III; Gregg, *Free-born John*, op. cit., pp. 309–10; Hughes, pp. 29–30.

matter of a rent due from Epworth, and the rest of the level, which had become forfeit to the state for the delinquency of the second Duke of Buckingham. Enraged commoners had rescued livestock distrained upon former participants' lands by the rent collector and his assistants on 5 June 1651, and at the end of the year Captain George Wood (an agent of the committee for advance of money) had made preparations at Hatfield to collect the rent and arrears by military force after futile attempts at persuasion. On 6 January 1652 Captain Wood, ignoring Noddel's warning the previous night that the inhabitants 'were resolved to pay no money', had entered the Isle of Axholme with a troop of seventy horse and six infantry and, over the next five weeks, had terrorised (according to Noddel) the inhabitants into submission while their property was distrained for rent arrears. Wildman first appeared as the commoners' counsel before the committee for advance of money on 14 May 1652 and, in the following month, Noddel and John Thorpe put the Epworth case reciting their title, confirmed by the recent Vavasour verdict, and hence denying that any rent was due for those grounds. Wildman continued to urge this case before the committee throughout the summer, but by the time the matter had finally come to a hearing, on 12 January 1653, he was apparently no longer acting for them and, with Noddel back in the Isle, the commoners' side went unrepresented. The hearing was consequently adjourned to the following term when Noddel, who had been ordered to produce his authority from the inhabitants of Epworth to prosecute the business, appeared to urge the commoners' case without success.[44]

As the commoners' hopes of a successful outcome to their association with Lilburne and Wildman were fading, the participants were mounting a counter-offensive through Parliament. On 16 January 1652 investigation of the events of 1650–1 was referred to the same committee which had examined the Haselrig and Primate affair, and Say and Darley ensured that an appropriately one-sided report was produced. Meanwhile, all those who had been in any way involved in those disturbances were explicitly excluded from the Act of Oblivion. Noddel's reply to the Say and Darley report's bias and deficiencies was entrusted to the Lincolnshire MPs for reference during the anticipated debate, but Parliament was dissolved by the army before

[44] P.R.O., S.P. dom. 19/99, fols 100–1, 111; 12, fols 47, 122, 270, 322; 11, f. 368; 28, fols 170–1, 173.

the report's submission. The report therefore fell to the consideration of the council of state which, in July 1653, accorded it official endorsement, ordered that the participants were to be settled in possession of their 7400 acres in Epworth manor, with the assistance of that part of the army quartered nearby, and awarded a special commission of oyer and terminer to deal with the rioters and assess damages with a view to compensation. This was, however, merely a paper victory for the participants as the order does not appear to have been put into execution, thus leaving the commoners in possession of the 7400 acres, and former rioters immune from trial and punishment.[45]

It was only to be expected that the commoners of Epworth would react negatively to any further attempts to bring them into line with the rest of the level, as when commissioners of sewers tried to levy taxes upon improved lands for the maintenance of drainage works. Goods distrained for nonpayment were rescued by commoners in crowds of two or three hundred, and the collectors and their assistants were assaulted and threatened with death if they returned.[46] The commissioners were consequently obliged to entrust the task of collecting tax arrears, or levying distresses, to Nathaniel Reading, esquire, probably the least scrupulous of that band of fortune seekers attracted into the fens in this century by the prospect of rapid wealth and advancement. The choice was apposite for Reading possessed the qualities of character, especially courage and pertinacity, and the experience necessary for meeting the challenge of the Epworth commoners. He had been brought up in London, where he had received a legal education, before embarking upon a tour of Europe in the course of which, if the story is not apocryphal, he had imprudently become secretary to Massaniello during his Naples insurrection and had only narrowly escaped execution when it was quelled. Returning to England, he established a reputation as a legal adviser and first ventured into the Hatfield Level around 1650 to help collect rents due to the state for the delinquency of the second Duke of Buckingham. For a brief period he became legal adviser to the commoners until persuaded to assist the participants free themselves from the power of commissioners of sewers by procuring a

---

[45] Hughes, pp. 29–30; *The great complaint*, p. 273; *Commons' jn.*, vii, 73, 87; *Cal. S.P. dom.*, 1651–2, pp. 106–7; *The declaration of Daniel Noddel*, p. 269; Spittlehouse, *The Case and Appeal*, p. 1; P.R.O., S.P. dom. 25/69, f. 298; ibid., 70, fols 297–8; ibid., 18/38, f. 102; ibid., 126, f. 57; Notts. U.L., H.C.C. 6002, f. 24.

[46] Notts. U.L., H.C.C. 6002, fols 24–6, 59; P.R.O., S.P. dom. 18/129, f. 144VI.

parliamentary ordinance. Reading was granted one-fifth of their 7400 acres but, when the promised ordinance failed to materialise, the participants tried to reverse the grant and thereby drove him back into an association with local commoners as a legal adviser. He reneged on the commoners once again (and not for the last time) on 28 April 1655 when he reached an agreement with Sir Arthur Ingram and other commissioners to subdue the commoners, in return for a salary of £200 a year and an assurance that they would indemnify him and meet all his expenses. Between 1655 and 1663 Reading's periods of employment as collector of Epworth tax arrears totalled about five and a half years, but some of the participants were to claim in retrospect (when estranged from him in 1678) that he had originally used his position, as 'a great favourite of the powers in those times', to secure the office of collector in order to collect, 'with great outrage and armed violence', over £2000 which he simply embezzled.[47]

Within a few days of Nathaniel Reading's appointment as collector, the trial of strength between himself and the commoners of Epworth had begun. On 27 and 29 October 1655 Reading distrained large numbers of the commoners' cattle, horses and sheep and impounded them in the yard of Hatfield manor, an action that brought commoners galloping to Hatfield intent on rescue around midnight on 29 October. With the help of a Hatfield constable and his son, Reading's men put up a stout resistance but they were hopelessly outnumbered and outmanoeuvred; while five or six rioters were distracting their attention by feigning an attempted entry, others crept round in the dark to another part of the yard and gained entry through the fence. In the ensuing fracas the constable was so badly wounded that he afterwards required the attention of a surgeon, and one of Reading's servants was wounded in the thigh with a pitchfork. The rescued livestock were driven back to Epworth by the rioters and returned to their original owners. The number of rioters involved in this episode may have been greater than the estimated forty or fifty dimly perceived by the watchmen in the surrounding darkness; over a hundred were said to have departed from Belton, mostly riding two to a horse, and the forty-two rioters indicted at the Barnsley sessions

---

[47] Notts. U.L., H.C.C. 9111, fols 9–10, 127–8; ibid., 8939, f. 4; ibid., 6002, fols 24–33; H.L.R.O., Main Papers, 19 October 1660 letter of Lord Castleton and other commissioners to Sir William Morrice; 5 April 1675 certificate of John Millington of Morton, Nottinghamshire, esquire; 2 November 1678 answer of Sir Anthony Vanvalkenburgh, bart., and other participants in the Level of Hatfield.

were said to have been accompanied by 100 others. The vast majority were Belton men, but there was a small contingent from the town of Epworth and the odd one or two from Owston, Butterwick and Kelfield. Members of the more substantial section of peasant society participated in the rescue alongside their poorer neighbours and, although none of the local gentry became directly involved, two of them were said to have given the rioters encouragement. Peter Bernard had allegedly threatened that if Reading returned to the Isle 'he would have 4 men to lie in wait to beat him and lay him along and did swear 4 times or more he would do the same', and Robert Ryther had sent one of his servants to join the rioters.[48]

Some attempt had been made to gain assistance from neighbouring towns prior to the rescue, and a Butterwick yeoman had subsequently sent along four men. But the fenmen's sense of solidarity may not have been as strong, or as constant, as first impressions would suggest for the response to the call for assistance was far from impressive. Added to which, the commoners' opponents could rely upon a small number of local informants who apparently had few scruples about furnishing the kind of evidence which brought their neighbours into so much disrepute. Vital information about the Hatfield rescue was contributed by two local husbandmen, Timothy Steward of Epworth and Francis Briggs of Belton, who had already testified to the commoners' detriment before the Say committee and yet, surprisingly, managed to remain among those whom they had harmed to turn informant once again. Steward had been a rioter and opponent of works himself in 1645 and 1649, only later to abandon his fellows and become one of the participants' principal witnesses. Others had also broken the bonds of local loyalty, like the venal Richard Glewe in his betrayal of Noddel, William Wrootes in his willingness to lease land from the participants, or Francis Thorley of Epworth who had been the Dutchmen's first local pinder and had 'thereby purchased the evil will of many of his neighbours (though they did not absolutely show it)'.[49]

When the rioters set out for Hatfield on 29 October, mainly armed with clubs and staves (although a few carried forks, swords or pistols) their intentions were quite clear. An Epworth yeoman, with six

[48] Notts. U.L., H.C.C. 6002, fols 46-7, 49-50, 52, 54, 61; P.R.O., K.B. 9/871/344-5.
[49] Notts. U.L., H.C.C. 6002, fols 48, 50-1; P.R.O., K.B. 29/296/69-69 dorso.

horses distrained, vowed that 'before he would give a penny to lease them he would loose his life', and a Butterwick labourer, with two calves at Hatfield, had similarly resolved that 'he would venture his life but he would fetch them back'. On their triumphal return early the next morning, most of them went to Belton to celebrate the success of their venture with food and drink. Underlining the point of the rescue, a Belton yeoman, Peter Clarke, was said to have pledged that the commoners 'will not obey any Order that comes from the Commissioners for they had no power to Levy any Scots and . . . so soon as Mr Noddel came down from London they would pull down the Church at Santoft'. Twenty-seven of these offenders were eventually fined amounts varying from £3 6s 8d to £100 by sewers commissioners at Doncaster on 24 January 1656, with two Belton yeomen who appeared to have played a prominent part in the organisation of the rescue, Robert Bernard and William Ellis, receiving fines of £100 and £40 respectively.[50]

Further attempts at levying distresses in the Isle were fiercely resisted by commoners allegedly prepared to carry their defiance of authority to the point of open rebellion. On a visit to Belton shortly after the Hatfield rescue, George Starkey, a Thorne gentleman, had been alarmed at the seditious thoughts of four townsmen he had spoken with on the subject of the distraints. His reminder that the Protector and his council had ordered them was dismissed with the words, 'that if his highness were there they would make no more matter of him then of an ordinary person' and they scoffed at his warning that the Protector might use the army to restore order, challenging 'that if his highness would make choice of 100 men 100 of the Isle aforesaid would fight with them for their possessions'. And when further questioned as to whether they were prepared to rebel against the Protector, the townsmen bluntly declared 'that they had Rebelled against a better man and would not care to Rebel against him'.[51] Reading was not prepared, like his predecessors, to retreat in the face of threats and intimidation and, on 4 December, he distrained some horses found grazing on Belton common which he again impounded at Hatfield and which were again rescued the next

---

[50] Notts. U.L., H.C.C. 6002, fols 48–51, 53–4, 64–5; P.R.O., K.B. 9/871/344–5. There are no obvious reasons why other rioters were fined heavy amounts like one hundred marks or £40 and £50, unless the commissioners had discovered varying degrees of activism when they were examined before them.

[51] P.R.O., S.P. dom. 18/129, f. 144V.

day by Epworth and Belton men. On 19 December he returned to the Isle with the sheriff to levy another distress but this time about forty or fifty commoners mobilised quickly enough to prevent their livestock from being driven off to Hatfield and replied to the sheriff's order in the name of the Protector to lay down their arms and depart with 'scandalous and opprobrious Language' about the Protector's person.[52]

There were three consecutive days of upheaval in January 1656 which attracted support not only from the more substantial commoners, but also from some of the lesser gentry. Peter Clarke, a Belton yeoman who had already earned some notoriety for his involvement in the riots of 1650–1 and for his later public declaration that he would defy the commissioners' tax levies, was said to have been behind the rescue of 400 distrained sheep on 19 January. He had reportedly alerted the town of Belton and dispatched 'some lewd persons' to rescue the sheep from the collector. Eighteen mainly humble Belton inhabitants were subsequently fined for their part in this rescue, seven of whom had taken part in the Hatfield rescue of 29 October. One of the local gentry, Robert Ryther, whose servant had also been at Hatfield, was accused on this occasion of having lent his own sword, belt and horse to one of the labourers for his assistance. The sheriff's customary call to keep the peace in the name of the Protector allegedly provoked the words, 'the Lord Protector the Lord go shite or he may send soldiers to quiet us which shall be while they are present but when they are gone we will be as ill as ever we was'. The day after the rescue (a Sunday) two guns were fired off in the streets of Belton between 7 p.m. and 8 p.m. to rally the townspeople after two of the rescuers, who had spent some time drinking in a local alehouse, had resolved to rescue some more distrained sheep, but this was possibly a case of drunken bravado as no action ensued.[53]

With Noddel back in their midst, on Monday, 21 January the church at Santoft came under renewed attack as Peter Clarke had predicted. Two other members of the local gentry, Robert Ryther and Thomas Vavasour, helped Noddel organise this riot. Ryther and one of the probable organisers of the October Hatfield rescue, Robert Bernard, were said to have sent word that morning to a Belton man and his wife 'to go to Santoft or they would pull down their house, and

[52] Notts. U.L., H.C.C. 6002, fols 49–50, 52, 61.
[53] Ibid., fols 60, 65–6.

lay it on a heap and appraise it and sell it for the rich had appeared and done so much that they durst do no more and the poor should do something'. Whether or not they acted under duress (or simply used it as an excuse afterwards to escape retribution), the Belton couple did in fact join a gathering of about twenty-five others, including Noddel, Ryther and Vavasour and other experienced activists. Before leaving for Santoft the company visited a number of Belton households seeking the loan of arms, but co-operation was not automatic for a widow categorically refused their request and, as further proof that not everyone in Belton was of the same mind, she subsequently testified against the rioters. The rioters of 21 January differed in one respect from their recent predecessors in that four of them were accompanied by their wives whereas, with the sole exception of one woman engaged in the rescue of 19 January, local upheavals had of late been exclusively male affairs. Once a body of rioters had been assembled, Noddel, Ryther and Vavasour departed from the scene and avoided any further open involvement as the rioters proceeded to Santoft carrying guns and other weapons. Reading had recently taken the church under his aegis and ordered its repair and cleansing, and so the rioters' first action was to drive away one of his men and two settlers by threatening to shoot them. After chasing the men for half a mile, the rioters returned to the church where they systematically smashed the windows, piled up the wood from the doors, pulpit and seats in the interior and set fire to it but did not fulfil their threat to demolish the building itself and sell off the stone and timber. Major-General Whalley had the responsibility for restoring order and conducting an investigation, and he produced another partial report for the council of state's information on 12 June. The latter accordingly instructed Whalley to prevent future trouble by disarming the commoners and assigning a contingent from his regiment to assist the sheriff or his deputies.[54]

Peace had, in fact, temporarily returned to the Isle after the January riots and, with the minor exception of an alleged assault made upon Reading at Belton on 1 March,[55] there was no further violence until the following summer. Noddel's return home may in fact have led to a change of policy whereby open confrontation with Reading and his

[54] Ibid., f. 60; P.R.O., S.P. dom. 18/126, f. 57; ibid., 25/77, fols 342, 840; ibid., 18/129, fols 144 144I-III.
[55] P.R.O., K.B. 9/870/37.

men was exchanged for the less hazardous device of pursuing them through the courts. In his enthusiasm to subdue the commoners, Reading had overreached himself and complaints over the way he was executing the office of collector resulted in his temporary suspension from office on 28 April. The self-righteous nature of Reading's reply to these charges must have nauseated those who had experienced his flagrant opportunism: 'since it pleased almighty god to engage him in the Level' he protested that he had 'by all Lawful means so prosecuted the just Interest and advancement of the same and so Impartially Provided for the security of the country that (had the Inheritance of the whole Improvement been his) he is not conscious to himself of being able to have managed either with more Integrity'.[56]

Epworth commoners engaged Reading and the participants, and vice versa, in legal battles for much of 1656 and 1657,[57] but the transfer of confrontation to the law courts did not signal the end of the commoners' resort to direct action, especially when judgements passed against them. When the news that a London jury had found for the participants in one recent trial reached the town of Epworth on 14 June 1656, John Dillingham of Mellwood, gentleman, was assailed with verbal abuse and menaces because of his acquaintance with Reading and, two days later, cattle were driven into the grass of his enclosed meadow. The latter action was led by James Mawe of Epworth and his two sons, in company 'with divers others of the Richest sort of the Commoners', who invited fellow commoners to do likewise. Dillingham warned the Protector and his council that 'it is generally the sense of the Commoners that they will defend their Common, with their swords which they say they may as Lawfully do as the Protector may the Government he hath taken upon him'. He became a virtual prisoner in his own home as he believed that there was a conspiracy, involving six disguised women, to kill him and afterwards hang up his quarters in several parts of the Isle, and he was unable to gain 'any relief in the usual course of the law the next Justice of peace either not willing or not daring to act any thing against the pleasure of the said Commoners'.[58] However, despite the occasional incident, like the wounding of a tax collector at Haxey on

---

56 Notts. U.L., H.C.C. 6002, fols 81, 150.
57 Ibid., fols 85, 88.
58 P.R.O., S.P. dom. 18/128, f. 80.

17 June,[59] the commoners generally appear to have been content to resume their offensive in the law courts, resting their case upon the strength of their title to all the commons within Epworth manor. Spokesmen for the towns of Epworth and Belton (including Robert Ryther, Thomas Vavasour and Robert Bernard) petitioned the court of sewers in July 1656 challenging the legality of the taxes laid upon the 7400 acres, and any distresses taken for nonpayment, principally on the grounds of title, but also recalling that the original contract between the King and Vermuyden had obliged the latter to meet all maintenance costs after the completion of the work and the participants, as his successors, inherited that obligation.[60]

From June 1656 until the Restoration the peace of the Isle was shattered by only one more riotous commoner outburst. On 24 September 1656, in an incident at Haxey bearing all the appearance of a spontaneous demonstration of hatred, Reading was assaulted by a crowd of over thirty men and women, yet Michael Monckton and a fellow justice declined to act when Reading urged riot proceedings.[61] The legality of a 1656 imposition of twelve pence an acre on the commons of Epworth was challenged in the second Protectorate Parliament, after local inhabitants had reportedly threatened collectors with swords and other weapons upon the pretence that they were 'Cavaliers'. But the participants were quick to remind the House of the tumults of 1650-1, and the involvement of Lilburne and Wildman, and how, after Whalley's report had concluded that they were 'very rebellious' and required suppression by military force, all those implicated had been deliberately left out of the Act of Oblivion. Major-General Whalley took part in the ensuing debate and, upon his recommendation, examination of the whole business was referred to a committee.[62] Although no further riot accusations were raised against the commoners until 1660, there were, ironically, three riot indictments found in quarter sessions in the spring of 1657 against Reading and his men, probably arising from further attempts to levy distresses.[63] The renegade Timothy Steward of Epworth appears in two of the indictments having been taken into Reading's service,

---

[59] Ibid., K.B. 9/870/36.
[60] Notts. U.L., H.C.C. 6002, fols 132–3.
[61] P.R.O., K.B. 9/869/288 gives 44 rioters; ibid., 871/394 gives 30 rioters.
[62] J. T. Rutt, *Diary of Thomas Burton, esquire* (reprint ed. by I. Roots, P. Pinckney and P. H. Hardacre, New York, 1974), i. 199–200.
[63] P.R.O., K.B. 9/875/401–2, 417–18, 530.

perhaps as a reward for his earlier usefulness to the participants. By May 1657 Axholme commoners were prepared to contribute towards the repair of drainage works on the assurance that the money raised would be used solely for that purpose and that a new expenditor would be appointed in the manor of Epworth.[64] Yet even in periods of relative calm there were occasional reminders of the potentially explosive nature of the situation in the Isle. In September 1659 one of the Collector's assistants was murdered in Haxey Carr but neither the circumstances of his death nor the identity of the murderer were disclosed and apparently no one was proceeded against for the murder.[65] The continuance of a fragile peace in the Isle largely depended upon both sides abstaining from provocative acts, but the restoration of Charles II was taken by the participants as a signal to recommence their campaign for the recovery of losts lands, thus ushering in another phase of violent confrontation.

The intervention of Lilburne and Wildman into the affairs of the Isle of Axholme did no service to either the fenmen's or the Levellers' cause. The former's association with the Levellers deflected attention away from the question of title, and on to radicalism and subversion, at the precise moment that a crucial legal verdict had at long last passed in their favour and ensured that they derived no benefit from it.[66] And the Levellers' association with riotous fenmen, engaged in levelling enclosures and destroying property, focused attention upon the most damning charge raised against them, that of challenging property rights and advocating communism. In reality, the Epworth agreement cautiously entered into by Lilburne and Wildman was quietly conventional in the sense that it involved no revolutionary schemes of landownership; both men set themselves up as local men of property prepared to defend at law the right of their fellow freeholders, and other commoners, to enjoy peacefully the commons of Epworth. But their local ally, Daniel Noddel, may have envisaged a more ambitious and more radical outcome to their association, if any credence can be given to some rather questionable evidence, and he remained after their departure to continue the struggle as commoners defended their title by force against the agents of a regime established and maintained by force.

[64] Notts. U.L., H.C.C. 6002, f. 181.
[65] H.L.R.O., Main Papers, 10 July 1660 certificate of the sheriff and justices of Yorkshire to Sir William Morrice.
[66] Holmes, *Lincolnshire*, pp. 211–12.

7   The Restored Undertakings

THE Restoration of Charles II was not followed by a general revival of pre-war drainage schemes, despite the King's fulsome praise of them as 'of so great a benefit and honour to the nation', and his frequent entreaties to the Commons shortly after his return that they accord fenland drainage priority. Only those schemes that had succeeded in attracting some support from local landowners won the endorsement of Parliament whose statutory authority had now to be sought by drainers who had previously relied upon executive favour and conciliar coercion. Neither prerogative courts nor prerogative undertakings were restored at the Restoration; the efforts of Sir William Killigrew and Sir Henry Heron in April 1663 to repudiate the claim that their interest originated in 'Court or prerogative power' failed to convince enough Members of Parliament that courtier-dominated enterprises merited revival, and the repeated appeals of undertakers and their descendants made little impact upon representatives of a political elite which welcomed Charles II's restoration, but not reminders of the excesses of his father's personal rule. In the Isle of Axholme the war of attrition between participant and commoner continued unabated after 1660, and into the next century, oscillating in its accustomed way between direct action and protracted legal battles. The violent responses of the commoners to these restored undertakings were of such magnitude as to place them at the forefront of rural riots in the post-Restoration period.[1]

Courtier-dominated undertakings

Sir William Killigrew, Sir Henry Heron (the third son and heir of Sir Edward) and their fellow undertakers in the Lindsey Level entertained great hopes at the Restoration of recovering their lands and of even completing the original project by extending works as far as Lincoln. Two Bills were prepared for this purpose in August 1660

[1] Holmes, *Lincolnshire*, pp. 226–8; M. Beloff, *Public order and popular disturbances, 1660–1714* (1938), pp. 77–80; P.R.O., S.P. dom. 29/52/1, p. 9; 72/46, p. 5.

and May 1661 but, after a smooth passage in the Lords, they failed to make much progress in the Commons where a Lincolnshire MP, Sir Charles Hussey, voiced local opposition. An attempt by the King and privy council to resolve the differences between undertakers and commoners in the interval between the first and second sessions of the Cavalier Parliament also proved fruitless. When Parliament re-assembled in March 1663, Charles made a special point of recommending that the Commons take action for the preservation of the Lindsey Level, but two further Bills similarly failed.[2] The Lindsey undertakers repeatedly sought parliamentary approval in the reign of Charles II, introducing Bills nine times between 1666 and 1678, but the consistent opposition of Sir Robert Carr (who replaced the late Sir Charles Hussey in 1665) and his fellow Lincolnshire knight of the shire ensured their demise, and the same fate attended a 1685 Bill. Their heirs continued to press for parliamentary recognition of the Lindsey undertaking in 1698, 1700, 1701, 1705 and 1711 but encountered no more success and hence remained permanently dispossessed of the former fenland estates.[3]

The efforts of courtly undertakers to retrieve lands in the Holland Fen, and the East, West and Wildmore Fens also proved futile. A Bill recognising the interests of Sir Anthony Thomas's son and heir in the latter group of fens gained the Lords's concurrence in 1661 but failed to attract sufficient support in the Commons. In Michaelmas Term 1661 George Kirke and other surviving participants tried to revive the decree of 11 August 1637 and regain possession of their lands but, with the sole exception of Wildmore Fen, the commoners apparently continued to enjoy the whole of their former commons for the rest of

---

[2] A. R. Maddison, *Lincolnshire Pedigrees* (1903), ii, 488–9; *Lords' jn.*, xi, 149, 153, 160, 193–4, 201–2, 226, 253, 255–6, 286–7, 292, 353; *Commons' jn.*, viii, 202, 275, 281, 283, 285, 288, 291, 306, 319, 325, 402, 408, 417–18, 425–7, 429, 435, 452–3, 455, 457–8, 463, 473–4, 477, 517, 525–6, 528, 533; H.L.R.O., Main Papers, 30 August 1660 draft Act for draining Lindsey Level; 3 September 1660 petition of Sir William Killigrew and other undertakers; 14 May 1661 draft Act for Lindsey Level and annexed petition; P.R.O., S.P. dom. 29/72/46.

[3] *Commons' jn.*, viii, 654; ibid., ix, 20–1, 27, 29, 51, 60–1, 64, 70, 76, 79–80, 82, 84, 86, 92, 101–3, 118, 126, 129, 162, 184, 190, 193, 195, 198, 206–7, 222–4, 306, 313, 326, 330, 345–6, 363, 367, 374, 381, 390, 394, 421, 443, 445, 453, 455, 482, 490, 725, 738; ibid., xii, 185, 240; ibid., xiii, 186; ibid., xv, 27; *Lords' jn.*, xvi, 606, 618, 625, 632, 650, 653; ibid., xix, 235–6, 256, 263, 277, 289, 297; Holmes, *Lincolnshire,* pp. 228, 235, 239; C. Robbins (ed.), *The diary of John Milward* (Cambridge, 1938), pp. 128, 140, 185, 246, 254–5.

the century without any further disturbance of their traditional economy.[4]

Wildmore Fen was the scene of rioting in 1663–4 after workmen had been instructed by the surveyor general, in April 1663, to repair fences around 4000 acres formerly allotted to Charles I as improvement. On 1 May, shortly after work had been completed, some of the fences were thrown down by local commoners, and over three hundred of them subsequently petitioned against the Lords's order of 3 June for the King's quiet possession because of the fen's crucial importance for their survival.[5] The commoners also secured the indictment of some of the workmen at a Horncastle quarter sessions on 13 July for riotous entry and unlawful enclosure, and others involved were indicted for ejecting the commoners' livestock from the 4000 acres. Included among those thus deprived of pasture rights were Sir George Southcott, baronet, George Langton, esquire, Theophilus Hart and three other gentlemen.[6] But the Lords reaffirmed their order of 3 June and, on 22 July, the King instructed the sheriff to put it into effect and Richard Peck, gentleman, was dispatched to supervise the work of enclosure.

Two or three hundred Wildmore commoners advanced on the King's enclosure on 6 and 7 August to throw down fences, demolish a newly built house (and burn all its contents) and assault its three occupants. A group of rioters who remained there afterwards were said to have made flags out of sheets and to have chosen Theophilus Hart as their 'captain'.[7] Hart of Mareham-le-Fen, gentleman, was married to Hannah the younger daughter of the late Nehemiah Rawson, a distinguished opponent of the drainers prior to the Civil War, and, like his father-in-law, had been a fervent parliamentarian, reaching the rank of major under Cromwell, and had been a

---

[4] *Commons' jn.*, viii, 326, 333, 349, 369; Albright, pp. 59–60; Darby, *Draining,* pp. 80, 147; Thompson, *Collections,* pp. 148–50, 154; *The Case of the Adventurers in the East and West Fens* (undated).

[5] *Lords' jn.*, xi, 534–5, 553; H.L.R.O. Main Papers, 3 June 1663 affidavit of William Garret, citizen and stationer of London; 8 July 1663 petition of the freeholders and owners of land within the soke of Horncastle.

[6] P.R.O., K.B. 9/895/211-2, 214–15, 217–18, 220–1, 223–4, 226–7, 229–30, 232–3, 238–9.

[7] *Lords' jn.*, xi, 566; P.R.O., P.C. 2/56, f. 515.

petitioner for the King's trial.[8] Such a record was hardly likely to endear him to the post-Restoration privy council, yet Hart was eventually discharged having convinced the board that he had not been actually present during the riots. However, the behaviour of the sheriff of Lincolnshire, Sir Edward Dymock, earned the board's censure, and the King's particular displeasure, for his response to the call for assistance had been to arrive on the scene, observe what was happening and then leave without one word of restraint, thus positively contributing to the rioters' boldness. On the other hand, Sir Edward had proved more amenable on the previous 4 July when Theophilus Hart had requested a warrant for the arrest of one of the King's labourers for trespass. Hart and three other supposed ringleaders were sent for by serjeant-at-arms and the lord lieutenant, the Earl of Lindsey, was instructed to prevent further disturbances as they were 'Commonly forerunners of greater Mischiefs'. At his board appearance on 4 September Hart insisted on his innocence and was discharged after entering a bond of £400. But the other three suspected ringleaders had still to be arrested and the brother of one of them was said to have obstructed the hearing of evidence by securing the arrest and committal to Lincoln gaol of Richard Peck himself and one of his witnesses, and other suits were being threatened against Peck over the enclosure. These suits were almost certainly aimed at securing a legal verdict on the question of title, but the refusal to accept bail (reportedly on Hart's advice) clearly obstructed a thorough investigation of the previous riots and led the board to take appropriate action to ensure that no witness was prevented from appearing before them. Witnesses' depositions were subsequently transmitted to the attorney-general who recommended that the rioters should be prosecuted at the next Lincolnshire assizes.[9]

Although cleared of complicity in the August riots, Hart had to face fresh charges raised by the serjeant-at-arms originally charged with securing the ringleaders' arrest, who was principally concerned for his fees. The serjeant accused Hart of obstructing his efforts to convey

---

[8] A. Garner, *Colonel Edward King* (Grimsby, 1970), appendix iii, 47; P.R.O., P.C. 2/56, f. 515.

The Hart and Rawson families were closely connected. Theophilus Hart's youngest brother, Daniel, married Abigail, another of Nehemiah Rawson's daughters, and Theophilus' son and heir was named Rawson Hart (Maddison, *Lincolnshire Pedigrees*, op. cit., ii, 464–5).

[9] P.R.O., P.C. 2/56, fols 515–17, 546, 548, 558, 588, 612, 627; K.B. 9/895/235–6.

to London two ringleaders he had arrested after a lengthy search, thereby forcing him to seek help from the mayor of Boston and causing additional expense in horses and guards. Because Hart was said to have threatened to deprive the serjeant of his fees, the two arrested leaders were ordered to remain in custody until the serjeant's account had been settled in the belief that they and their fellows were supported 'by a Common purse'. Yet if such a fund existed, neither of the men apparently drew upon it for they were still in custody on 29 April 1664, having lamented their inability to pay fees totalling £260 in the previous December. An offer to pay the serjeant £20 within about three months if they might be allowed to go home and raise the money from among their friends had been rejected by the board which refused to accept anything less than £100 before their discharge. When they tried to secure their release by writ of habeas corpus, the board condemned the manoeuvre as a serious contempt and ordered the serjeant to confer with the attorney-general about ensuring their continuance in custody pending full compliance with the board's orders.[10] Renewed attempts were made to enclose the King's 4000 acres in 1664 but as fast as Charles's tenants erected fences, the commoners threw them down again and military help was needed to restore order. In February 1665 a Bill 'for settling and improving' Wildmore Fen was introduced into the Lords but it progressed no further than the committee stage, and the commoners were probably ultimately successful in safeguarding the fen from enclosure for the rest of the century.[11]

The Ancholme Level

In sharp contrast to the reception they accorded former courtier-dominated enterprises, post-Restoration Parliaments looked with favour upon drainage schemes for the Ancholme Level and the Great and Deeping Levels, which had succeeded in attracting varying degrees of local landowner participation. A Bill confirming Sir John Monson in possession of his 5827 acres, introduced into the Commons in May 1661, reawakened commoner opposition principally in the towns of Winterton, in the north, and Bishop Norton, in the south of the level. Opposition in Winterton was led by Thomas and William Place (the sons of the Winterton juror who had

10 P.C. 2/56, fols 630, 633, 646, 657; ibid., 57, f. 80.
11 Darby, *Draining*, p. 80; *Lords' jn.*, xi, 659, 668, 670; P.R.O., P.C. 2/57, fols 152-3.

refused to sign the verdict of 31 March 1635) who opposed the Bill even after it had received the royal assent on 19 May 1662.[12] In the following October workmen employed on the banks of the old river were interrupted by several commoners led by Thomas Place who, acting as the commoners' solicitor, took a note of their names and threatened to sue them for working there and, when that did not suffice, pelted them with clods of earth and threatened to bring fellow townsmen to drive them away. Thomas Place similarly took the lead on 29 December when more than a hundred townsmen constructed a dam to block a new drain in Winterton and the drain was blocked again on the following 9 March, but this time by only two Winterton yeomen. Men from the same town also made a breach in a dam constructed across the old river to flood works downstream. The Place brothers were still actively involved in August 1665 when they assaulted one of the undertakers' tenants and his wife and impounded their cows.[13] In the same year William Place and other leading Winterton men brought an Exchequer action against Sir John Monson over 120 acres of Winterton common which he had resumed possession of in 1663, claiming it as part of his allotment. Sir John had involved the commoners in hefty legal expenses by bringing actions of trespass and ejectment when they disturbed his possession and had hired men to prevent his livestock from being driven forth. Yet the commoners claimed that the grounds were vital to their survival; that no grounds in Winterton had been returned hurtfully surrounded in 1635 because Thomas Place, senior, had refused to add his signature to the jury's verdict; and that the grounds could not be improved and had in fact deteriorated since work began. In a majority verdict on 4 October 1666, six of the eleven commissioners charged with investigating the matter for the Exchequer rejected the commoners' claims and came down unequivocally in favour of Sir John's undertaking. However, the remaining commissioners submitted a diametrically opposed minority report vindicating the commoners and confirming that the inhabitants of Winterton had been prejudiced, not bettered, by the undertaking.[14]

The commoners did not succeed in halting the work of redrainage

---

[12] *Commons' jn.*, viii, 248, 252, 257, 296, 369, 374; *Lords' jn.*, xi, 395, 398–9, 406, 473; P.R.O., E. 134/17 Chas. II/East. 14; Lincs. R.O., Monson 7/17/42.
[13] Lincs. R.O., Monson 7/17/46; P.R.O., K.B. 9/894/369–70; ibid., 904/141–44; ibid., E. 178/6301.
[14] P.R.O., E. 134/17 Chas. II/East. 14; E. 178/6301.

in the level which was completed by Sir John, in alliance with some of the most substantial local landowners, at the cost of a further £9000. Opposition to the drainage of the Ancholme Level had always been a far more muted affair than that encountered in other levels, with an absence of rioting on a scale comparable with the tumults experienced elsewhere. Part of the explanation for this is probably to be found in the relatively modest scale of the enterprise, but the central reason is almost certainly the fact that it attracted support from a substantial section of the chief landowners in the locality and hence aggrieved commoners would confront not 'foreign' undertakers, but their own manorial lords when they sought to defend their commons. It is true that a handful of local gentry voiced opposition to the Monson enterprise, but they were greatly outweighed by their pro-Monson fellows which could only have served to restrain the lower orders from more serious or extensive violence.

The Great Level and the Deeping Level

Parliament could devote little time to regulating the affairs of the Great Level before 1663 and, in the interval, temporary maintenance Acts were passed to safeguard drainage works pending a permanent settlement.[15] When commoners began expressing their dissent in petitions addressed to Parliament in May 1661, Sir John Maynard, junior, joined with them to continue his late father's anti-adventurer stand.[16] Opposition was also expressed in more positive ways, including the cutting of banks and unseasonable opening of sasses and sluices, prompting an intervention by the Lords on 18 May 1661, and by the privy council a year later, forbidding future disturbances of the adventurers' works and possessions until a final parliamentary settlement.[17] Despite the King's personal adoption of a reconciliatory role, debate on the eventually successful Bill brought out into the open the rival claims of the existing, or new, adventurers and the old adventurers, or those who claimed under the original 1630s undertaking of Francis, Earl of Bedford.[18]

[15] *Commons' jn.*, viii, 145, 147, 149–50, 157, 163, 186, 192, 195, 250, 258–60, 299, 322–3, 335, 346, 358, 360, 400–1, 416, 427, 429, 432, 435; *Lords' jn.*, xi, 148, 150–1, 168, 171, 313–14, 317, 331, 461–4, 470.
[16] *Commons' jn.*, viii, 258–9. Sir John Maynard, senior, died on 29 July 1658 and was buried in the churchyard of Tooting Graveney. His son and heir, Sir John, junior, was knighted on 7 June 1660 and died on 14 May 1664 (*D.N.B.*, xiii, 156).
[17] *Lords' jn.*, xi, 258–9; P.R.O., P.C. 2/54, f. 159; ibid., 55, f. 638.
[18] P.R.O., P.C. 2/56, f. 341.

The general drainage Act of 27 July 1663 formed William, Earl of Bedford, and his associates into a corporation for the Great Level and, drawing heavily upon the ideas of its repudiated predecessor the 1649, or 'pretended', Act, structured its government and laid down its procedure in a form that survived in its essentials until the corporation's disappearance in 1914. The King was given 12 000 of the 95 000 acres of land set aside for the adventurers, all of which was subjected to taxes for the maintenance of the level. Mindful of the hostility the Act would arouse in some quarters, penalties were stipulated for those who disturbed enclosures; they could be convicted upon the testimony of two witnesses before two justices and would forfeit £20 for each offence, half of which was to go to the informer and half to the person, or persons, disturbed in their possession. Fines would be leviable by distress upon the offender's goods or, if the latter were insufficient to meet the penalty, he was to be committed to a house of correction or common gaol, without bail, and detained there at the justices' discretion.[19]

Parliament looked with corresponding favour upon drainage proposals for the Deeping Level and an Act of 2 March 1665 repealed the original grant to Thomas Lovell and empowered Edward, second Earl of Manchester, and his associates as drainers. They were originally given a seven-year deadline, but in March 1670 the Act was amended to allow a further three years as work was still far from finished. A supplementary Act to improve the drainage of the level was committed in the Lords in February 1678, and in June 1685 an attempt was made to gain their assent to a Bill incorporating the Deeping undertakers. Although theoretically the level had been drained, a considerable part of it continued to suffer from flooding and mounting tax arrears accumulated by owners of inadequately drained land led to the eventual sequestration and sale of nearly half the taxable lands.[20]

The first specific report of anti-enclosure rioting in the Great Level to reach the privy council after the Restoration concerned Peter-

[19] Darby, *Draining*, pp. 78–9; 15 Charles II, c. 17 'An Act for settling the drainage of the Great Level of the Fens called Bedford Level' in *Statutes of the Realm*, v, 499–512; *Commons' jn.*, viii, 447, 450, 453, 484, 491, 504–7, 509, 512–13, 532; *Lords' jn.*, xi, 548–9, 555, 561, 572, 574, 579.
[20] Darby, *Draining*, pp. 81, 144; *Commons' jn.*, viii, 322, 607–12; ibid., ix, 60, 63, 89, 91, 130, 133, 139, 141; *Lords' jn.*, xi, 636–7, 660–2, 670, 676; ibid., xii, 239, 310–11, 313, 319, 322, 351; ibid., xiii, 136–7; ibid., xiv, 31, 34, 53, 61–2, 64, 66.

borough Great Fen where, at the beginning of April 1667, ten commoners from neighbouring towns drove away workmen digging enclosure ditches for the Earl of Exeter and reversed their work. Having been brought before the board on 5 June, the rioters were bound over for their appearance to an information exhibited by the attorney-general in King's Bench.[21] More serious violence directed at the enclosures of Henry North, esquire, in Mildenhall Fen (Suffolk) was reported to the board in May and July 1669. Local commoners had allegedly levelled his enclosure banks during the night on several occasions; servants instructed to guard the enclosures had been driven away, assaulted and almost killed; a recently erected house had been burnt to the ground; and several horses and steers had been slaughtered. Three suspected Mildenhall ringleaders, Henry Warner, esquire, William Coe, gentleman, and James Howlet, yeoman, who were examined before the board in the royal presence on 16 June, impressed Charles as having been 'secretly Instrumental' in planning the riots and were consequently ordered to enter securities of £400 and provide sureties for bonds of £200 each for their future good behaviour (with no time limit stipulated), failing which they were to be proceeded against at law. But as the board was considering how best to proceed against the supposed ringleaders, reports reached them of two further riots: between 11 p.m. and 12 p.m. on 6 July, about thirty Mildenhall commoners, armed with swords and guns, set upon and put to flight (with a single gunshot resounding in their ears as a warning) two guards employed to keep a watch over North's enclosures before sawing in half the posts and beams of a recently built house; and two days later, about a hundred rioters chased away eight or nine guards and then proceeded to demolish a house and throw down enclosure banks. None of the offenders were named before the board on this occasion, the cover of darkness in the first riot and the wearing of vizards by some in the second hindering detection.[22] Further disturbances occurred in Mildenhall Fen in 1684 when land was again enclosed as improvement by the lord of the manor acting under the 1663 Act and local inhabitants challenged his action initially by legal suits partly financed out of a common fund. Henry Warner again provided local leadership and shouldered much of the burden of commencing suits against the lord of the manor, at

---

[21] P.R.O., P.C. 2/59, fols 430, 439, 475–6.
[22] Ibid., 61, fols 311, 325, 356, 358.

considerable personal expense. The contest eventually produced violence on both sides, with the lord's servants expelling the commoners and their cattle, and the commoners creeping back at night to throw down his fences. As no offenders could be identified, damages of £53 were assessed upon the inhabitants of Mildenhall and neighbouring towns which Warner met himself and subsequently encountered considerable reluctance when trying to recover some of the outlay from fellow commoners.[23]

Works and enclosures in the Deeping Level were subjected to a devastating attack in January 1699 by an estimated 1100 rioters drawn together from Pinchbeck, Spalding, Crowland, Cowbit and other places nearby. Assembled 'under colour and pretence of Foot Ball Playing', they were said to have done a possible £100 000 worth of damage in demolished windmills, houses and barns, uprooted trees and levelled banks. The situation was regarded as so grave that, with even more destruction threatened, the sheriff of Lincolnshire was ordered to raise the *posse comitatus* to suppress the rioters and several were later apprehended and proceeded against. The Deeping violence threatened to spill over into adjacent parts of the Great Level after a paper had allegedly been posted upon March bridge announcing a football match and other sports planned for around 14 March on Coates Green near Whittlesey. Under this guise, local commoners were expected to imitate their fellows in the Deeping Level, especially as several of them had been overheard assuring others that 'the Captain or chief' of the Deeping rioters would be attending their match, but the board's warning to local officers to prevent all potentially riotous gatherings in or near the Great Level apparently prevented an outbreak of rioting. In the following June several Crowland commoners drove hundreds of cattle into enclosures in the Deeping Level and guards were posted to watch from specially erected booths against attempts to impound them. The sheriff was again ordered to suppress the rioters by force after they had defied the proclamation of local justices to disperse.[24] Two years later the privy council received intelligence of preparations being made for a riot in fens near Market Deeping; the plan hatched in May 1701 involved the gathering together of large numbers of commoners by distributing verses inviting them to participate in levelling enclosures

[23] Ibid., E. 134/36 Chas. II/Mich. 44.
[24] Ibid., P.C. 2/77, fols 293–4, 309, 350–1; ibid., S.P. dom. 32/11, fols 117–18.

and destroying drainage works during the next holiday period.[25]

The Hatfield Level

When upheaval returned to the Isle of Axholme in May 1660 it took the form of a confrontation whose drama and scale was reminiscent of the very first local encounters between drainers and commoners. With the King newly returned to his capital, and the participants anxious to call upon the support of the new regime, Reading and his followers assisted the collector on 31 May in levying distresses for tax arrears in the Isle. Over fifty commoners, armed with guns, forks and clubs, descended upon Reading and his men shortly after the first cattle had been distrained and, dragging them from their horses, wounded several. Reading's caution against violence, as he was there in the King's name to execute orders of the House of Lords, court of sewers and other authorities, brought the alleged reply 'that they would obey neither King, nor Lords, nor Laws'. Reading and his men fled to the town of Hatfield followed in hot pursuit by rioters whose ranks had swollen by this stage to perhaps as many as two or three hundred. At Hatfield the rioters broke into the pound and rescued cattle which had been distrained earlier, but they transferred their attention to the house of Captain John Hatfield when they learned that the collector had taken refuge there and only abandoned their siege when Hatfield warned that he would send to Doncaster for a troop of horse.

Not all of the rioters immediately returned home; some retired into a local alehouse for about an hour to drink, and presumably mull over what to do next, and a number of them later issued forth allegedly to murder one of Reading's men, a Hatfield labourer called John Patterick, in the yard of Hatfield parish church. A Hatfield constable tried to arrest two suspects, Robert Ryther and George Gilby, after most of their fellows had left for home, but both men put up violent resistance: Ryther brandished a knife and pistol at the constable, vowing that 'he would be the death of him and if he ever met him he would have both his flesh and his blood'; while Gilby struck him, drawing blood, tore his coat and proceeded to drag the wretched man around the house by his hair. Robert Ryther of Belton, esquire (the son and heir of the Robert Ryther of belton who had been closely involved in the earlier anti-drainer struggles), was to be one of the

[25] Ibid., P.C. 2/78, fols 208–9.

leading figures in the post-Restoration tussles between commoners and participants and became connected by marriage with two other leaders, Thomas Vavasour of Belwood and Robert Popplewell of Belton.[26] On the very day of the coroner's inquest into Patterick's death, a commoner was reported to have replied to the assertion that Reading and his associates were acting in accordance with the King's laws with the words, 'If these be the King's laws, God's curse light upon his Heart, for that it was likely he would be a Traitor, as his Father was, and wished him hanged.' A number of Axholme men, including Ryther and Gilby, were eventually apprehended for Patterick's supposed murder and some of them were sent to York Castle to await trial. Around this time, Michael Monckton was also said to have declared that 'the action of the Islemen concerning the riot was lawful and justifiable and that they would maintain it'. The coroner, Joseph Beale, did not enjoy Reading's confidence as he failed to treat the accused commoners with the severity Reading favoured and was allegedly bribed to enter into a charade whereby he pretended to send some of them up to York 'but they stayed upon the road till the coroner came to them and he then released them and (as some of them confessed) for £10 in gold and a horse'. But Beale did send for the remainder of the accused by hue and cry, a procedure rendered inoperative by the failure of Thomas Wakefield, one of the Belton constables (the other being the veteran activist, Robert Bernard[27]), to co-operate. Not only did Wakefield fail to carry out his duties, but he had also reportedly urged the murder of Reading himself, assuring any willing to do it that they need not fear retribution for there was 'nothing done against him that killed the fellow in Haxey Carr'. The raising of a hue and cry would almost certainly have led to violence for a crowd of armed commoners had gathered at Santoft church where they were to remain for several days. John Amory (the defendant in the Vavasour Exchequer action), who had earlier assisted Reading and the collector, was waylaid by some of these commoners and was so terrified as they paraded around his house with guns that he abandoned his family for fear of being murdered like John Patterick.[28]

[26] Stonehouse, p. 324; Maddison, *Lincolnshire Pedigrees*, op. cit., iii, 841–2; P.R.O., E. 134/1 and 2 Jas. II/Hil. 25.

[27] Lincs. R.O., Belton in Axholme town book: constables 1660.

[28] H.L.R.O., Main Papers, [undated] copy of the petition of the farmers and tenants of the Level of Hatfield to the King; 21 June 1660 affidavits of Nathaniel Reading and John Amory; 10 July 1660 certificate of the sheriff and justices.

The above account of the events of 31 May and their sequel relies almost exclusively upon the testimony of Reading's witnesses whose clearly partial evidence was subsequently summarised in a certificate presented to the secretary of state in July 1660. The certificate's narrative of events significantly opened with the participants in peaceful possession of their 7400 acres before the Civil War and proceeded to recall the commoners' seizure of their grounds in two stages, their defiance of authority, and some major violent incidents, including the murder of one of the collector's assistants in September 1659, before closing with a full account of the events of 31 May. The document was obviously geared to securing the new regime's support for the participants, just as the Say and Darley report had been designed to rally Parliament's support, hence while the latter focused upon the commoners' abuse of Parliament, the post-Restoration document recounted anti-monarchical utterances to the extent of rewriting the script for rioters in 1650–1 who were now said to have scoffed at the dispossessed 'go and complain to their rotten King'. Reading could have had no illusions about the kind of reception he would get when he ventured into the Isle on 31 May to distrain the commoners' goods, and had plainly been preparing for a fight by recruiting men in parts of Nottinghamshire away from the fens and providing them with horses and arms. These recruits were given a firm assurance that they would be covered by the court of sewers' indemnity in executing its orders and Reading had even engaged a surgeon to attend to them if the need arose. It is by no means inconceivable that Reading had deliberately set out to provoke violence in order to gain a tactical advantage by projecting the commoners as riotous and traitorous subjects so shortly after the return of monarchy. There was decidedly much more to the killing of Patterick than Reading's witnesses disclosed. William Lockier, described as a ringleader of the fatal assault, was shot through the right thigh, allegedly by Reading, in Hatfield that day and about a week later died of gangrene, and John Patterick was named in a subsequent murder indictment as having been one of Reading's accomplices, pointing to the possibility that his own death occurred in the affray following the wounding of Lockier. The way in which Patterick met his death is consistent with this interpretation: stave blows administered to the head by two Belton labourers were said to have been responsible, rather than the more openly murderous intent of a gunshot or a stabbing. Reading was obviously concerned about the consequences

for himself and his men that would follow Lockier's death; he dispatched his surgeon in an attempt to save the man's life who conveniently shifted the responsibility for the death on to fellow
commoners whose own surgeon had failed to treat the wound
correctly and who had forbidden Reading's surgeon to search the
wound more than once on the grounds that it was past curing.
Reading was indicted for Lockier's murder at a Lincoln sessions on
10 September and one of his alleged accomplices, a Nottinghamshire
tanner called Hugh Girdler, was later arrested in East Retford and
imprisoned at Nottingham for about six months, despite the offer of a
£1000 surety for his appearance at the next assizes. In the meantime
the indictment was removed into the King's Bench, where Reading
secured an acquittal, and this judgement was subsequently produced
at Lincoln assizes to secure likewise Girdler's acquittal. The participants' informations concerning the May riot and slaying of Patterick
were also transmitted into King's Bench by order of the House of
Lords, and on 24 September the two Belton labourers were indicted
for murder at York and twenty-one others, including an Epworth
gentleman, John Mawe, junior, were named as accomplices.[29]

Tension continued throughout the summer with the settlers'
church at Santoft yet again subjected to desecration and destruction
in August. A dead cow had earlier been hauled into the church and
buried by Epworth commoners in the place formerly occupied by the
communion table. The building had apparently been re-equipped for
worship when, at the beginning of August, windows were smashed
and interior furnishings destroyed once again by commoners who
vowed that they 'would not obey any order that should come down
either concerning the Church or land', and on 13 August sheep were
driven into the church which became infested with maggots picked
out of their wool. Such persistent attacks were almost certainly frontal
assaults upon any scheme for carving a foreign settlement out of
commonable fenland, of which the Santoft church constituted the
centre and signified permanence. An appeal to the Lords to restore
order produced their directive of 23 August requiring the sheriffs of

---

[29] Notts. U.L., H.C.C. 9111, f. 10; ibid., 6002, fols 478–9, 485–6; P.R.O., K.B.
9/886/252–56; H.L.R.O., Main Papers, 10 July 1660 certificate of sheriff and justices;
ibid., [undated] petition of Simon Mawe, gentleman, William Tong and Robert
Bernard; *Lords' jn.*, xi, 75, 95.

the respective counties to take steps to prevent future riots in the level.[30]

Victory in the first round of the post-Restoration struggle in Axholme went to the participants when, about Michaelmas 1660, possession of the 7400 acres was delivered by the sheriff and confirmed by an order of the Lords on the following 20 December. Efforts were also made to obtain parliamentary confirmation of their title and a Bill to that effect had completed all its stages in the Lords by December 1661.[31] Reading employed a large work-force to re-enclose the participants' grounds yet their peaceful enjoyment of them was short-lived. In May 1661 commoners seized and detained livestock belonging to the participants' tenants, who were forced to pay for their recovery, and Misterton and Stockwith commoners joined those of Epworth in harassing tenants and setting guards over the grounds. Another participant appeal to the Lords produced a re-affirmation of the earlier order on 24 May but it was accorded the same contempt as its predecessor. However, there could hardly have been a more maladroit, bordering on deliberately provocative, act than entrusting the reading of the May order in Epworth parish church to John Amory, French settler and defendant in the 1651 trial of title, who had it snatched from his hands as he was reading it out to the congregation after the service. In July, as rioting spread north-wards to Thorne, the privy council intervened to protect the partici-pants' interests in Axholme by ordering the indictment of rioters at the next assizes.[32]

In the following August, Axholme commoners backed up their resolve to defend their title with vigorous action. Epworth townsmen led the way when, about the beginning of the month, Edmund Mawe and more than forty others rounded up over 150 head of cattle found grazing in the disputed grounds and impounded them at Epworth,

[30] *Lords' jn.*, xi, 139; H.L.R.O., Main Papers, 23 August 1660 affidavit of Elizabeth Foster.

[31] *Lords' jn.*, xi, 197, 201, 211, 218, 258, 281, 316, 334, 343.

[32] 'Depositions from the Castle of York' in *Surtees Society* (1861), xlviii, 175 note; P.R.O., P.C. 2/55, f. 299; H.L.R.O., Main Papers, 19 October 1660 letter of Lord Castleton and several other commissioners to Sir William Morrice; 24 May 1661 petition of the participants of the Level of Hatfield Chase to the House of Lords; 7 March 1662 petition of the participants, purchasers of improved lands within the Level of Hatfield Chase; 10 March 1662 affidavit of John Amory of Hatfield, Yorkshire, yeoman.

and shortly afterwards Thomas Vavasour, Thomas Wakefield (a former Belton constable), Peter Clarke and at least thirty other Belton men followed their example. The commoners refused to allow replevins and instead demanded payment of arbitrary sums for the livestock's recovery backed up by the threat of slow starvation as the pinder had been instructed not to feed them. A number of Epworth men, joined by reinforcements from Belton, were selected a few days later to mount a guard in each street in Santoft, and other towns within Epworth manor, armed with clubs and pitchforks. One of the agents employed by the collector of taxes for the court of sewers abandoned several recent distresses out of fear of the Santoft guards, having had 'long experience of the violence and barbarous usage of the said Inhabitants of the said Manor toward the Collectors of the said Court in pursuing and wounding of them'. The same guards also drove cattle through gaps they had made in the participants' fences to destroy completely their ripening crops of corn and flax, and when Reading read out the Lords's order they were violating, they exclaimed that 'they cared neither for the King, the Lords nor Laws, they would keep their ground in despite of them all'. Other commoners engaged in pulling down part of a windmill (rebuilt after its previous destruction) similarly cried out, 'down with the possession of the Participants Farewell Order of the house of Lords'.

Thomas Vavasour was later identified as the prime mover behind these recent events having, with the assistance of fellow townsmen, Richard Kingman (or Kinman), gentleman, Thomas Wakefield and Richard Mawe (all three former constables), organised a levy in Belton of 3d a week per head of livestock from all commoners in order to pay each guard 12d a day for his services. Vavasour and Mawe were said to have personally collected this money from each Belton household, issuing a stern warning to one (presumably unco-operative) townsman that his home would be pulled down if he did not keep guard like his neighbours. A few of the rioters were later convicted at both a private and a quarter sessions, but the smallness of the fines imposed, and the existence of a 'common purse' organised by Vavasour and his associates to meet the costs of prosecuted rioters, served only to stiffen their resolve and left the participants virtually without remedy. When the sheriff and his men, at the participants' insistence, tried to disperse the guards on the following Michaelmas a crowd of between fifty and sixty commoners fell upon them, seriously wounding a bailiff, and pursued them for a considerable distance.[33]

Several of those implicated in the August riots and the attack upon the sheriff and his men were by no means newcomers to that kind of activity, and Vavasour's long record of advocacy of the commoners' cause requires no further comment. At least six had been involved in the disturbances of 1650-1, and three others in the Hatfield rescues of October 1655 and January 1656. John Thorpe and Thomas Hill of Epworth, and Peter Clarke of Belton, men at the forefront of the August riots, had previously acted as trustees for their fellow commoners in negotiating the 1651 agreement with Lilburne and Wildman. Clarke had also earned special attention for his defiance of commissioners of sewers in 1655-6 and for having organised the rescue of distrained sheep on 19 January 1656. Two of the three former Belton constables, Richard Mawe (elected 1651) and Thomas Wakefield (1660), had earlier demonstrated that their primary allegiance lay in protecting the interests of their fellow commoners rather than enforcing the law. Mawe had been an offender in 1650-1, and Wakefield had more recently frustrated an attempt to apprehend those suspected of involvement in the murder of Patterick and had allegedly urged the townspeople to kill Reading too. Significantly, therefore, some of the natural leaders of society at the parish level were numbered among the offenders of August 1661.[34]

The above account of the events of August and Michaelmas 1661, like the narration of events on 31 May 1660, is almost exclusively derived from sources patently hostile towards the commoners – in this case from the participants' petition of 7 March 1662 to the House of Lords, and the affidavits of Reading and three associates. This appeal was obviously intended to prompt their lordships into proceeding against the commoners as riotous and seditious persons, who treated the orders of the House with contempt, while conveniently ignoring the whole question of title, and to press home this advantage the need for urgent action was stressed on the grounds that crops sown in 1662

[33] H.L.R.O., Main Papers, 7 March 1662 petition of the participants of Hatfield Chase; 10 March 1662 affidavit of Francis Barghe of Retford, Nottinghamshire, yeoman; 10 March 1662 affidavit of John Amory of Hatfield; ibid., affidavit of William Tompkinson of Hatfield, yeoman; ibid., affidavit of Nathaniel Reading.

[34] Lincs. R.O., town book of Belton in Axholme. These include two Belton gentlemen, Thomas Vavasour and Richard Kinman, and four other men (three from Epworth and one from Belton) of sufficient substance to appear on the subsidy rolls (P.R.O., E. 179/140/750-51).

would otherwise be at hazard. The commoners, on the other hand, remained unshakeably convinced of their title after the Restoration and had not interpreted the Lords's order of 20 December 1660 as excluding them from the Epworth fens; hence when they drove off and impounded livestock belonging to the participants and their tenants in August 1661 they were defending their title against the aggression of Reading and his men, as their predecessors had against the original drainers. They were later to secure another verdict giving legal recognition to their title and four verdicts at a Lincoln assizes against the participants for seizing and driving away the commoners' cattle. The timing of the participants' petition to the Lords (7 March 1662) may also have been significant. Thomas Vavasour and three other prominent commoners had been in London for about three months awaiting an opportunity to present the Epworth case against a Bill which had come down to the Commons from the Lords for settling the question of the participants' grounds, but the latter had not complained about the commoners' actions earlier having deliberately held back, it was claimed, until the Lords were pre-occupied with more urgent matters so as to deprive Vavasour and his fellows of their freedom and put them to great expense. Although sureties were offered for their appearance, Vavasour and twenty-three others were sent for by serjeant-at-arms on 10 March 1662, and he and twelve others subsequently yielded themselves up as prisoners; they remained in custody until 12 May when, with Daniel Noddel acting as their solicitor, they were released on the understanding that they paid their fees and entered bail for their future appearance and good behaviour. Nevertheless, the prisoners apparently returned home without satisfying either condition and were rearrested for contempt, and the Lords committed Vavasour and Peter Clarke close prisoners until they rendered obedience to the former order. These proceedings involved some commoners in considerable expense and several had allegedly incurred costs of nearly £300 and were still continually threatened with re-arrest. Vavasour probably incurred heftier expenses than most; indeed the financial drain upon his estate of the struggle with the participants may have been responsible for the eventual sale of the family property at Belwood.[35] May 1662 appears

---

[35] H.L.R.O., Main Papers, 10 March 1660 affidavit of Nathaniel Reading; 10 March 1662 petition of Thomas Vavasour and others to the House of Lords; 12 May 1662 order for the release on bail of Thomas Vavasour and others; 28 March 1663 petition of

to have been the last occasion on which Daniel Noddel acted for the commoners and from that year until shortly before his death, on 6 April 1672, he was employed as steward of the manor of Epworth under the crown lessee, Sir George Carteret, baronet. On the evidence of his inventory, Noddel died in far from prosperous circumstances, with a total valuation of £41 4s 8d (plus £20 in debts owing to him) and a modest seven-room house with a barn and stable. His second son and heir, Joseph Noddel, showed no interest whatsoever in the cause that his father had so energetically espoused, and the family's fortunes declined further as a result of Joseph's perpetual involvement in litigation.[36]

The Hatfield participants did not succeed in gaining parliamentary recognition of their interests; their attempts in 1661 and 1663 to secure legislation confirming them in possession of their grounds both failed.[37] By the end of 1663 the tide had begun to turn back in the commoners' favour. Epworth commoners agreed in that year to have their differences with the participants settled by arbitration and secured another verdict against them concerning their title, and around this time relations between Reading and the participants were seriously ruptured with his claims for salary and expenses being met by their charge of embezzlement.[38] The participants did proceed to enclose 2000 acres in Belton in June 1664, and a number of former tenants (including a sizeable proportion of foreign settlers) moved back to plant crops, only to have them harvested and expropriated by local commoners. Freshly reaped rape was seized in late July or early August by armed Epworth commoners, who threatened to return for the corn when it too was ripe, and on 30 September Robert Ryther,

Thomas Vavasour and Peter Clarke; 31 March 1663 petition of Vavasour and Clarke; 1 June 1663 petition of above a thousand householders, tenants and inhabitants of Epworth; *Commons' jn.*, viii, 326; *Lords' jn.*, xi, 404, 443, 445, 456, 485, 500-2; Stonehouse, pp. 339-40.

Robert Ryther, senior, who was connected by marriage with the Vavasour family, was one of the purchasers at the sale of Belwood.

36 Stonehouse, pp. 239-40 note; Joseph Noddel, *Christ's Crucifixion* (York, 1715), pp. 162-5; P.R.O., E. 134/2 Jas. II/East. 31; Lincs. R.O., Cragg 5/1/41-2; ibid., Misc. Don. 403/4/7/2; ibid., 403/6/1/3/2-3; ibid., 403/4/19/2-3; ibid., Bishop's Transcripts, Owston 1672; ibid., Inventories 220/98.

37 *Lords' jn.*, xi, 258, 281, 316, 334, 343; *Commons' jn.*, viii, 326, 333, 342, 441, 446, 470, 476.

38 Stonehouse, pp. 103-4; H.L.R.O., Main Papers, 1 June 1663 petition of above a thousand householders, etc. of Epworth; 12 June 1678 Reading v. the commissioners of sewers for the Hatfield Level.

Thomas Vavasour and Robert Bernard helped supervise about sixty other Belton and Epworth men drive away numerous cartloads of oats, wheat, rye, rape-seed and flax from the Belton enclosures. The full spectrum of local society was represented in this action from the gentry (three from Belton and two from Epworth) to the humble labourer, and many had been engaged in previous disturbances, but the most remarkable aspect of these events is the possibility that Reading might have done an about-turn and joined forces with the commoners. According to the participants' later allegations, Reading had assisted the commoners in throwing down enclosures and carting away the tenants' crops and had even participated in the share-out of the crops.[39] The year ended with yet another fruitless attempt by the participants to gain parliamentary recognition of their title to grounds in Epworth and Gringley.[40]

At the 1666 summer assizes held at Lincoln, Epworth commoners opened a legal barrage against the participants and obtained several verdicts confirming their title. The Mowbray deed, produced in support of an action brought by Thomas Vavasour against John Bradborne, a leading participant, was declared by the presiding judge to be a bar to further improvement of the wastes of Epworth manor. After 1666 the participants virtually surrendered all their grounds to the commoners, with the notable exception of 2 acres at Santoft on which stood Reading's home with its outhouses, garden and grounds. Reading refused to capitulate and at various times took on not only local commoners, but also participants and commissioners of sewers. On 19 August 1668 twenty-five men, mainly from Hatfield, Belton and Epworth, allegedly invaded his Santoft home, terrorised his family and wreaked destruction in his outhouses and garden for about six hours. Among the attackers were Robert Ryther, Robert and John Bernard, and other principal Axholme commoners, but this incident was not simply part of the commoners' long-standing feud with Reading for the accused also included John Bradborne of Hatfield, gentleman (who had presumably relinquished his Epworth claims), and a number of his associates, tenants and servants.[41] The

39 P.R.O., P.C. 2/57, f. 175; ibid., K.B. 9/902/3–5, 34–42; H.L.R.O., Main Papers, 2 November 1678 answer of Sir John Anthony Van Valkenburgh, bart., and other participants in the Level of Hatfield.

40 *Commons' jn.*, viii, 573, 575.

41 P.R.O., K.B. 9/911/180; ibid., E. 134/1 and 2 Jas. II/Hil. 25; ibid., 2 Jas. II/East. 31; ibid., Mich. 35; Notts. U.L., H.C.C. 8939, p. 4; *The Case of the Commoners of the Manor of Epworth in the Isle of Axholme in the County of Lincoln* (169–?).

whole affair was probably related to Bradborne's conflict with Reading over attempts to levy sewers' taxes, but the spectacle of men like Ryther assisting a participant in an action directed against Reading is hardly less remarkable than the possibility of Reading's earlier alliance with the commoners. The assault made upon a Dutch settler by about eighteen townsmen at Wroot on 8 November 1669 was probably part of the more familiar commoner hostility towards such intruders.[42] In the same month Reading refused to acknowledge the repeal of an Epworth law of sewers and began distraining commoners' cattle for nonpayment of taxes and, when challenged, he was said to have sworn 'the Curse of Egypt light upon the Commissioners and the Participants and the Devil take all the Tenants . . . if he lived two years longer they had lost the Lincolnshire land and they should loose the Yorkshire land too'.[43] Reading's determination to collect these taxes was almost certainly related to his earlier claim from commissioners of sewers of over £2000 owing for his salary and expenses which their collection would help defray. For the next ten years he was engaged in protracted, and at times violent, disputes with John Bradborne and others for distraining their goods in Hatfield and elsewhere in the level outside of the Isle of Axholme. His home was stormed in January 1670 by Bradborne and about forty neighbours, and in March 1672 he was reported to have been shot in the legs at Santoft by one of Bradborne's servants.[44] He also clashed with commissioners of sewers in 1678 over money he still believed due to him for his services and was supported by the House of Lords. After reaching a final agreement with the commissioners in 1680 over the money, he set about distraining goods belonging to Bradborne's tenants and others whose lands were charged with tax arrears earmarked for him.[45] A further chapter had been added to Reading's colourful career in the previous year when he had been engaged as legal counsel to the Catholic lords imprisoned in the Tower at the time of the Popish Plot; he had been sentenced to the pillory, fined £1000 and imprisoned for a year after being found guilty of suborning witnesses on the other side.[46]

[42] P.R.O., K.B. 9/921/281.
[43] Notts. U.L., H.C.C. 6003, fols 74–5.
[44] *Surtees Society,* xl, 174–6; P.R.O., K.B. 9/921/278–80, 288.
[45] *Lords' jn.,* xiii, 246–7, 269, 287–8, 722–3, 754; H.L.R.O., Main Papers, 12 June 1678 Reading v. the commissioners of sewers for the Hatfield Level.
[46] J. P. Kenyon, *The Popish Plot* (1972), p. 152; *Surtees Society*, xi, 175 note; Notts. U.L., H.C.C. 9111, f. 128; *H.M.C., Ormonde MSS.,* new series vol. V, pp. 31–2, 68;

Reading was prepared to take on the commoners once again in 1681. He procured a writ of assistance out of the Exchequer on the grounds that Robert Ryther, senior, who was now the commoners' principal leader, had threatened to pull down his house because it stood on common land. But he had a more ambitious scheme in mind than the protection of his home and, extending the writ to cover the possession of the whole 7400 acres, he began trying to exclude the commoners. The impounding of Belton commoners' cattle by Reading's men led to proceedings at Spital quarter sessions on 14 July presided over by Robert Ryther and another local justice, and a complaint to the Exchequer about the unwarranted use of their writ brought an order restraining its applicability to Reading's house and premises only. But Reading also succeeded in gaining an Exchequer reference to the deputy remembrancer, Toby Eden, of his assertion that Ryther and his associates had been parties to the 1636 decree, or claimed under such parties. Despite Ryther's emphatic denial, Eden produced yet another long narrative of events in Epworth with a pronounced pro-drainer bias upon the basis of which the writ was this time officially extended over the whole 7400 acres. Several of the sheriff's men consequently drove livestock from the disputed grounds in August 1682 and delivered possession to Reading for enclosure, but the commoners reacted by pulling up the fences, turning in cattle and indicting Reading and his tenants at assizes and quarter sessions for encroaching upon their commons. Robert Ryther was identified as the driving force behind these manoeuvres and he was bound over, following his examination at Santoft, to appear before the Exchequer in January 1683 to answer for his contempt in breaking the 1636 decree and disobeying a writ of assistance. He had apparently instructed a servant, Henry Ellwood, to drive his cattle into Reading's enclosures and assert common rights there in other ways, and when Reading's fences were re-erected Ryther and his neighbours had broken them into pieces before turning cattle into the grounds. Money had also been collected in Belton (with some contributing allegedly under duress) to meet the costs of suits concerning the grounds and pay their solicitor, John Pinder.[47]

The Trial of Nathaniel Reading Esq., for attempting to stifle the King's Evidence as to the horrid Plot (1679).

Reading was possibly a victim of perjury in this matter (Hunter, *South Yorkshire*, i, 168).
[47] Stonehouse, p. 104; Notts. U.L., H.C.C. 9111, fols 387–9; P.R.O., E. 134/34 and 35 Chas. II/Hil. 13; ibid., K.B. 11/8.

The need to spread the burden of legal costs must have been felt particularly acutely in the next few years as commoners and participants waged battle in the Exchequer. The former, who had persuaded John, Earl of Mulgrave (the owner of lands in Butterwick) and George, Lord Carteret, to associate their names with the commoners' defence of title, continued to stand resolutely by the Mowbray agreement and refuted the participants' claim that it had been overtaken by the subscription of the most substantial Epworth commoners to the 1636 decree.[48] Throughout this period Reading and the commoners remained locked in conflict as he continued to distrain the commoners' livestock, and they retaliated by overturning his attempts at enclosure and attacking his Santoft home. Robert Ryther was on the bench at a Spital quarter sessions on 17 July 1684 when seven indictments were found against Reading and his men for impounding horses and cattle in his yard at Santoft which had been found grazing in fenland pastures at Haxey, Belton and Epworth, and two commoners were also said to have been assaulted at Epworth on 27 June and prevented from removing a cartload of hay off the commons. Further seizures of livestock in May–July 1685 resulted in another batch of indictments being found against Reading and his men at quarter sessions, and three of them were accused of having opposed a sheriff's bailiff when he came to execute replevins. His wife, Sarah, had joined in the action at Santoft in the previous May and June when she and two other wives had pelted some commoners with stones and set the dogs on them. Around harvest-time the commoners began to hit back by seizing Reading's horses and carrying off his oats, and on 20 May in the following year over thirty of them, led by Robert Ryther, filled in his enclosure ditches around West Carr in Belton. Ryther was accompanied by his eldest son, Baptist, and servant, Ellwood, as well as three other Belton gentlemen, one of whom, William Kingman, was listed exactly one year later among the Belton inhabitants accused of a riotous attack upon Reading's home when the surrounding walls and fences were demolished, the windows broken and the orchard badly damaged. Fourteen of the thirty-four accused had been involved in the previous year's levelling, but the two incidents differ in one respect – the 1686 incident had been exclusively male while nearly a half of the 1687

[48] Notts. U.L., H.C.C. 9111, fols 399–400; P.R.O., E. 134/1 and 2 Jas. II/Hil. 25; ibid., 2 Jas. II/East. 31; ibid., Mich. 35; ibid., 3 Jas. II/Mich. 42.

rioters were female. Four of the women accompanied their husbands, like Anna, the wife of John Swinden, yeoman, who brought along her daughter. Swinden had apparently been involved in misdemeanours prior to the attack on Reading's home and a warrant had been issued for his arrest, but the constables of Belton had refused to execute it. Similarly, the chief constable of Epworth, Edmund Mawe, was to refuse to perform his duty and arrest William Kingman and other offenders in the following July. In an action clearly designed to underline the question of title, around midnight on 30 June just six Belton men, three of whom were gentlemen (including the two Belton constables who had refused to arrest Swinden), removed the horses and cattle of two of Reading's tenants from his enclosures and impounded them at Belton until they were replevied. The eighteen inhabitants involved in the attack upon Reading's house, and the assault upon his wife, daughter and servants, on 30 July also constituted a comparatively modest crowd. Ryther and two other local gentry were named as having been implicated in the attack, one-third of the accused were women and there was a significant carry-over of personnel from earlier incidents, including John and Anna Swinden. After leaving Santoft the rioters were also said to have driven livestock into over 40 acres of oats at Belton. Ultimate responsibility for these actions was laid at the door of Ryther and nine gentlemen from Belton, Epworth and Owston, who were believed to have masterminded the attacks and raised local funds to meet expenses, but when two of the gentlemen were sent for by the lord chief justice's warrant on 30 September, Ryther failed to fulfil his duty as a justice and bind them over for their appearance.[49]

By the end of the decade strife-weary participants and commoners appeared to be edging towards some form of accommodation. In 1688 representatives of both sides agreed to refer the whole matter to the arbitration of Sir Thomas Hussey, Sir Willoughby Hickman and others who on 6 April awarded the commoners 750 of the 7400 acres plus one-half of the remaining 6650 acres (a grand total of 4075 acres) discharged of all sewers' taxes and arrears, and gave the remaining 3325 acres to the participants who were to meet the cost of maintaining the drainage works. This award did not find general acceptance among the commoners, especially those of Misterton whose claim to part of the Epworth commons had been ignored, and

[49] P.R.O., K.B. 11/10/part 1; ibid., 11; ibid., 13/pts 1 and 3.

it was not observed. After an Exchequer hearing on 13 April 1691, both sides were urged to attempt another agreement and by 5 May new terms had been arrived at whereby the commoners of Epworth manor would receive 1000 acres, and those of Misterton 664 acres, leaving 5736 acres to be equally divided between the participants and the Epworth commoners. The participants' share was reduced, therefore, to 2868 acres yet they were still burdened with sole responsibility for maintaining drainage as well as safeguarding the commoners against any claims that Nathaniel Reading might advance to any part of the 7400 acres. The agreement was decreed in the Exchequer on 14 May 1691 and, as a first step, a commission was issued for setting out the commoners' 1000 acres. Immediate difficulties arose as Epworth and Belton commoners conflicted with those of Haxey and Owston over where the 1000 acres should be located and the final division and allotment of grounds was not agreed until 18 October 1692 (and was confirmed by Exchequer decree on 20 February 1693). However, the agreement of May 1691 was far from receiving general applause in the Isle where some denounced it as being on a par with the 1636 decree as an act of betrayal by trusted spokesmen with no mandate to act as they did. The commoners had been represented in London by Robert Ryther, senior, Robert Coggan, John Maw, Robert Whiteley and John Pinder, their solicitor. Prior to his departure for London, the latter had evidently been expressly forbidden to entertain any proposals for an accommodation with the participants, at an Owston meeting of principal commoners from all parts of Epworth manor, and had been directed to proceed to a hearing of the cause. Having consented to the 1691 agreement, the commoners' representatives returned to a hostile reception in Epworth where the vast majority of commoners (ten to one according to one witness) were said to have been implacably opposed to it and to have been dismissive of the argument that it was necessary in order to signal an end to conflict within the Isle. John Maw later claimed to have been duped by Pinder into not opposing the agreement and denounced him, Ryther and Coggan as having succumbed to bribery. Pinder had allegedly been given 1000 guineas, and Ryther and Coggan granted 100 acres and 50 acres respectively out of the participants' allotment for their betrayal of their fellow commoners, and particular obloquy was heaped upon Ryther for his supposed treachery in revealing the commoners' secrets to their enemies. The allegedly irregular and fraudulent conduct of Ryther and the rest was subsequently exposed

in an Exchequer Bill exhibited by several commoners in an unsuccessful attempt to get the decree reversed.[50] By the time of his
death in October 1693, Ryther had lost the confidence of most
Epworth commoners and if anyone succeeded him as local leader it
was not his son, Robert, junior, the deputy recorder of Lincoln, but
his son-in-law, Robert Popplewell of Belton and Temple Belwood,
and his fourth daughter, Catherine, Popplewell's wife.[51]

Far from bringing an enduring peace to the Isle, the 1691 agreement opened another protracted period of violence as commoners
manifested their rejection of it by uprooting the participants' newly
erected fences and damaging tenants' crops, with Nathaniel Reading
and one of his four sons, Thomas, joining in the attacks for a brief
period. There are several possible explanations for Reading's erratic
behaviour at this point: he had been abandoned by the participants as
part of the price of reaching agreement with the commoners in 1691;
there was still friction over money owed for his earlier services; and
there was always the possibility that he was acting as an *agent
provocateur*. Whatever the reason, his son Thomas helped several
commoners pull down sections of fence recently erected around Wood
Carr prior to turning in cattle and, after their repair, Nathaniel
Reading helped throw them down again, paying some local boys 6d
on one occasion to make passage ways through the fences for cattle.
Later, with the approach of harvest, Catherine Popplewell, allegedly
spurred on by her husband, recruited a crowd of Belton men, women
and children to make bonfires of the fences and destroy the crops.[52]
However, by this stage Reading had made his peace with the participants, reluctantly agreeing to accept a six-year lease of grounds in
Epworth manor in lieu of the money owed him, and had erected
several miles of fences and ploughed up about a thousand acres. The
commoners' response was immediate and violent: Reading, his sons
and servants were assaulted and he was shot at, his crops were set on
fire, his cattle slaughtered and, finally, his Santoft home was pulled to
the ground. Catherine Popplewell was again singled out as having
played a leading part in these outrages, for which she and others were
indicted at a 1694 Lincoln assizes but escaped with only moderate

[50] Notts. U.L., H.C.C. 9111, fols 390–94, 399–402; P.R.O., E. 178/6802; ibid., E.
134/5 Geo. I/East. 18.
[51] Maddison, *Lincolnshire Pedigrees,* op. cit., iii, 841–2, 787–9; Stonehouse, p. 324.
[52] P.R.O., E. 134/5 Geo. I/East. 18; Notts. U.L., H.C.C. 9111, fols 11, 406.

fines in return for Robert Popplewell's pledge to work for peace. In pursuance of this objective, mediators drew up an agreement modifying the respective allotments which was accepted by two representatives of the participants and thirty-one principal commoners who agreed to make a joint approach to Parliament for a confirmatory act. Yet Popplewell's enemies claimed that once he had succeeded in averting stiff assize sentences, he not only renegued on his pledge but actively encouraged the commoners to engage him as their solicitor to get the decrees reversed. Attacks upon enclosures and buildings continued unabated as offenders avoided detection either by operating at night or by wearing disguises during daylight incidents, before disappearing into a sympathetic and protective community. A Bill was therefore introduced into the Commons to extend the provisions of the statutes of Merton and Westminster to cover offences committed by disguised persons during the daytime so as to make neighbouring towns liable to distraint if they failed to bring rioters to justice within a reasonable time. The commoners condemned the Bill as further evidence of Reading's deviousness given the magnitude of the task of keeping a constant watch upon the fences and the very real possibility that Reading or his servants would covertly pull down the fences themselves and then lay ruinous blame on the commoners.[53]

Reading's continued residence at Santoft occasioned one violent encounter after another, culminating in the dramatic destruction of Reading's rebuilt house and the surrounding property. On 12 October 1696 John Reading (another son) and two servants were assaulted at Santoft by twenty-eight Epworth and Belton men, and there were similar incidents at various times during the first half of 1697 in the same neighbourhood. A large crowd of Belton commoners also asserted common rights in Wood Carr by ripping up fences and driving in their cattle, and one of them, Alexander Pitts, later testified to the existence of a common fund. Pitts himself had been engaged by Robert Popplewell (whose own services were provided for out of the fund) to prevent Reading or his servants impounding the commoners' cattle and had received payment from a

---

[53] Stonehouse, pp. 105–7; Notts. U.L., H.C.C. 9111, fols 406–7; *An Answer to the Case of the Commoners of the Manor of Epworth . . . Published in Opposition to the Bill for making the Statutes of Edw. 1 and Edw. 6 against Destroying Improvements more Effectual* (169–?); *The Case of the Commoners of the Manor of Epworth in the Isle of Axholme* (169–?).

Belton constable. Upon his conviction at Lincoln assizes, Pitts was fined forty marks and imprisoned when he could not pay the fine until Popplewell entered a £40 bond for his release.[54]

By far the most serious incident occurred around midnight on 15 April 1697 when Reading's new home was burnt to the ground by, according to his own and his servants' account, a group of disguised commoners. They were said to have crept up to the house while its occupants lay asleep in their beds and thrust torches under the thatch and, when the household awoke to the flames and made for the doors, they found all the keyholes had been stopped up with clay, and only narrowly escaped death by pulling out one of the window bars and squeezing through into the garden. The commoners, on the other hand, placed the actual responsibility for the fire upon Reading's servants whose wood piled up for brewing on the previous night had accidentally caught fire and ignited the thatch, and accused Reading of trying to turn this accident to his advantage by making torches and thrusting them under sections of unburnt thatch so that he could represent it as another grave commoner outrage. The available evidence gives few pointers as to which account of the burning down of Reading's house is closer to the truth. In Reading's favour it has to be recalled that only a few years before a group of commoners had demolished his previous home and within a couple of months commoners did in fact devastate what was left standing on the site. On the other hand, there can be little doubt that Reading was capable of the kind of devious act envisaged in the commoners' account and there are some surprising inconsistencies in his witnesses' accounts of how the household escaped the flames.[55]

Reading claimed that the burning down of his home had been followed by further attacks on his household and property in May: around midnight on the 24th a gang of disguised commoners allegedly shot at and threatened his servants vowing that they would demolish the house they occupied (close to the charred remains of their former home) and on the 25th they returned to make bonfires of his fences and materials accumulated to build some temporary accommodation for his family, and then filled in sections of dyke that protected his corn from flooding. The privy council offered a pardon

[54] P.R.O., K.B. 11/18/pts 1 and 2; ibid., E. 134/5 Geo. I/East. 18.
[55] Stonehouse, pp. 108–9; P.R.O., E. 134/5 Geo. I/East. 18; Notts. U.L., H.C.C. 9111, fols 11, 407–8.

on 3 June to any offender who was prepared to inform on his fellows and Reading added the incentive of a £20 reward. Yet later that month another crowd of disguised commoners marched on Santoft to pull down Reading's outbuildings (and expropriate their contents), destroy his orchard and gardens and burn his farming implements, and returned to Belton that evening to celebrate by dining on his pigs and poultry. The commoners did not confine their attention to Reading's property but also demolished houses belonging to several participants around the same time. When an accusing finger was pointed at Robert Popplewell as riot instigator, the gravity of their offences was such that he was obliged to dissociate himself completely from them and their excesses. Some of the ringleaders fled the county to escape punishment and, branded as outlaws, never dared return, while others were indicted at the Lincoln assizes. Popplewell was again forced to request the intercession of two Lincolnshire gentry to escape the full rigours of the law and, through their good services, an agreement was reached on 28 February 1698 whereby the commoners undertook to pay Reading £600 compensation in return for his staying all legal proceedings against them.[56]

At some stage in 1697 negotiations had taken place at Hatfield between a group of commoners and participants aimed at achieving a permanent settlement of their differences, and the latter had apparently been prepared to accept either a reduced allotment of 1200 acres or an annual payment of £200 if they relinquished all their Epworth claims, but the commoners had refused to countenance even these greatly reduced demands. The participants could not have enjoyed a very strong bargaining position for, by the turn of the century, most of the grounds allotted them in 1691 were still being enjoyed as common lands. By 1709, however, the commoners were evidently prepared to lease Wood Carr to Thomas Reading for seven years at an annual rent of £200 and to add extra land at no extra cost when he complained that they had struck a hard bargain. Robert Popplewell negotiated this lease on the commoners' behalf adding the stipulation that the first £500 of rent was to go to Thomas's father to compensate him for the damage done to his property by the commoners.[57] There was further serious rioting in the Isle between

[56] P.R.O., P.C. 2/77, fols 25, 31; Stonehouse, pp. 109–10; Notts. U.L., H.C.C. 9111, fols 12, 407–8.
[57] P.R.O., E. 134/5 Geo. I/East. 18.

1712 and 1714 until Robert Reading (who like his brothers had embarked upon a military career) stationed part of his own regiment there to protect fences and crops in Wood Carr.[58]

After nearly ninety years of turmoil, peace was finally brought to the Isle in the wake of the Riot Act and the commoners' final legal defeat. Nathaniel Reading died at Belton in June 1716 at the ripe old age of over a hundred, leaving the last confrontation with the commoners in the Exchequer to his sons, Thomas and Robert, as lessees of the participants' lands, which ended with the dismissal with costs of the Commoners' Bill in 1719.[59] Nevertheless, the commoners had achieved a large measure of success as the whittling down to 2868 acres of the 7400 originally awarded the participants demonstrates. And the Mowbray charter continued to be a cherished document, with the commoners of Epworth as late as 1776 still laying claim to the advantages it accorded them, although peaceful relations had long been established between them and the participants.[60]

The fenmen's defence of their common rights and traditional economy had achieved a great deal by the end of the seventeenth century. Courtiers who had ridden roughshod over property rights, local interests and established conventions governing drainage procedure, prior to the Civil War, found post-Restoration royal favour no longer enough to secure the revival of their claims and they remained permanently dispossessed of their fenland acres. Participants in the Isle of Axholme were eventually forced to concede over three-fifths of their original award to commoners who had never forgotten the strength of their title under the Mowbray charter. In other levels, however, the involvement of local men of considerable substance enabled former undertakers, or their descendants, to appeal successfully for parliamentary backing and thereby secured an authority and permanence for their enterprise that no Stuart king could have given.

---

[58] Notts. U.L., H.C.C. 9111, fols 12–13; Stonehouse, p. 110.

[59] Stonehouse, p. 110; Notts. U.L., H.C.C. 9111, fols 13, 380–411; ibid., 6004, fols 355–6.

[60] J. Korthals-Altes, *Sir Cornelius Vermuyden* (1925), p. 138.

Conclusion

IN their defensiveness, conservatism and restraint, fenland riots in the seventeenth century shared common characteristics with many other popular disturbances in early modern England.[1] The fenmen were primarily concerned with preserving their commons from wholesale enclosure, and their traditional economy from transformation, and their actions directly reflected these priorities. Violence was directed in the main at property, rather than persons, as appears to have been the case in enclosure riots in the early sixteenth century, and food riots and other forms of popular disturbance in the early modern period as a whole.[2] Any challenge to authority or government inherent in the fenmen's actions was incidental, for their struggle produced little in the way of a heightened political consciousness among the great mass of fenland commoners. They moved along well-worn channels of popular protest by wherever possible claiming royal sympathy, once the King was apprised of their plight, and affirming their absolute obedience to his will,[3] or, in the early 1640s, to the authority of the House of Commons, and rarely concerned themselves with the wider social, political or constitutional issues their actions raised.

An anxiety to keep within the law, if at all feasible, or to minimise their transgression and the consequent penalties, if not, was responsible for some of the more restrained features of the commoners' violence, such as the careful division into groups of two

---

[1] R. B. Manning, 'Patterns of violence in early Tudor enclosure riots' in *Albion*, vi, 1974, pp. 131-2; P. Clarke, 'Popular protest and disturbance in Kent, 1558-1640' in *Economic History Review*, 2nd series, xxix, no. 3, pp. 378, 380; J. Stevenson, *Popular disturbances in England, 1700-1870* (1979), pp. 309-16; Sharp, pp. 7-8, 32, 84, 86.

[2] Manning, 'Patterns of violence in early Tudor enclosure riots', op. cit., p. 133; G. Rudé, *The crowd in history* (New York, 1964), pp. 254-5; Stevenson, *Popular disturbances in England, 1700-1870* (1979), pp. 312-13; Sharp, p. 32.

[3] D. G. C. Allan, 'Agrarian discontent under the early Stuarts and during the last decade of Elizabeth' (London University M.Sc., 1950), p. 171; Clarke, 'Popular protest and disturbance in Kent, 1558-1640', op. cit., p. 380; Stevenson, *Popular disturbances in England, 1700-1870*, op. cit., pp. 311-12; Sharp, p. 48.

so as technically to avoid a riot charge. The latter device was employed in other disturbances in this period despite the fact that it was evidently classified as 'a cunning riot' in Star Chamber and as such severely punished.[4] The participation of women in a significant proportion of fenland disturbances may have owed something to an awareness that a relatively lenient attitude was adopted by legal authorities to their sex, as well as a belief in some circles that women and children under the age of discretion were immune from punishment for riot if they acted without male instigation or direction.[5] Although not openly articulated in the fens, female rioters elsewhere in the early seventeenth century were said to have acted in this belief, like the women who rioted at Rotherham in 1606, 'the most of them thinking themselves lawless because they were women', or those who levelled an enclosure in Dorset in 1619 upon the assumption that there was no legal remedy against women and boys for such an offence. In actual practice, however, such an immunity was probably not observed; Star Chamber ruled in 1605 that husbands were to pay the fines and damages resulting from their wives' participation in riots, even if the offence had been committed without their prior knowledge (although, significantly, in the case giving rise to the ruling, the fines imposed on female offenders were set at one-half of the male rioters' fines), and nine Axholme women faced crushing Star Chamber fines in 1631.[6]

Fenland disturbances drew forth some of the larger crowds of the century, involving 100 rioters and many more in a considerable number of instances, while in Kent, by comparison, the numbers of those involved in riots during the period 1558-1640 probably never exceeded a hundred.[7] Large-scale riots tended to be seen by the authorities as possessing a military organisation, as some disturbances

---

[4] E. Kerridge, 'The revolts in Wiltshire against Charles I' in *The Wiltshire Archaeological and Natural History Magazine,* no. CCVI, June 1958, pp. 65–6; Allan, 'Agrarian discontent under the early Stuarts and during the last decade of Elizabeth', op. cit., pp. 32–3; Sharp, p. 234; B. L. Harley MS. 1226, f. 27.

[5] See, for example, W. Lambard, *Eirenarcha: or of the office of the Justices of Peace,* 4th ed., 1599, pp. 184–5; yet Lambard recalls one notable exception to this in Star Chamber.

[6] C. Z. Wiener, 'Sex roles and crime in late Elizabethan Hertfordshire' in *Journal of Social History,* viii, 1975, p. 39; M. Campbell, *The English yeoman under Elizabeth and the early Stuarts* (Yale, 1942), p. 86, note 80; Sharp, p. 36; P.R.O., STAC. 8/247/10; ibid., 293/12; ibid., 295/11; J. Hawarde, *Les reportes del cases in Camera Stellata 1593 to 1609,* ed. W. P. Baildon (privately printed, 1894), p. 247.

[7] Clark, 'Popular protest and disturbance in Kent, 1558–1640', op. cit., p. 379.

may indeed have had,[8] but the suspicion remains that the authorities may sometimes have been too ready to impute a military aspect to such riots. Much of the explanation for the scale and persistence of fenland, or indeed of other, major disturbances in early modern England is probably to be found in the extent to which members of the local governing elite condoned or actively encouraged violent behaviour. The frequency with which the fenland gentry assumed the leadership in opposing the drainers leaves little doubt as to their central role, and the importance of the gentry in encouraging, initiating and frequently assuming the leadership of popular disturbances has similarly been noted in studies of other enclosure riots in the sixteenth and seventeenth centuries and of food riots in the eighteenth century.[9]

This interpretation of the importance of the gentry's role in fomenting and guiding some of the larger-scale and more persistent rioting in this period has recently been challenged by Buchanan Sharp in his study of riots in the forest areas of western England in the period 1586–1660. Dr Sharp refutes the notion that disaffected gentry, and other men of substance, were behind the disorders he has investigated, and accuses historians of having been too ready to accept as fact the groundless fears expressed by authorities who were convinced that the lower orders, without the instigation or leadership of their social superiors, were incapable of the kind of coherence and organisation such disturbances possessed. The virtual absence of gentry involvement, and the relatively few yeomen who participated in the forest riots, is explained by him as arising from the fact that the Crown's disafforestation proceedings, far from being an example of arbitrary enclosure, were a good case of enclosure by agreement in which the property rights and interests of the gentry and the more substantial commoners were recognised and adequately compensated. When some freeholders and substantial copyholders

---

[8] Cf. Rudé, *The crowd in history*, op. cit., p. 251; Kerridge, 'The revolts in Wiltshire against Charles I', op. cit., p. 66.

[9] Manning, 'Patterns of violence in early Tudor enclosure riots', op. cit., pp. 121, 127; Kerridge, 'The revolts in Wiltshire against Charles I', op. cit., p. 72; Allan, 'Agrarian discontent under the early Stuarts and during the last decade of Elizabeth', op. cit., pp. 98–9, 108; E.P. Thompson, 'The moral economy of the English crowd in the eighteenth century' in *Past and Present*, no. 50, February 1971, pp. 94–5.

Instances of active gentry involvement, however, may have been exceptional and a feature almost exclusively confined to major disturbances (Clarke, 'Popular protest and disturbance in Kent, 1558–1640', op. cit., p. 380).

opposed disafforestation they did so for tactical reasons, to increase the amount of land granted to them as compensation by a recourse to law, and their opposition was not of a kind that would result in rioting. Those who did riot were the virtually landless rural artisans and cottagers, the very people most dependent on the commonable resources of the forest, who either possessed no legal title to common rights there (and hence no legal claim to compensation), or their tenements, which gave them such entitlement, were so small that they received paltry compensation. This section of society provided their own leadership and organisation, and articulated their own grievances, without outside assistance from their social superiors.[10]

Dr Sharp is undoubtedly correct in pointing out the dangers inherent in a necessarily heavy reliance upon accounts of popular disturbances produced by authorities engaged in their suppression and prevention, and historians working in this field ignore such a warning at their peril. But his main conclusions are not upheld by this present study of fenland riots for, although the authorities were obsessively concerned with discovering disaffected members of the local elite behind the riots, and some unfounded accusations were occasionally levelled at substantial figures who were later exonerated, members of the fenland gentry and more substantial commoners did play a remarkably prominent part in the disturbances. Fenland drainage and enclosure, unlike the disafforestation proceedings described by Dr Sharp, was by no means always carried out with a scrupulous regard for property rights and local interests; and legal processes, as Epworth commoners could testify, failed to provide a safety valve against violence. Members of the local elite were to be found in the drainers' camp, and local differences in attitude to drainage and enclosure did at times divide the better from the poorer sort of commoner, with the divisions in Sutton providing a prime example, but no clear-cut social division in attitude to the fenland schemes existed on the forest model. This is partly confirmed by the absence of expressions of hatred for men of property in the fens, with Sutton significantly proving a notable exception, in contrast to sentiments approaching class hatred uttered by forest rioters.[11] The generality of fenmen had no immediate reason to feel hatred for the gentry as such because individual gentry associated themselves with

10 Sharp, pp. 5–6, 126–55, 261–3.
11 Ibid., pp. 8, 265.

the fenmen's cause and thereby afforded some counterbalance for those who allied with the drainers. In actual fact, fenland rioters in the seventeenth century, like many of those involved in eighteenth-century disturbances,[12] generally did not articulate political or social sentiments beyond those specifically related to their immediate grievances.

The reaction of a whole region of England to a policy of drainage and enclosure personally endorsed by the Crown helps to explain the collapse of Charles I's personal rule and the eventual outbreak of civil war. Many of the features associated with the implementation of the fenland schemes tended in the direction of an absolutist form of government in which the Crown, with the connivance of influential courtiers and government officials, undermined property rights and silenced opposition by blocking the aggrieved parties' recourse to law and employing conciliar courts to bring dissidents to heel. But the Stuart state lacked the kind of police powers needed to deal with the scale of violence and the intensity of opposition fenland enclosure provoked, and on the wider issue of safeguarding property from violation by prerogative power and courtier exploitation many of the political elite could find common cause with indignant fenmen. The summoning of a Parliament raised expectations that fenland grievances, like other excesses of the personal rule, would be speedily remedied and, when the Long Parliament assembled, the commoners' appeals for justice, combined with direct action in the fens, helped to raise the political temperature. In Parliament, fenland affairs occasioned a constitutional clash between the two Houses and, in the country as a whole, the riotous levelling of fenland enclosures helped convince a growing section of the political elite that anarchy lurked around the corner and only by rallying to the King could order be preserved.

The vast majority of fenland commoners remained virtually oblivious to the great issues debated at Westminster in the months leading up to the outbreak of the Civil War. The chief significance of the political crisis for most of them was the ideal opportunity it afforded to level enclosures and regain their commons, and if they demonstrated any political allegiance it was secondary to and often in pursuit of the regaining of those lands. There is no real evidence that the generality of fenmen had been politically educated by their

---

[12] Stevenson, *Popular disturbances in England, 1700–1870,* op. cit., p. 314.

experiences in the 1630s, and the political and constitutional points made by their most articulate spokesmen, like Sir John Maynard, were addressed to fellow members of the political elite and made little, if any, impact upon the consciousness of the fenmen themselves. Like their forest counterparts,[13] the fenmen's main preoccupation, as the English Revolution ran its course, remained much the same as it had been in the 1630s, the defence of an open fen, and the official favour extended by successive political regimes towards fenland drainage ensured that it would remain so. In a sense the 1650s made their keenest impact upon fenland commoners in the availability of military forces to restore order and protect works and enclosures, and any idea that the fens developed revolutionary potential at the beginning of the decade, with the intervention of Lilburne and Wildman, deserves all of Dr Sharp's censure for an uncritical reliance upon unsubstantiated official reports.

The fenmen's persistence was rewarded with victory in the long term in all those schemes where a courtier group had had a dominant interest. After 1660 fenland drainage was debated openly in Parliament and a position of confidence or intimacy with the monarch was no longer sufficient to secure the revival of earlier claims. Any new proposals to drain the East, West and Wildmore Fens in the eighteenth century foundered on local opposition and a comprehensive scheme was not put into operation until the beginning of the nineteenth century.[14] Renewed attempts to enclose parts of the Holland Fen in the second half of the eighteenth century led to disturbances in 1768 when a crowd of commoners seized and tore up enclosure papers and scattered them through the streets of Boston. An anonymous letter hurled through a window in the following year proclaimed 'An open fen for Ever', and trouble continued until 1773, with ricks set on fire, sheep hamstrung and gates into the fen destroyed, and a grazier actively involved in this resistance was proceeded against as late as 1770 under the Black Act.[15] After the second decade of the eighteenth century, Isle of Axholme commoners called a halt to their lengthy dispute with the participants and con-

---

[13] Sharp, 8–9, 247–51, 264.
[14] Darby, *Draining*, pp. 80–1, 151–2, 233–4, 236–7.
[15] J. Thirsk, *English peasant farming* (1957), p. 214; E. P. Thompson, 'The crime of anonymity' in *Albion's fatal tree: crime and society in eighteenth century England* (1975), eds D. Hay and E. P. Thompson, p. 276; E. P. Thompson, *Whigs and Hunters: the origins of the Black Act* (1975), p. 247.

tented themselves with the large measure of success they had achieved in considerably reducing the latter's intrusion. Commoners within the Ancholme Level were, in contrast, entirely subjugated by Sir John Monson and his fellow undertakers but, by the end of the seventeenth century, the condition of the level had deteriorated badly leading to complaints about the failure of the undertakers and their descendants to maintain vital works.[16] Where the commoners' resistance had failed, nature was eventually to prove more successful and by 1700 all the surviving schemes were experiencing serious problems arising from a combination of outfall difficulties and the progressive lowering of the fenland surface as the peat dried out and wasted away.[17]

[16] *Commons' jn.*, xii, 120; xiv, 447, 464, 471; xvii, 282-3, 297.
[17] Darby, *Draining*, pp. 94-103, 104-14, 119, 144-5.

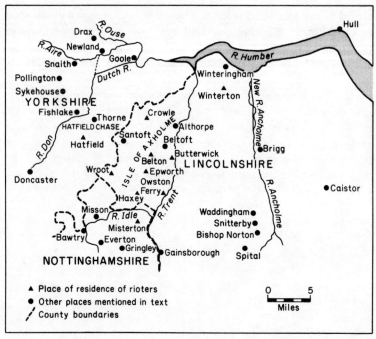

Map 2   Geographical origins of rioters in the Hatfield and Ancholme levels

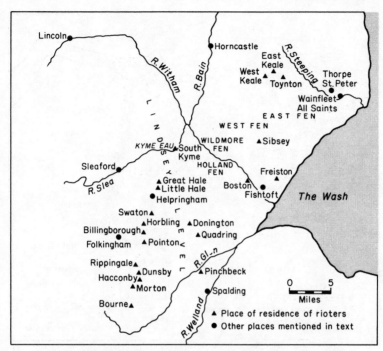

Map 3 Geographical origins of rioters in the Lindsey levels, the Holland Fen and the East, West and Wildmore Fens

Map 4 Geographical origins of rioters in the Great and Deeping levels

Index